*The Art of Appreciating*

# MORE

*By Peggy Halevi*

# THE ART OF APPRECIATING MORE

Copyright © 2020 by Peggy Halevi
First edition April 2021

All rights reserved, including the right to reproduce
this book, or portion of it, in any form.

The Art of Appreciating MORE co-creator:

Book Manager: Uri Halevi

Library of Congress Control Number: 2020921592
ISBN 9780984328895

Published in The United States of America by: Halevi Publishing

PRINTED IN THE UNITED STATES OF AMERICA

ANOTHER PUBLICATION FROM PEGGY HALEVI IS *THE ART OF APPRECIATION* 2010

Discover *MORE* at: WorldofAppreciation.Com
Email: More.Book@Halevi.Com

*The Art of Appreciating MORE*

I AM in great Appreciation for
my ability to hear the Omnipresent Voice Within,
for my husband, Uri, whose loving support enlightens,
for our daughters,
Tasha & our son-in-law Sean, & Michelle and her fiancé Peter,
for our Art of Appreciation friends
for my many spiritual teachers,
for knowing Universal Laws exist,
for the readers of this book,
for those who do not read it & for everything.

We are the Space of Appreciation in-between a Shared Heart

*The Art of Appreciating* MORE

## Introduction
### By Peggy Halevi

Appreciating MORE.

This is the Art of Appreciating MORE, that I often call "THE MORE BOOK". There is something special that happens to me when I use the word "MORE". When I type or write it, I want to capitalize MORE (although I restrain myself from doing so in the text of The MORE Book, as much as I could). It, MORE, even as I type it and when I speak the word I often immediately sense MORE as part of what is good to be a part of in life. My ears and eyes hear and see the word "MORE" very easily. Incidentally, I experienced this about the word "Appreciate" which led to my first book, *The Art of Appreciation*. After writing *The Art of Appreciation*, and then publishing it, I had a sense of accomplishment and joy, even while feeling openly vulnerable and publicly exposed. Over the past years some people have mentioned that The Art of Appreciation Book helped them in some ways. Some people say it helped them be happier. It is a book about appreciating into your life. Now, I publish the MORE book to share the results of appreciating into my life very deliberately. Therefore, it is a book based upon appreciating and if it happens that someone benefits from reading it, I would like that happy feeling. Happiness is a very good feeling.

I am a "sensitive" person, and parts of being so makes me seemingly shy, although, I do find, under the right situations, I am anything but shy. I am a bit uncomfortable and unfamiliar with receiving too much attention, so shy comes to surface to look around. I do not require attention to be happy. This book is meant for people to read, not for me to become known, but for themselves. I think most people feel a bit intimidated

*Introduction*

with others reading their personal thoughts. I have found that personally sharing is a good experience and, as I will mention often in The MORE Book, we all have so much MORE in common than not.

Truly much has changed since writing and publishing *The Art of Appreciation*. However, I find the fundamentals of that book are the same ones I still hold and practice. I am ever improving my Law of Attraction knowledge with experience. Knowing the Law of Attraction and really living The Law of Attraction are two different things. I, thankfully, stay on top of remembering to practice the principles of The Law of Attraction, although, I am far from all-knowing. I am very appreciative for where I am in my life-wisdom based upon The Law of Attraction. I keep in mind the positive quality of my thoughts often and it greatly increases joy. Wisdom is connected to discipline and I am wise to create from my heart, mind, soul and spirit of joy.

Over my lifetime I've discovered things that built upon other previous things and yet, as to my spiritual life I've found MORE a blending and growing overtime rather than a turning away from or releasing myself from initial spiritual concepts. I, definitely, have a greater understanding of life. I am not religious, although I have been and for that I am in great appreciation. *The Art of Appreciation* provided the basics of the Law of Attraction that remains constant. You can read the MORE Book without having read *The Art of Appreciation*, although it is the solid foundation on which *The Art of Appreciating MORE,* became.

I love people and I am so happy thinking about society and the way Humans behave, yet I am not terribly social. There is a world of difference between wanting to be with people and actually being with people to fulfill self-comfort and needs, especially during the COVID Pandemic. I love people and I think I need people. Yes, I do need people. I do not need people for me to be happy though there are people who make me so happy. It is important for my happiness that others are happy too. I attract all types of people and many of my skills are sensitive to other people's emotional needs. I truly believe that that characteristic is also connected to my being a female, although if you argue the point that females are MORE sensitive than most males, I will put that down and accept whatever you think as right for you and what I think is right for me. The longer I live the less I identify with gender anyway, and, trust me, that is a very good place to finally achieve in a lifetime. I know that equality has nothing to do with gender, and I hope you do too.

The COVID time has rewarded me with such hopes and insights, into myself, of course, and also into my fellow Human Beings. This time of transitioning has been an eye-heart-soul-life-opening-experience for all of us. We are making it a better world for the experience. What I've discovered during this pandemic has been incorporated into this book, because it was held up in publication because of it and hence it became apparent that it was to be included into it as well. Who would have known!

There is no way in knowing accurately what percentage of the population around and across the Earth are Law of Attraction aware. It is apparent that many are sitting on the fence and come in and out of awareness of their self-thought and the implications regarding this knowledge. It must, by nature, be increasing, which is a very good thing for mankind. It is impossible for this awareness to decrease as once recognized, it cannot disappear, even if distracted from or forgotten from time to time. Curiosity, inquisitiveness and an eagerness to

learn are such wonderful inspirational directions and I am so much a willing student of life, hence, it comes easily to me and I wish this for others also.

I believe that this is an important Time of Transformation for Humans.

> *Human's biggest transformation is being conscious of what we are thinking, and the second biggest transformation is then taking personal responsibility for what we are thinking.*

The center of the More Book is the story of the Lavender Scarf. It enfolds the manner in which the Law of Attraction taught me manifestation which is an essential component of MORE. Learning how to manifest is an achievement that is accompanied by wisdom and strength. Revealing the connections to bring me wisdom are in the Lavender Scarf chapter. Wisdom cannot be handed over easily, hence the story assists.

I write often from the listening and hearing place Within[1] that I know to be My Inner Being's love. Across my personal decades, the Voice Within Me and what might be considered My Own Voice have leveled out and are MORE a genuine continuous Presence of Love, than something of or not of me. It is all of Me. There is a great freedom in this writing. I've improved my listening and I am (seriously) braver at sharing. We are all equals. I am hoping that this book will be well received. I thank you for reading it.

---

[1] Within: Within with a capitol W, is often used as a proper noun in this book. This Within is the Voice Within or my Inner Being (IB).

*The Art of Appreciating MORE*

# Table of Contents

*Chapter 1 Permeate & Radiate ................................................... 1-1*

*Chapter 2 What You Think Matters................................... 2-59*

*Chapter 3 Coincidence & Synchronicity ..................... 3-91*

*Chapter 4 The Path of Least Resistance................................ 4-129*

*Chapter 5 Appreciating Leverage............................................ 5-151*

*Chapter 6 Appreciating Relearning ......................................... 6-193*

*Chapter 7 The Manifestation of the Lavender Scarf............ 7-217*

*Chapter 8 Jury Duty Judgment Day ......................................... 8-275*

*Chapter 9 Appreciating Is a Tool ............................................. 9-297*

*Chapter 10 Appreciating Non-Physical Awareness........... 10-313*

*Chapter 11 Appreciating my Inner Being ............................ 11-343*

*Bibliography .................................................................................. 363*

x

*The Art of Appreciating MORE*

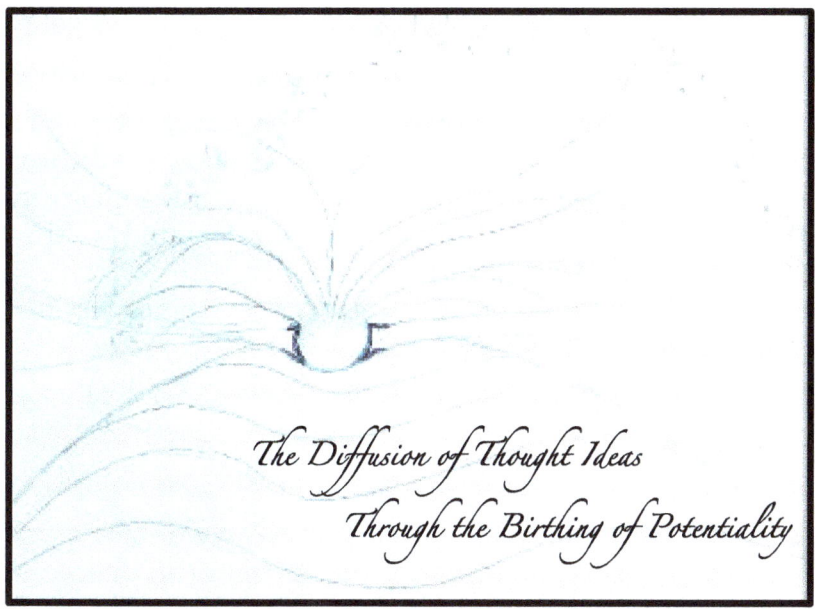

## Chapter 1  Permeate & Radiate

I appreciate the words *"Permeate & Radiate"* that came to me while in a lovely looming misty hillside garden near the sea in Ventura, California many years ago when I was much younger. I appreciate so much about this happening to me. It was a mild-weathered day. It was about an hour before the evening lights would dusk a cooler relief on this ancient slope. I cannot recall the date or month, or now, the year. I had been tending to my land-lording on our property there which was once upon a time a part of the Old San Buenaventura Mission Ranch Tract and held much settlement history and now and for years gone and to come, it was our family investment property. I felt healthy, responsible and alive with creative ideas whenever on this hillslope or in either of the two old houses that sat there for now longer than

a century. It was a beautiful enchanted property and from anywhere upon it or inside of its houses that were window-considerate, you could look out and down upon the bustling town of Ventura, the deep blue Pacific Ocean just down the street entertaining sail boats afar and the city pier with its fishermen and sea captivated walkers, and into the horizon you could see the untamed Channel Islands and beyond. The view could take your breath away. Often, actually more than seasonally, the early morning and late evening cool adventure-telling sea fog would forecast change and control over this land and all on it. It was where I was presented a visual visitation in the form of an optical aberration that appeared as a mighty, huge, and most beautiful Angel, probably an Archangel.

Its height and magnitude varied waveringly as if it was still becoming and it was ever-adjusting to the degree necessary for me to retain a clear enough focus to see it and, simultaneously, exchange a solid confidence, as in a two-way reassurance, that this was a very good, welcomed and friendly encounter to be happening. There was no fear on my part, only rather a calmness and quiet that felt as if time had entered slow-motion and then reframed "now" into a true-stop. Nothing else mattered. There was a continuum of mutual respect and love for something I currently did not have to completely understand to sense enough meaning into my reality and it, which began to feel more like a relationship than a substance, felt kindly familiar. My heart though, was beating faster and louder and my body was almost out of itself. Special moments in life are like that; providing for less than a full comprehension and delivering a great comfort and relief.

There were many things about this happening that seemed unusual, and at the same time, there arose a great admiration for this moment had seemingly finally come for my well-timed-astonishment, and I was willing, and it was a spiritual mystical blessing.

This softly illuminated vapor-like image, that was definitively a seraphic auroral form, gave to me, in an instance of a breath or a blink, the meaning of those words, "Permeate & Radiate". This knowing exchange wanted me to remember, these endeared words, as if they were keys that could unlock something I had forgotten. I just knew that it was agreed upon that these words could "trigger" a heightened enlightenment onto me. The understanding of it came in full essence as I fell dreamishly absorbed and helplessly floating to my knees and quite tenderly I planted myself to the earth in wonder, awe-frozen in the then, stilled-time, by this Graced Magnificence. Right there, where my knees met the earth, was adorned and woven a deep moist mossy growth that looked like a patch of rug made by nature. I intuitively knew this super-natural eternal entity well and this pure love, knew me well too.

I immediately came into a reverence and a refreshed clairvoyance, that empowered me to open-up and become more than I was. We walked my mind, heart and soul into this holy ground of gifting to me an awareness long overdue. I could not move, nor would I dare to do so, for this moment in time was orchestrated as much by me as by this Spiritual Being. I felt so pleased to have not missed it.

Much understanding and wisdom was conveyed to me in that time that I felt and witnessed this eternal love's presence. I was asked, rather than told, to allow these words into my heart and awareness;

> "Permeate and Radiate".

## Permeate & Radiate

To further inform me as to the direction I was to take to instill a practiced process of love into my life and onto those I would come to meet thereafter, I was gifted with a powerful appreciation of this knowledge, albeit, I knew there was much for me to follow-up on to satisfy re-direction.

I felt so honored. This great and loving Voice without verbal sounds, clearly told me internally and most profoundly to offer this knowing and sighting to others who might believe perhaps in Angels, and who might believe in more than what is most apparent. Most people only believe in what they can see and touch. This was a view of some kind of rare real light of love. I think most and myself included at times might have missed its substance and warmth.

In that, through many years, I was careful about to whom I told the story of receiving those words or about the warm light of this translucent Angel's Form upon me and only when I had confirmation of others their belief in Angels did, I attempt to describe my experience to anyone. It had to be perfectly timed and only when they held interest in knowing and open-minded enough to receive. Seemingly, only certain special people, to me, came to hear this story, although everyone I meet is special in many ways. They were required to be believers. I especially loved telling it to others when in that dreamy ancient hillslope garden. And make no mistake, that garden grew in miraculous ways and furnished the story with aromas and colors to affirm that heaven does exist on earth.

I also painted, on stones, those two words and strategically placed them, as reminders to myself mostly, in the general area of the garden, whereby I knelt and where this quasi-form floated effortlessly above me, such

# The Art of Appreciating MORE

that I was looking up into the sky long after it was no longer seen as there by me. Somedays, I would quickly and happily genuflect in that place or I would just stand there and absorb more love which lingers forever when awareness is touched into a heart. Love being invisible, was always there awaiting my arrival and receiving. It is always there still.

I now am given space and freedom to allow these Blessed Words into this book, to become available to all here, reading it, as such. Believe it or not, as you wish. What these words have come to mean to me have assisted in my life in great, positive and powerful ways. They teach and remind me, over and again, that change happens and, through change comes much joy and, in the experience of both; change and joy, it is completely my responsibility to create what I will. We are all endowed with this richness that is created from what we can know to see, if we choose to allow.

I did not know the meaning of, or ever before use the word "Permeate", when it was gifted to me on that fine holy day or holiday. A bright lighted blast of comprehension penetrated my heart with a familiar resonance that vibrated into a capsule of enlightenment that opened my ability to be still and hear. I felt, and it came to be true that, I would come about to grow with this word "Permeate", and that time would exemplify it for me, as I was ready to allow it into my knowingness, seemingly once again.

I felt that I previously had appreciated the meaning of Permeate, although, my life had drifted me away from consideration of its influence upon me through a faded memory and numerous life distractions. Right then, in that garden of soft twilight images and spiritually uplifting shapes that conveniently brought the misty comforting sea-fog along with it such that it could be camouflaged in plain sight, I was reminded rather than taught, and exactly on-time what I intended, with a little help from my friend, to embrace into my long-time life experience. It was a key.

Across a lifetime, I have felt Reminders, like this, although different, come to me to embolden my spirit to lift up my soul into the consciousness of my mind and to rise up. Often these Reminders are bestowed upon me when I have been demonstrating and becoming drenched or overwhelmed in self-doubt and in need for a boost of confidence.

Permeate was first interpreted to me in the thought of going through something to become a different something and perhaps even an improved something afterwards, such as the way water percolates through boiled water to become filtered through as desired coffee. Coffee still contains water, although, it is now coffee too. It is more than water. There was a process involved in the change too.

Radiate on the other hand was a word I felt very familiar with and used more often but not regularly. Permeate not so. They were now being provided to me together. They belonged together to create an essence, as there is no one word that can do that. Radiate is easier for me to comprehend as it is a glowing form of results that comes from within our own spirit, as is inspiration. Many people and many things Radiate. Heat and light radiate out from within places and/or Beings. The idea of Radiate has evolved through my years to mean more than it did on that day. It was close enough in my natural awareness that it blended immediately with Permeate. Many forms of Radiate can be seen as well as felt. It is beaming out. I have evolved in all ways and anew I become part of the process to Permeate and Radiate.

It came to me, so that I might grow.

I have adjusted my understanding of this process of deep spiritual consequences as;

*Spiritual Thought Diffusion.*

The combined results are seemingly more visual than what goes on during a permeation or even how something comes into a glow from not being a glow. In this understanding they, permeate and radiate, are joined as if married to each other in love and appreciation for each other's participation in influencing each other in positive manners. The Covid Pandemic is a permeation.

Permeating and Radiating includes the ability to change self to benefit what is outside of self. It is the perfect expression to introduce "Compassionate Awareness and Behaviors". All of mankind's changes and shifts are now involved in recognizing the responsibility to care about one another. There have been many signs of this need to alter our spirit of self by increasing the experiences of self, such that we can easily offer more of self to others who are ready, willing and able to receive. We need never concern ourselves with making another person; ready, willing and able. We are here to be aware of the consciousness of others and self and to be compassionate towards others. This is a benevolence we are each capable of implementing and encouraged to yield. Kindness is a goodness that touches the souls of

others. Kindness is a prerequisite to a participation of appropriate degrees of loving one another. The deeper the concerns of others, the wiser and stronger enlightened ones need to establish themselves.

At this time, with the quick essential requirements to change, we all can reposition our kindness to include identifying the changes that are part of our surroundings, in self and in others. Being "the change" you want to happen is a good thought that can stabilize the increased amount of changes that are here and to follow. When we surrender to the changes, we can learn to shift.

<u>We are going through Changes and are experiencing the miracle of the transformation into potentials.</u>

<u>And so, it is.</u>

*What is it that we can do to serve others in ways that are most meaningful?*

That is a good question to ask.

*The answer varies depending upon the life experiences we encountered and own at the time we perhaps are extending our skills, assets and desires to be of service to others. Charity is a hero's walk and we are all our own heroes in ways only we know. It is a good time to notice where you can make a difference in the lives of others and while allowing others to find their way without taking responsibility for them or away from them. That totally reminds me that one might restrain from given others advice, if they are not asking for it. A teacher can only gift a student knowledge if that student is wanting to learn.*

# The Art of Appreciating MORE

*To help anyone, is always connected to their truth in accepting assistance, rather than your willingness to be of service. If they are asking of you; it is most likely you have the answers they are looking for in a wise response. Likewise, when someone is asking for help and you can do so, it is most likely you have the ability to help. There is a pleasure in being part of the solution regardless of what you put into the mix to create it; if it is something of yourself that is good, if it is nothing that too is good. Do not judge yourself or others by the "service" rendered. Be thoughtful and kindness will follow. Caring appropriately for others is what compassionate consciousness is and we are being opened to this more readily. Know this is happening to you and to many others. Participate at your personal will and watch the way love grows for everyone.*

<u>Changing includes</u>
<u>Letting-Go and Moving-On</u>

Now quite a while ago, I felt a real impulse to move. Indeed, "impulse" rather than "inspiration", because it felt too uncertain to be an inspiration. Inspirations come about and when they do, they take hold of you. Inspirations are the best. This was not inspiration. There is a rich wondrous awakening when inspired. This felt a bit like that thought of "moving" was undermining my sense of habit and comfort. Like a teenager's opposing reaction toward authority's patterns given specifically to them and supposedly for them and their good; I felt unleashed and unwilling. It felt surprising, immature, and untamed.

Initially, I very much didn't want to think about it ever-less do it, especially not yet, and not now. I was comfortable where I was. I wondered how it got there, this feeling to move away to someplace else. I was very cozy, no I was more than cozy, I was cushy and plush-comfy in my house and home, life and times. It made financial sense to be here too, since over the years we invested wisely in updates and upgrades rendering a magnificence often the envy of our neighbors and friends for our effort and outcome. Truly, the value of our home was connected to its comfort and it had appreciated in value three times over. We could not seemingly ever afford a house like this were we buyers. Here we were living in it and it was grand. I was blank minded trying to determine why then I felt so strongly about leaving this obviously wonderful home for I was not sure of where it was or why I knew I'd eventually find a new and better way of living. I did find comfort in that though, not as my living-reality. It was but a thought with no evidence to back it up. I knew it to be part of my life and without doubt in my destiny.

I mentioned my unsettling feeling to my husband, Uri, and he didn't get it either. We loved this house of great times, memories, interesting stories and, most importantly, positive loving outcomes. We had so many successes living here for all these years. We raised our amazing children, who are now amazing young adults right here, and, we knew every inch of this place. It was a special evolved place that was our house and home. Neither of us had ever lived in one place as long as we had here where life was so dependable. Over the coming months, I could not deny that there was an increasing gnawing at my sense of stability, and I was beginning to notice things that were not at all on the surface of life that whispered; 'It is time to move on.'. This feeling will prove itself over and repeatedly over again to be a sampling of the great many changes that were to follow and that, incidentally, are to continue. We are all a part of what seemed initially a calling for me to follow. It felt so personal. Now, I must say that little did I know that I was included inside of a whirlwind of what can, looking back, be sort of temporal in nature and while universal. This message telling me it was time to move on, felt imperative.

What? "No", I was so content here. Everything after all these magical near thirty years was in place and all place was where it was supposed to be. I loved each season here, each memory here, every morning here and I was securely brought into my safe clean comfy bed each night feeling a wonder of joy and grace for this life, we had created here. This house was of abundant joy and great comfort. This house and property gave us the familiar streams of light that we knew as if a part of ourselves. Our fruit trees, that were planted many years ago, were rich in harvest and bearing so much goodness and timeliness. It was so; the moment I needed a lime, orange, lemon, avocado, guava, tomato, or many other garden living freshness', it was there bringing me and my cuisine great health and pleasure. Everything here was in order and thriving, but perhaps me for these insistent thoughts of moving-on. I was not even too certain if that was it either. I felt great and I had a lot of confidence in myself. What was going on? Something, but, what?

I loved my house and home. I knew Uri loved it too. Why then, did I also feel an odd and novel liberated emotion of noticing and an apparency, like a twitch, towards why it was time to prepare to move? No! I love it right here. Please, I so want to stay. The feeling to move grew stronger and stronger and now it was just there all of the time. In a matter of about as much as six conflicted months, I had turned the corner on resistance, and I knew I had to move. It is the perfect definition of the Law of Attraction and the way what you think about continues to grow until there is an inevitable results and direction. I felt a fight within that was taking me over and making me realize that I had choices and I had direction, and I needed to recognize what was what and I was required within myself knowingness to reduce my stress and fight and be less stubborn. As I mentioned, Uri didn't get it either. As while I was already fighting within myself, we even began to, not argue, but converse about it and it yielded it more attention. It was an uncomfortable time although looking back at it, I'm so glad it happened. As time wore me into submission and great difference, I started taking myself and my feelings more positively and seriously.

Was this that "mid-life crisis" one hears about?

*No, I didn't want to go.*
*Yes, I wanted to stay.*
*No, I could overcome this thought of moving on.*
*Yes, I can be open to the possibility.*
*No, there is too much to let go of here.*
*Yes, I can change.*
*No, I am so used to everything here.*
*Yes, changes are healthy and natural.*
*No, I do not want to change.*
*Yes, I have to find out more about these feelings.*
*No, I like it here.*
*Yes, I can open my mind and heart to just take a look at this idea.*

It went on and on like that for what seemed like a long time. It went back and forth. Eventually, I felt momentum.

*The Art of Appreciating MORE*

Therefore, when I did give into this feeling, I started to see things that I didn't think I wanted to see. I addressed discontentment more and more often. I was discontent and I knew I needed to feel more content. I needed to feel happier. I noticed that I started to feel happiness when I thought about an alternative future. Different things around me triggered me to think more deeply and that opened my perspective of the life and surroundings that I had so truly, until then, come to feel a certain amount of pride in having created over these many years. I was secure, and even though in that knowing I was now detecting that security, and some of the other valued components that made up my environment, might not be enough to carry me into and through my next and last thirty or More years. Still, how could I ever change all this life into a new one. Indeed, I wanted to live in a secure and safe place. There were some overlining factors towards managing and maintaining happiness that were surfacing as priorities that needed to be re-addressed. After all, these arriving years are to be our Golden Years. We were getting ready to retire. That's a big change. I loved it here though. I did feel an unsettlement in the almost over-familiar place I called home.

It didn't start out of any reason I could realize, for if it did, I surely would have corrected it as promptly as possible, as I had been doing all these years. If I was feeling this need to change my lifestyle, there had to be something wrong with me. Perhaps this was happening because I was not working a nine to five job, having agreed to stop working now. In other words, I had voluntarily taken an early retirement. In my professional working years, I was often called a catalyst for change. I

adapted quickly and energetically to new technologies that were in the forefront of application. I loved the latest ways to do software engineering and designs. I was a master at computer technologies, languages and methodologies. I loved to implement new ideas and I loved to discover new and better ways of software engineering. And now, although the situations that made my leaving my last job made a lot of sense, things were different and perhaps a job could occupy my wandering thoughts. Over time, though it proved impossible to actually find any type of job, so maybe I was suffering for a lack of being needed. I was too old and too experienced, but that's another story. The big story here is that I was changing the way I felt about where I was living and I knew the reasons had more to do with other things, albeit, being home now gave me more freedom and time to think about my life course from now on.

I loved my house though and I had remained satisfied living here for many years. We seemed to always make it work and to improve living here throughout all these years. If we needed a new faucet, doorknob, light fixture, garden fence, coat of paint, or even on a grander scale a new kitchen, bathroom, or convenience, we would just do it. We were always changing our environment to suit the changes we were experiencing in our lifestyle and interests, and it had worked so well. We experienced meaning for us to permeate and radiate in our lives. We changed to suit needs and desires and there was a joy in so doing. Our results were positive, and our path was positive, as well. One is connected to the other. I felt there were only a few changes left here to correct, and small they were, hence, it felt like a perfect place to stay. So why, as I started to conjure-up thoughts of being someplace else that I felt, though, where I might go would be better for me and for us. Was this a midlife or even later than midlife crisis? Could I just put these thoughts aside and go on here? Uri was not fond of them either. He didn't feel a need to move. Nor were our children happy with my thoughts of moving out of the house they loved and grew up in. This place represented stability and joy, family and love to them, and to me too. I kept feeling stronger and stronger about making a move to this illusive someplace better.

I was spiraling inwards and outwards, like breathing in and out, somehow feeling I belonged somewhere else and that this was the time to begin the momentum of changing or pivoting towards it, although I also felt that it didn't make sense to uproot and additionally, I felt there was no rush. Hence, I didn't know how to actually go with it. I didn't know how to flow towards it.

I was wise enough to know that if I could allow and be happy, direction would come. I felt I would know the steps to take to accomplish this, what was feeling more and more like a need rather than a choice. I could feel the massive amount of energies it would take to move-on, and I felt tired even before starting. I kept saying to myself that if it is meant to be, I would find my way easier. I wondered if I had enough energy to actually create in this no-place-in-particular direction and I had no idea where to start in addition to being reluctant about it. I thought we were to spend the rest of our lives living right here in our comfortable house and home of our past wonderful family years. We had been designing it to serve us well in our older years. We thought it would be a great place to retire.

As time went on, a thought developed as bits of pushing me forward thoughts. I had pulls on me to stay and now I began to feel pushes on me to get out of this place. My InnerVoice reminded me that it is a wonderful state of being emotionally to be at, to love where you are before moving on. It was not because I didn't love what I had; it was because I loved myself enough to let it go. Moving-on was so filled with wonder to me, because I know that my thoughts and feelings were good and appreciative so why then did, I begin to see and feel things changing.

I would look at our neighboring houses and notice that many had actually changed-out more recently, for newer and younger families with smaller kids and babies and seemingly there were larger households which was a sign-of-the-times in California as houses cost a lot of money; above the average price in the USA. The immediate households, more often, reflected a new family model. I'd look around and I would think that I did not want to grow old here. I felt this in the same vibration as I had when I recalled as a younger me thinking that I didn't want to grow up to be like my parents. I am so me and not anyone else. I am unique and as much as others are too. I didn't have to stay here for the rest of my life. I could permeate and radiate from here to there. I also felt, though I had no proof, that there was someplace better suited for us.

A change happened, and I started to notice reasons to leave. It was not friendly enough for me to stay here for the rest of my life. Soon enough Uri would retire, and I was home full time now and this neighborhood was on the hillside where it was hard to take a walk especially as we would get older when walking would be most valuable for wellness and we would have more time, after Uri's retirement to take walks and to take on activities that did not depend on the hours either before or after normal working hours. Again, like other times, we found an easy solution to continue loving where we lived and drove to the park or the ocean front promenade to take our early evening constitutional

# The Art of Appreciating MORE

walks, even now prior to Uri's retirement. Our walks were so enjoyable, and the environment was so beautiful, the weather was generally mild, and the scenery was natural and pleasant. We both held a sense of pride that every house in this above-average priced hillside 70ies tract housing area was looking-pretty and well-kept, even manicured. Still after so many years of living there I didn't know much at all about my neighbors and no one recognized us.

I began noticing that we could be a better match to our neighbors and friends. I might say that my closest neighbor, would sometimes hide from conversation and avoid just the typical coincidental meeting each other as we both started to bring our garbage bins down from our houses to the street on those night before pickups. One evening, Uri was taking the bins down as I sat at my desk which included a magnificent ocean horizon view off of the hillside, actually breath-taking, and also included seeing the side area fence and gate of our neighbors right across the street. She was standing in her bin area and was unlocking her gate when I noticed she looked up and into the direction where Uri was opening up our side gate to bring down the bins for tomorrows pickup. I thought that it will be nice to see them greet each other. To my complete surprise I saw her quickly back up, close her gate, lock and hide from Uri's view. It was the weirdest sight to understand could happen. We were both always so polite and supportive of this neighbor who we knew for nearly thirty years. She was not unfriendly towards us ever, or so it seemed. We were friends. We had dined with her and her husband. She had witnessed some documents with a notary at our house. We had sat with her and her husband in their kitchen chatting or our living room and enjoying each other's company many times. We knew and loved each other's grown children. Go figure, here she was hiding from Uri. I saw that for a reason. Things go on in one's personal life sometimes that we really don't want to share with our neighbors or friends. I felt a sense of rejection or lack of interest. I, also, felt a bigger sense of alignment and clarity being conjured up. Perhaps, the actual reason she might be avoiding us was that her husband and also our friend was diagnosed with a form of cancer that was hard to combat, although he was fighting for his life and she was alongside of him fighting their living cause together. We didn't though know this was happening on that day. Now he is gone, and she has uprooted just prior to be near their son, and his family. They would rent their house across the street eventually. *Oops,* I am getting ahead of myself.

It was a good neighborhood. It also was pretty reserved from developing neighborly friendships. The landscapes and lot lines were difficult to connect to your neighbor's directly. Every house had a fairly large approximately one-half acre lot. The properties were on progressively higher or lower spaces relative to each other. I think so many neighborhoods are like that all over the USA. It's not that we don't like each other, it is we do not have or take the time to get too involved with each other's lives, so avoidance is the best behavior to take-up and keep not giving to each other friendships. There are already a lot of connections between people at work or school, so home tends to be a little more personal and void of neighbor drama. It seemed weird to me that there were a lot of people around, yet few to speak to or actually know.

After I stopped working and started to go into my retirement time, I recognized that staying home could be a lonely place to be. Fortunately, I knew how to keep myself "busy". One of my last jobs was a remote work experience, so I had acknowledged the importance of being independent from others. In fact, that job's title was; Independent Verification and Validation Agent. I worked on my own and directly reported to a Naval Captain. Now, there is a bunch of ego. Shall I continue! I knew how to do things on my own and I liked it. The biggest thing I got interested in doing was learning to love myself and learning that made me know that I was never alone or lonely. Not really. In my self-appreciation I became more and more aware of my appreciation for everything surrounding me. On a scale of one to ten, I was at least a nine-point-five in the happiness range.

Our family house, there on the hillside with its magnificent open ocean view that contained so much to delightfully daydream into for so long was a perfect place to raise our family, to be creative in the garden and hillslope, to manage successful careers, to host parties, and to be happy together. As I mentioned, initially, it was hard to find concrete reasons to move. We had incrementally prepared this house to serve us for the rest of our lives. We were getting older. Our house was a ranch style house and we converted two of the bedrooms into one large airy office for us to set up our computers and a conference area and a supply area. It was a well thought out office that we could share for many years to come. It could accommodate the future.

That is how it was then and looking back I know that my feelings about moving started as little thoughts that were a bit uncomfortable and seemingly unnatural. They grew, and I thoughtfully managed them such that I could be more of a participant than being pushed or pulled, and, hence, I became invited into being a deliberate creator by these circumstances. I was, indeed, permeating and radiating. It took three years to find our retirement house and home. We did it. And in so doing time came and went and once again, changes happened.

# Permeate & Radiate

I am ever grateful for the coming into knowing and appreciative of the timing and the miracles along the way.

Wisdom influences logic with a resulting of a better understanding. We did, along the way, agree, eventually, to take the journey to move-on. It took some time to compile our journey after reaching what felt like could be a new and adventurous goal. Time is a re-newished-entity once wisdom acquires a domination within thoughts and, of course, physical direction. Being alive longer does make its benefits known only as much as the wisdom of experience is encouraged to surface with a strength that provides clarity. Wisdom only comes to those willing to embrace its knowledge. In other words, not all older people are wise. We are!

Many find the surrender into wisdom far too adventurous and deny wisdom to benefit their increase. And so then, what are the influences wisdom, knowledge and experience have on willing people? If you are interested in being wise or if you are looking for the communion with your similar-minded compatriots, then you are in the right place. Firstly, in acknowledging this arrival within (which is the coming to know you are wise), one can begin to address the uneasy feelings of approaching the unknown with a more trusting directing authority. Wise people are less influenced by the ways they previously felt to be part of a well-defined destiny. Wisdom comes from the asking. Ask for it and want it.

I am a wise person. In fact, I am a very wise person. I am wiser than ever and growing wiser daily. I love this me, who shatters the wisdom's of my ages into this amazing

## The Art of Appreciating MORE

world I am so very wise to take ownership of as mine. I am now, more on my own than I ever was before now. And by that, I mean that it is me who is thinking for myself more of the time. I have freedom to think. I have and continue to let go of other's thoughts for me to think, behave or become what they want of me. I find less regulations in my choices and behaviors and I am less concerned with the right or the wrong of my path. I am wiser in knowing that it is all really very good and simple. Some might be turned-off to such a self-conversation as if braggadocio and to them I say, that attitude of thinking about another person as conceited or boastful, is more from your ego justification. It is good to construct oneself in positive ways and, it is true that the more you appreciate the more to appreciate comes into your life. Hence, when appreciating yourself, trust me, more to appreciate about yourself will rise to notice. It's a good thing. Let it come to you. Be unashamed to confront your value and your increasing value. My InnerVoice reminds me to identify with what is my worthiness. That is a worthwhile focus. Learning to love oneself, being appreciative of oneself and knowing one's worthiness are all specific and unique relational states of being. To permeate through these life-gifting aspects of self-awareness relinquishes wisdom that radiates into others through self. It truly provides trusted direction.

My feelings count. Mistakes are ridiculous to believe in. I am as perfect as I can think myself to be and the more readily, I apply that type of non-judgement to myself, and for the record to others, as well, the more I enjoy the journey I am on and the more I appreciate others their journey's too. I am free to be me. I think I have always felt my freedom. Now I know my freedom better. It is an awareness of self. I've always been free. I constrained my freedom into the freedom society dictates as being just enough. I kept an acceptable freedom. I lived the permitted amount of freedom. I've learned that freedom defines acceptability not the other way. I no longer feel constraints. I, as so too you, were born with this freedom I now activate into my life-stream with a greater confidence, and not, may I add, a moment too soon. I am so fortunate that I am young enough to appreciate this characteristic about myself in a time space large enough to create so much more than I've ever thought I could. Most valuable is that my creations are easier and in-balance with what I want to be focused upon.

For example, I am Happy, Healthy, Wealthy, Worthy and Wise now. I am enabled to quantify these aspects of my life as well. I could say that I am More Happy, More Healthy, More Wealthy, More Worthy and More Wise and that is More accurate. In that quantity, I have chosen to be "More than enough" Happy, Healthy, Wealthy, Worthy and Wise. I have identified the range of the quantity to be More than enough. More wasn't enough and enough didn't expand on the More, hence I am more than enough. I have more than enough. I overflow with more than enough. I love that space in all the forms of abundance that I appreciate into my life. I only want More than Enough. Some want far too much; I want and have More than Enough. And so, it is.

Uri and I eventually both became equally inspired to move from our Family Home, and from our jobs of long threads and actually retire, as it is known. We are less satisfied with the word retired because it seems like a 'tired again' type of sounding word. It sounds like it must be time to go to sleep as the youthful ones can take care of themselves without any of our assistance. When thinking deliberately about it, it, retirement is something else, if you want it to be. It is that we have figured out how to live with a plentitude of more than enough and without the need of having a job working for someone else. We advocate to all younger people, spend time and thought, planning and creating your retirement years to be financially sound and prepare the way by living a happy life and by creating a vision of joy and freedom into your retirement years. The earlier you can retire, the better, although we didn't realize that until we did it and for some, perhaps retirement is something that declines their understanding of self-worth. Some people feel busy is important. I discovered that it is easier to be busy, than to decide to be happy. In our adaptive retirement expressions, busy became an understanding that holds onto something make-believe and self-important. Now, retirement is more like a freedom rather than a finishing-up of something or other because of being tired of life or life is tired of your contributions. Retirement is a great freedom although with freedom comes responsibility. With retirement you can re-evaluate your wellbeing. Every aspect of life changes and changes are good for people. Time is your friend in retirement and once you retrain yourself to appreciate this amazing freedom without feeling guilty for achieving it, well, the sooner you can apply into your life this amazing personal freedom to be more yourself. I imagine the same feeling comes from having wealth and, to be honest, in designing our retirement years successfully it was good to consider ourselves wealthy. Be wealthy by design or default and retire into doing what utilizes your strengths. It is important to allow yourself the space to design even more freedom into your new space and to know you can do, be or have anything you want in life. In retirement we are more aware that we are responsible for our own happiness. We are wanting a new word to define our classification in this society and retired is too extinguishing. We are still seeking a better way to speak of retirement;

Independently wealthy seems to fit. Although our wealth is something other than only money it is self-propelled joy.

We are alive with a desire to participate in doing what we really want to do. And although it took three years to find the place we did and retired into, it was a long and wonderful arrival and it was still perfectly timed. All together we are so excited about our outcomes. In the days, weeks, months and years that we felt momentum often wobble us about, until when we knew this was it, it was a time to learn to trust in self-direction. All during our relocation journey we said things to each other and our children, who were on their own yet who were very curious, if not concerned, about our courageous changes that we seemed, perhaps from the outside, to be forcing upon ourselves, we'd say things like;

> "We will know it when we find it." or
> "It's coming our way soon.", or
> "We just know we have to keep searching because we know we will find our way."
> "We know that everything is working well for us."

Oh, and we really felt the truth in those feelings. We had faith in our journey, and we knew the outcome would be great. We were creating our future and it was usually fun. We knew this uncertain future was a perfect unfolding. Additionally, it was, without a doubt, an improvement over what otherwise was to be the environment of our coming up years. There were times of doubtful wonder, though, we knew above all doubt-leanings that, of course, we are in a momentum of finding. We knew to continue seeking and the only part of not finding what we wanted that bothered us, was that we were not allowing it faster by wanting it to hurry up.

We were also learning to appreciate all aspects of the journey. Yes, we knew it would work out. We seemed to be wanting for it to happen faster, even knowing our slightest apprehension or impatience brought forth their own ramifications, usually delaying things a little, which in turn we appreciated. Our timing is always perfect, even in a desire to reach goals. And let me explain, these ramifications from impatience or doubt, were from someplace other than guilt for our behavior or thoughts. These were ramifications that were intended to assist us into the best results. The ramifications began to blend themselves into the solution. It seems easier now to take control of "doubt" by turning away from it as soon as recognized. We had this opportunity on-hand to practice controlling our thoughts into more pleasant outcomes, than learning where we did not want to relocate. Once we were on the decidedly relocation path, which took a few years to totally commit to, the momentum was unstoppable and although encouraging with good feelings was also filled with bumps. We found in the adventure many things and many feelings along the way. It was a brilliant time to discover our connection to Source and to allow. It is, after all, the journey rather than the goal that proves in the final analysis most valuable.

I will start at that place where we were before finding ourselves comfortably resituated and take you also on our journey. I intend, gently, that you will experience this journey of ours with your own experiences loosely-coupled to and around ours; for we are all so much more like each other than not. I sincerely believe that experience is our greatest teacher, and still, reading and comprehending what others do is a vicarious experience and can assist in judging your own direction choices by judging others theirs. It is a good thing to incorporate into experience. We all share so many of the same desires and dreams and perhaps even in that thought we can actually sense that oneness, so much like glue holding our civilization together. Value in this reading is the knowing that within that belonging of oneness there is the individual spirit that shapes and shades our most prominent urges to travel our own way. Our uniqueness is the flavoring of humanity that makes us so colorful in all ways, that contrasts us next to each other and that influences us in ways we can only appreciate truly if we understand the vibrational gifts of wellbeing, we all contain. We are all very intelligent and capable. We are equals. Diversity is a strength.

We were so much smarter together, Uri and I, regarding the deliberate path we could arrange into existence in our goal to move-on and out of Ventura, California. Initially, it was a complicated idea and it consumed us into many hours of appreciation creations followed by writing messages from our Within, which guided us along our path to learning where to move and also learning so much more about ourselves. I will write about our systematic route, incrementally, as I know it was easier for us to utilize the processes we did and sharing them with others will assist in refining what already proves to work well. To assist me in defining our process, which could very well work for others, I placed "Appreciation Statements" that I think of as mine at the end of each chapter of this book. Perhaps it will assist you to do the same and experiment with conjuring out of yourself statements that feel like that Voice within is talking to you about. Regardless of what your goal might be at any given space and time, this process can work well. For us it was finding a place to move to where we might well enjoy many years to come.

Emotionally, it is a big step to move after thirty years, or even five years. I think that life choices are always affording everyone the option to grow, or not, but mostly to grow, and, life choices, likewise, are always affording everyone the opportunity to grow easily and in joy, or not. It is always a personal choice. Life doesn't have to be hard. We each can adjust our thinking to appreciate that fact into personal existence and then see the difference in the paths that open. The pandemic insisted we change. We had to do so. It was easier to agree with the COVID changes. And changing too doesn't have to be so hard. That is good to know as the things that we can depend upon staying the same can assist us to experience deep stability. Choosing to move-on actually brought with it a deeper respect for our willingness to enter the unknown, knowing all is good.

Mostly everything is constantly changing, hence developing stability within the constancy of change is valuable too and holds a degree of stability in us being aware of those changes. The momentum is free-forming and although many aspects of change feels like the same thing to us, such as the rotation of the planets, or the solidity of the Earth, in truth, they are always moving slightly differently than the moment before and after now, and so it will always be. Things change and in many ways. The global virus was proof of that fact. There are only a few permanent things that do not change in our time space reality and they are really important to reflect upon and often. This cannot be overstated. They are the grid of our posture and grace.

## My List of Constants:

1. I AM, YOU ARE and WE ARE.

*Permeate & Radiate*

I sincerely believe that this is imbedded deep within all souls, whether known or not. Acknowledging the existence of self, others and our being here together is a constant entity form of reality. Although we may not be here, as such someday since we and others "die", that is the point I am trying to make. We are everlasting souls who are here now as we know ourselves and others to be. In being an everlasting soul, we continue after death. You do not have to know that YOU ARE in order for me to know that I AM. Knowing or not doesn't change what is. If you believe that you are always going to be you in some form, you can believe that is a dependable constant. We are eternal Soul Beings. That is such a steadying thought for me to remember and reflect upon often. It feels so good to believe in that and although I have no way to prove it as so, I have no way to disprove it either. I have chosen to believe this mainstay of my life. I also feel the truth of it. It resonates with me. I sometimes feel messages received by me stating that in being a Human Being in this particular time, I cannot even imagine the total me that I am. Our Human minds cannot perceive that size ordination. However, I can accept that as probable. I am unable to fathom the grandness of myself and or others, all being equal and equally capable, I can appreciate that I AM. I can expand that in good faith that; YOU ARE and WE ARE too.

We also, are each capable of knowing more of our greatness, if we only really knew how. Sometimes I feel that "stretching" my self-awareness is a vital exercise for improved health and understanding. Taking a few moments daily to sense, as much as possible, our grandiose-ness is a prodigious form of posturing ourselves into a better future. It is a simple thing to do, and while some might view this exercise as a selfish one, remember that while most everything is changing and if you can possibly change the constants in your life to be strengthened in understanding on a personal level, then appreciate that reflecting upon self-existence is a very special capability we each have, not to reset constants, rather to strengthen our personal awareness of our constants.

## 2. The ONE is the ALL and the All are the ONE.

To me, we indeed are part of the ONE also, everyone and thing is of the ONE. For me, this ONENESS constant makes it easier to love one another and to treat each other as we want for others to treat us. We are connected and together in this constant. Wherever our inter-personalities conflict negatively, that is a cause of being unaware and there are still many, too many, particulars that separate us from homogeneously respecting our ONENESS, and, in fact, it is impractical to anticipate that everyone is into this ONENESS concept. It is okay, yet, in this statement of my understandings of constants, I respect what others feel too. We do not have to hold ONENESS as our personal believe to respect others do or not. It's not a judgement call. It is a position that I take. I am not going to attempt to convince anyone to believe as I do. We each have choice. We can learn and react to indifference by purely accepting that there are wondrous reasons why we see and evaluate things uniquely. It is not so that we can have negative conflicts, and it is not so that we can have positive conflicts, it is more so that we do not judge another for being different. We are all equals. We are all unique. We are all uniquely equals.

It seems apparent to me that Humanity is experiencing a shift in our consciousness that includes mindfulness of each other. It began prior to COVID, which has stimulated shifting. I feel the shift personally and I observe it in others also. We can look forward to a higher consciousness of mankind, now or whenever. I certainly sense things leaning towards sometime in the not-too-distant future. I see and feel degrees of this daily in ways that feel reassuring. The shifting is not a constant, it is a momentum. The ONENESS is a constant and I suppose that if and or when more humans come into this knowing, then our abilities to change will increase in quality and quantity.

Be open-minded with yourself here and ask yourself about what the quality of interactions and respect for each other is required to look like when we are all here on Earth living in a world of peace, harmony, equality and kindness? It is a stretch of my imagination to see a new dawned civilization of significant harmony, although it is clear to me that changes do happen, and I experience them, and I see them in others, and I stretch. Seemingly to me, we have to learn to get along with each other as we progress into an advanced thinking, advanced technological race of humans. Imagine the year 3000. What do you think it will look like? Will it look like some of those sci-fi movies where the Earth is scorched and broken, and its inhabitants are mean dirty raged warriors willing to kill whatever moves in front of it for survival? I am thinking something else is happening. I am a great optimistic person, and I am a logical person and for the life of me I cannot imagine devastation on Earth. I can only envision a lot more harmony and kindness than we now experience. And even in my view of today's world, I see a great more goodness than is available on television, news, social media, internet etc. I do see a lot of exaggerations and down wrong lies. That will have to change. I believe in that premise. We can start by knowing self as an equal to every other Human Being.

*The Art of Appreciating MORE*

How can we do that? Now I ask you to think instead of a world in turmoil think of a world, and in the reasonably near future, where we are all interested in pursuing equality. We already know how to obliterate the planet and haven't. I am thinking there is a good chance we collectively want to improve Humanity. We are all working out the details as to how this happens. It's an image that we do not collectively focus too long upon because it feels odd, whereas thinking that sci-fi image is easier to think longer upon. That is a direction that can easily change and change the hearts of thoughts. Trust that Life, as we know it, is changing and into this betterment and then your choices are well aligned. You no longer have to be intimidated by being a kind person. It is the only choice that makes sense. All other directions will either come to acknowledge this or it will take longer to arrive at a higher collective consciousness. There are many facets to existing in a momentum of collective creative changes and they all start with you. You must first know your own equality and in so immediately you know others their equality.

Loving one another is a major component obtained through knowing the constancy of equality. We are all equal is a slight variation on ONENESS as a collective assumption. The changes that come to us that will eventually add up to the shifts in awareness, is to be distinguished from what ONENESS is; for love is in each aspect of all that is. To acknowledge this constant, many will be in respect for each other the way we are, not the way we want others to be. As I have said before, not knowing doesn't change the fact that we are ONE to believers. It is far better for each ONE of us to appreciate that option is valid to some, rather than deny this amazing connection and to appreciate that some do not see it and that is really the way the pieces of harmony are. It is not right or wrong for some to believe in

ONENESS and others not to believe in ONENESS. It is not the way it is known to be with religions, whereas you are a believer or not and if not, the believers will want for you to believe. If believed in or not, this ONENESS connection provides a certainty, to believers, that strengthens collective achievements and has no impact on non-ONENESS believers. ONENESS is not like the Borg from Star Trek, we are more like the Oak Tree, building branches of growth in the ONE that forms. Beyond natural thoughts, we are not anything like an Oak Tree, for we can change more thoroughly and quickly. There will probably never come a time when everyone believes in ONENESS. That's okay. There is enough goodness in life to be aware of different realities. We can respect our differences and restrain from judging others who are thinking differently. It is intended, as such. That is Love.

3. The Law of Attraction.

To me, the Third never changing thing is The Law of Attraction which stays forever the same in behavior and availability, although I am constantly learning more about it, so it seems bigger rather than different to me over time. Before I knew of it, it was there too; I just didn't know what it was and how to recognize it. The Law of Attraction is a simple knowing, only once realized, which is; "What you think about; you bring about, what you put out; you get back." The Law of Attraction was the hardest of the things that never change, for me to comprehend and appreciate, oh and then, apply into my life more deliberately. I think it is because there is so much dimension in its interaction with everything. When discovered and loved in appreciation and desire to know it better, it yields a gentle wisdom without of which I am only running my engines in slow motion and unattached to my potential and my manifestations as holy amazing.

This book is all about the Law of Attraction because there is not one simple way to express it into a learning caption that approaches its complex entwinement in all our lives. Sometimes it is through telling the stories and adventures, feelings and ideas, that the Law of Attraction can be better explained. Personally, coming into my very first awareness of the Law of Attraction has changed me forever and for that, I am in great appreciation.

4. Everything Else Changes.

The fourth stabilizer that I depend upon remaining the same all of the time is that; all else, except for those three previously mentioned things, are always and forever changing.

Change whatever you think you will to change. The mentioned first three constants, are the framework of life itself to me. They form a structure that is solid, and I am so grateful for coming to know this so clearly and sincerely. As clear as it is to me, I am certain I will come to know it better with more experience. You do not have to know everything about everything or anything at all. To know the fundamental Laws of the Universe will yield a great sense of confidence and bring about More as a result. Know also that all humanity is on a constantly changing unknown journey. The future is ours to create. It is our adventure.

When times, things, situations and thoughts seem hampered and dulled by the "now" that is being experienced, it is extremely helpful to remember that everything else is changing and so too now will fall into the future-now one second into the next. We cannot hold on too long to now, without refreshing our instant of being alive in this time space reality. I am experiencing a great joy in meditation in the now, however, and promote daily glimpses into that space where now brings to us itself. Meditation and quiet thoughts can promote a connection. The more one exercises meditation, the quicker one can obtain that relief of joining into the now. I, however, recommend meditations be short and sweet, refreshing and revealing. I feel that having "no thought" is good for self to approach, stand in it and then allow "all thought" to come into place. Meditation is dynamic and concurrent with the natural love gifted us through our desire to know. Experiment with meditation. It should be personal and, of course, changing. Breathing in thought for breath itself is a doorway into meditation experiences.

Beyond the unchanging aspects of life identified above, we, personally, can still only change the way we look at life as it occurs and understand, or not, life as it happens. Note that we can create into our lives that which we choose relating to the future. As, such, humans have found the ability to open our minds to more and more possibilities while recalling what was constant to lean upon and help us stand the way.

Law of Attraction creative minds also discovered, much to our amazement seemingly, that we could not get life wrong and that when we experienced coming into knowing what we did not really want, we began immediately upon a new invigorated journey segment as a result of that happening or coming to realize. This concept was, to me, a great relief. I felt more responsible to be less concerned with outcome. It was like taking steps away from where we could not fit ourselves comfortably and then taking a step into where we thought we could find out if we actually did fit.

Of course, even by definitions known, "the unknown" is constantly changing too - or so it would seem. We don't know what we don't know, and we don't know the unknown. That's the point of the unknown. Timing can become a friendly instrument in which one can evaluate the essence of experience. Intuition can apply here vigorously for some, yet, the unknown is exactly unknown, which is more or less of something or other. Walking into the unknown with full intent to know our way through places that might well be described as the cobwebs-of-the-mind more than not the right places, is the adventure. We could, in some varying diverse aspect, and in a growing part once understood, delineate our choices into our future in many subtle and rewarding ways. We know what things, rules, understandings, laws, change and which ones were always and forever constant. This is a great advantage especially put into practice.

All in all, our interests were zeroing in on what we favored and that yielded us insight as to what next to try out and test for true. We had so many years of minor changes required from us, whereas, our decisions were involving our daily needs. Here we were, rearranging our entire lives. The biggest mystery began by changing focus from finding a perfect place to be, to being in a perfect place emotionally to journey forth. We knew to feel good and then move-on. That remains a constant in many ways for us to take comfort in, as it is part of the Law of Attraction. We were pretty darn happy with our

## Permeate & Radiate

lives when we uprooted and due to that, we were bound to find a pretty happy future.
Abraham-Hicks[2] says;

> *"You cannot have a happy ending to an unhappy journey."*

or put in positive clarity;

> "You can discover happiness when you are happy."

If you are unhappy you will more easily reap more unhappiness. We were happy where we were and now, we wanted to change things, and we wanted to be and stay happy too.

"Hold true to what you are doing."
"Trust your instincts."
"Stay the Course."
"Go for it."

All seemingly good advice to appreciate and relate into experiencing.

On the other hand, I was brought up to believe that if something wasn't broken, why fix it. Nothing was broken and nothing needed to be fixed. It was that everything seemed to be ready to graduate from or ready to say it was finished. We had accomplished what we wanted to do. We didn't want to change the world, we wanted to discover what the world had in store for us. We are people who have for all of our lives wanted to improve

---

[2] Wikipedia says that Abraham-Hicks Esther Hicks (née Weaver, born March 5, 1948) is an American inspirational speaker and author.

*The Art of Appreciating* MORE

our lives and meet up with our resulting efforts to seek after more. Our direction of changes was to increase our happiness. This is the opposite of what politicians are doing, albeit they have convinced the majority of people otherwise. Politicians try continuously to fix what is really not broken. In fact, politicians habitually break things, insist you notice and request to assist them into breaking things more, and all this in order to have some type of what they think is control. There is coming a great and wonderful change in politics. It has to change because many more people upon finding their own choices appropriate and their own changes best for them will have less and less so a need to feel a dependency upon governments or politicians fixing their lives or any of their neighbor's. We can all do more to take responsibility for our thoughts, actions, and results. That is the best shift in our world from where we are currently. These changes and those shifts will be confusing and complicated for many people. Our changes will be different than our technological advancements, albeit we have a relationship with technologies and machinery that complements our improvements. Once increasingly more and more people find surer footing and turn the feeling of dependency into the glory of self-reliance, there will be a great parade of joy wobbling and wandering about for centuries to come. When we collectively accept and promote kindness, we will be rapidly on our way to a new form of society.

As changes happen and I find new needs I put myself into noting if I've thought about this or that change or desire enough to feel its direction required. When something comes about into my heart-mind that requires and, seemingly, or absolutely insists on my involvement, there is no stopping me from it. This is good, especially when I've contemplated it and its results. This is deliberate living.

It is a special mellowed-out and well-seasoned awareness to recognize this happening. It doesn't happen without looking for it to be there. I have free will and I get to choose my own thoughts. I am actually "being" that choice long before I consciously choose to be. There is then, within me, a truth of existence that awakens and rattles me into places that I must have agreed to be in, perhaps long before when I can remember. Otherwise, why would it feel so important and immanent.

In those special experiences, when being aware of them as different than because I am truly choosing total involvement and all my Being is taking me into it, almost over-willingly, I can begin to command my presence be rewarded more knowledge and wisdom for the orchestration and participation of the agreement itself. In that place, I find great love. *From where do I feel this great love?* From everywhere; inside and outside of myself. I feel loved by all that is. In my understanding that we are All One and in order to reap the benefits of doing what was mutually agreed into doing in another space of awareness, one must be enlightened to the open willingness as part of a destination of Oneness. We are more than we generally think we are. We are more than enough to do great things, to experience great things, to create greatness and to be aware of this status of life.

In other words, as I am here on earth longer and becoming wiser, I seemingly can detect more quickly and accurately, when something has gotten my attention very purposefully. I can, at that point, recognize that my giving-in to it can, if requested, provide additional options in which I can be more demanding or thorough, and I can request that the results be more beneficial to me. I ask for more wisdom. These places-of-diversion are gifts to play with too. The outcomes are flexible enough to manipulate or manifest as a participant in the creation rather than only being taken into the destiny-of-time. Being happy about the seemingly required exposures to life experiences and results, will indeed create happier results, and furthermore, being happy to participate can regulate the outcomes to include more of what is ultimately wanted. One, however, must be ready to receive more than enough or what is your defined enoughness.

It's an interesting proviso to register that result, the rewards to be made apparent to me, as part of more than I can control and still, now over, I am resolved to appreciate the love others have for me in so doing. It is a new path of Inner participation that I've become aware of in this wanting my giving-in to this Good-Golly-God-Force to lift me up and above what I previously understood. I love it so much. I know that when I appreciate something, even the slightest anything, within what otherwise feels like a contrast or wobble in my experiences that take me into a seemingly uncomfortable place or experience, I now search around for the goodness that grows from that experience sooner than I did before. It's a big step forward in creative and deliberate thinking. It might be less intuitive to wander my thoughts away from what is seemingly discomfort during the time I am in what is seemingly discomfort. This is a magic that can be a growth of opportunity to rise up faster and be in truer appreciation for all journeys I am experiencing. At this point in my life, if I am experiencing something that feels off, I now know that that "off-ness" is but my current interpretation of something wiser and more directly taking place to assist me along my way. I am not in fault. The experience is not in fault either. Others are not in fault. It is an intention playing out. Many people can accept that by now.

Things do work out. That is a grand wisdom in so having. What I am further experiencing is within that turning point of acceptance, there exists a space in which your personal desires have grown and knowing that, it is a very good time to request more understanding of it. I ask, believe and receive. This receiving includes more than I can possibly know, hence, it is an opportunity to be specific and how I deal with that is by asking, within the receiving, for a richer reward for my yielding back so much love to Source. Source loves me and I love Source. Between us there is a respectable relationship. I used to think Source, or God, only gave to me what I was ready to receive. I now understand that Source, or God, receives from me as well. When I am yielding to God, I am in Love with Life.

I ask, believe and receive and then in my receiving, I actually ask for more clarity. It is like I ask again and with more specifics. That quick conversation of desires coming forward during my receiving, is most connective and associates me with a bigger than self-creation momentum. I am so in love with the Source-Force and yes, I am so in love with myself. This Inner Connection is empowering and holy and everyone is enabled to experience this connection and any time we so desire.

When next you reach understanding regarding a "contrast" you are in, in that moment, speak to Source, I call it my InnerVoice, and talk it over and you will see that your part was very worthy. I'm less inclined to refer to this InnerVoice as God, however, many people relate to God as a higher Source, so when I refer to God, Source, or my Inner Being, it is all the same or a similar concept. I think the word God has been over-used and Inner Being is under-used. Source is a nice enough expression, albeit, when I ask for a name from my InnerVoice, it says it is that which has no name. Whatever serves you best to think about as that which has no name, in your awareness of your worthiness, it is well pleased and wants greatly to reciprocate with your new desires and needs, if but you will ask. Be then thankful and open yourself up to the riches that amount within your wanting to be a wiser and a gentler human.

We are all connected to each other in amazing ways and in these periodic surrenders into contrasts, which are always more enlightening than to struggle and wiggle a way through them in a fight to not be a player, I find a fulfillment of civility and a great love that goes in many directions and it arrives in total pleasure and personal satisfaction, the likes of which I've never known until now. It is, in so doing, I know of my greater Wisdom. Allowing is the receiving. We are either tuned into receiving or we are not. Either one, is available. Gift yourself the ability to receive and allow the love you deeply want, and you deeply are.

Being connected to Self is being connected to Source. Being connected to Source is being connected to everyone and everything. Remembering the uniqueness of Self in these connections, collectively and fluidly, can uplift the moment and increase the ability to translate and transcribe what seems unknown to self and most. Knowing Self as worthy of more than we ever can come into fully understand, opens the gates forward and into novel streams of coming into your most intended Being, the most you can be at the moment. Within this space of accepting self you will experience the cutting-edge of time. Trust it. Take a deep breath in and, likewise, out and give yourself permission to love yourself more. There is a place where you can love yourself more than enough. You are abundant.

Enlightenment is often coupled with an emotional and spiritual understanding whose time is right. Describing enlightenment comes to me in words that express the feelings of enlightenment rather than the physicality of enlightenment, which is like a warm ghost of misty fulfillment. Enlightenment when experienced defines more than enough as a passage into personal positive growth. Enlightenment is all so natural. In my experience, and, yes, I am an enlightened one, Enlightenment is a soft completing feeling rather than an amazing awareness finally arrived. I do not look for enlightenment, I receive enlightenment. It is often dreamlike, residing in that space when just before awareness arrives, which is different than being in unawareness. Softly and usually slowly, the light comes on, as a smooth dimmer mechanism wakes up the room in a soft adjusting manner. When the light lit is otherwise unobtainable thought, and in so this very special light fades on never to fade off again. Perhaps not too brightly, yet, one sees more in this new light and this "more" often begins, one might want to say, as a spark, although, not so sudden as a spark. The light is not a flicker either. It, the light of enlightenment, is softer and it catches my attention as a gentle realization that is a glow around something, and from within that something that easily defines itself in hues of love and completion. Enlightened is being in awareness of self and synchronously existing in our "We-are-One" knowing. Enlightenment is a spiritual technology.

*The Art of Appreciating MORE*

I imagine truly heightened enlightened ones are those that glow. Halos come to mind. I think self-professed enlightened ones have much to learn before our "halos" visibly glow around us and still more so before others can see them. I think in light of that, one has to have a halo to see a halo, yet I do not know if that is true. Having no halo, I personally experience perplexing incompatibilities that dull my light softer than perhaps the future of mankind will create in like circumstances. Enlightenment strengthens the questions contained in their being answered. Enlightenment, for me, comes as a normal feeling that I never recall seeking after, yet I am always open to the holy sense of timeliness in it. Nature has a way of helping us change. Isn't becoming Enlightened a form of arriving in awareness, as is happiness a form of joy that can bring laughter? And Enlightenment is a natural occurrence throughout our lifespan. It, though, seems somewhat vague in my capturing it enough to absolutely define it, albeit I want to. Most fortunate are we who embrace our natural Enlightenments. I think they are capsulated and intended to be activated exactly on time. It is our nature to wonder about being enlightened because it moves us along so tenderly in its nature. Technology and machinery are similar to experience.

It is said, "We are like Nature", yet I know; Nature is like Us, as much, in gentle and total ways as too are the rocks-of-walls actually man-made. We know them as garden-walls, yet they are usually built out of and away from our big cities, although big cities were once small towns of many stone walls. The older stone walls are comprised of the stones that were near there, like the way the apples fall close to its tree, so too do the old stone walls grow up from their surroundings. We are as those stone fences that became organically part of the environment; lent into our picturesque country-scape.

*Permeate & Radiate*

Robert Frost[3] wrote about the "Mending Wall" that kindly brings civility and boarders together; holding neighbors to their own. We deliberately mirror purpose into our creations, especially, it seems, while playing in elements available around us in nature. Likewise, we all build our lives one natural stone upon another in their rustic available forms, born of our own experiences, until we desire, from wisdom's gift, newly aware elements. We intuitively sense that the top of our life-wall, over, and beyond; there exists so much "MORE". Therefore, we remember to build our walls with gates to conveniently pass through when the time comes to gracefully move-on.

## What is there beyond what we have built thus far?

I dare say; there comes a time that building walls is unnecessary and adding on-top of another stone makes the existing wall unsteady and serves no longer its original helpful purpose.

"Change" is like that! Change, at times, requires a new approach, perhaps a different element, rather than to aptly add on-top of what we previously put there. These metaphors are intended to help us relate to levels of abstractions and allow our thought to compare forms together without judgement. Allowing Self to finally open our existing gate and go-on into our carefully created and previously chosen-by-self, pivotal life changes, introduces a choice to take a new, confident approach and then continue within a welcomed shift. The nature of these magical enlightened events are the becoming of More "Self".

---

[3] Robert Frost... American poet.

## The Art of Appreciating MORE

The Pandemic of 2020-2021 was an eye-opener, a mind re-arranger, and a heart reminder. It stood upon the boarders of us all and it connected us while separating us. It reminds me of the stone walls that stand to announce what is yours and what is your neighbors. It asked of us all to create those boarders between us for us all to appreciate what we have become. It enabled us to size-up the situation relative to self-endangerment and self-preservation. I might feel a halt-thought with the forces that bestowed this Pandemic upon us, as it was never feeling like a gift of gratitude and joy. I have a suspicion that so much more goodness will come out of this contrast, that it will be celebrated someday as perhaps an important time of changes that shift us into a better kinder humanity. In the silence of the moments of not knowing if infected by the virus germs of the Pandemic, we all took notice of our proximity to each other and moved enough away to allow the space intended to support our health and wellbeing and everyone else too. It was an awareness to me to look at others as in now a need to keep distance.

Emotionally, we had been sharply aware of each other, yet, not so much our distances between each other. In the request to keep a distance physically, we grew a bit closer emotionally. Sharing what is nothing, the space between, turned out to be the sharing that supported our love for self and each other. There is something there in that in-between nothingness. I found that by-product of the Pandemic interesting and I am enlightened by the extreme measure nature took to help us each find our way. A positive gain that we can extrapolate from the need for separation be-caused by the apparently new-normal created by the pandemic experience, is to find our own worthiness from a different viewpoint. Worthiness, as a form of deserving, rejects the pandemic, which feels like a chore and might feel difficult to accept negotiating. Therefore, the Worthiness gained has another meaning than deserving. Worthiness, as a strong stance to hold; as in the phrase "Not let your heart be troubled.", provides strength Within. It is easier than dealing with deserving. In our times that state we should not be troubled; we know there is something substantial to appreciate. Hidden between experiences and a novel path, we hold the choice to find goodness at the cost of otherwise settling for trouble.

Could we each have been assuming too much of the others in our life with our physical closeness? I think so. That is a very apparent results from this distancing. Missing a hug or a pat on the back is a noticed change that could very well help us have the space to reflect upon our own growth. When thinking about distancing space we can view it as a space we claim ours. It is closer to us. What could be beneficial in having this space? As children we are taught about our Guardian Angel. What if, as we have been increasing our self-awareness and self-consciousness, we are approaching an opportunity to relate in a closer way to that type of spiritual Being, such as our personal Angels. I think, if we can sense the possibility of our Guardian Angel, perhaps in our opening hearts of compassion, due to increasing our consciousness, we are ready to allow these forms of Angelic Beings to come more out of or through us. Perhaps it is also that our Spiritual Guides, Guardian Angels, or whatever are these Beings who we all sense do some form of "protecting" or "helping" us, are utilizing this separation space as a whereabouts in which they can be more included in the physical realm with us. I think that is a reasonable uncharted thought worthwhile thinking. The truth might well be that we need a little more space between us, to expand. Perhaps in the distancing more civility will emerge. Everything happens for a good reason. Let us understand that together. As in my consciousness of this required distancing I am more aware of my aura. It seems happy with this distancing. The wall built to comfort boarders is like that, I feel my abilities to sense the vibrations of connections to other people and other things, especially including the trees, the animals, the Earth, the temperatures of the air and breezes, and so many other articles of things existing outside of my sphere of space and self. I think a good name for it would be self-space. Being aware of this is easier while observing distancing.

Back to the moving Uri and I experienced. There we were and just as Uri was to retire that we took a first step which was to move out of our Family house and into our rental units with the dual intent to adjust to moving-on and to improve the rentals to increase their value before selling them for profit. Being there allowed us the opportunity to sell our Family house while living elsewhere familiar and in our town. It was a convenient natural steppingstone enabling us to adjust and feel purpose in so doing. Uri and I continued to redefine our path of least resistance such that we could find a mutually agreeable direction as to where we might move to and begin our retirement years. We utilized the remodeling tasks at our rental property we were residing in, as guideline markers to assist us into seeking after what we were wanting to find. As we completed a task in the remodeling of our rentals, we took a trip into another new area of terrain and real estate choices. These trips helped us recover from the effort it took to live at this temporary housing solution and from the work we were doing on the remodeling design and implementation. Taking small fact-finding trips was the only reliable current way we knew to learn about other places to consider living, other than on-line house shopping.

The remodeling was coming along so professionally stylish, practical, comfortable and beautiful and included landscaping as well as interior improvement upgrades. These houses were becoming high-end executive housing. The amount of work that had to be accomplished on that property was huge. It actually felt it was far too much to do at times, whereas our family house was on the market and ready-to-sell. We staged the family house with many of our existing furnishings and were designing the rental houses for final sale furnished too. Many nights Uri and I spent hours talking about a remodeling plan to get the rentals ready to sell also, and we would be emotionally ready by then too. It was nice in many ways to have these half-way houses to readjust away from our family house. I know we were and still are extremely fortunate, and the challenges that were required to prepare these houses for maximum sale value was felt. Making money is good and natural to us. We are practical disciplined people and we have an instinct to do the next right thing. The next best thing, in our experience, always produces profits and we acknowledge our part in that assumes our trust in what is fair and reasonable. We always have a return on our investments, because we always treat our investments with honor. We actually love making money and we love respecting our property. It is a good feeling to enjoy making money in all compartments of our exchanging with money and real estate was one way we could really participate with the outcome. We worked so hard enjoying it too.

We decided to hire out portions of the work, as we could. We also hired a talented and willing handyman, Ricky, who soon became a friend. I recall when we all met together and discussed our terms and conditions and the tasks that needed to be done, Ricky gave us a dollar figure on an hourly salary, and we did not agree with him. Instead, we gave him more than he asked for. Why did we do that? Because we wanted Ricky to enjoy working on the property and with us too and it helps to be appreciated. We appreciated Ricky working with us. It is a rule that one finds self-worth when others treat you with worthiness, and it does, however, additionally, strengthen self-imaging. We love being with others of high self-confidence and we knew Ricky was a worthy equal. We knew already that being generous works like being appreciative; the more we are generous and the more we are appreciative; the more generosity and appreciation increases unto us. It is law. It is always true. In that behavioral model, it is easy to share with others as equals and it feels right. I do not write about this to brag, I write to open up the truth as we experience it in the hopes that others will open up their hearts to equality in all ways. If it feels like enough money to pay yourself, it is the right amount of money to pay another working for you and then give more.

We really enjoyed working together with Ricky. Before we finished the work designed into completing before selling our property and physically moving-on, Ricky had an accident while driving to visit his mother and died. We were so surprised in wonder at his leaving. He was ready, though we were not ready to say goodbye. Even in our thoughtful sorrow, we were happy for the too short and helpful time we three spent together. Ricky used to say, we should just retire there at the little houses because they were so convenient, and they were glowing with pride and accomplishment into the neighborhood.

He left that on the property, as did we. Little miracles are always with us. It was a delightful miracle to contract with Ricky and in its way, it was a little miracle that Ricky had pretty much finished all the work we had commissioned him to do when he went off into a better place, as they say. There was no doubt this property was more desirous because of our improvements and, although this was not the place, we would live out our lives, we understood the appeal in it that Ricky saw too, and we did take comfort there and it was our home for those transition years.

This property had a lot of history. They had housed a great many people during our thirty-year ownership and the return on our investment was real. We appreciated our sense of business and our decision to purchase this property so long ago. It provided increase in our lives in many ways, including the sharing our dreams with Ricky. After Ricky died, Uri did most of the labor himself. It was wearing, for us both, to get to know someone and then to care about them as a person and friend, just to lose them so quickly. We had been working together for about a full year. We always got along so well and respected each other and the quality and attitude of work habits. Uri and I just wanted to take our time and emotionally work it out. All being as such, we knew there were reasons for our too brief encounter, and whenever I think of Ricky, I smile ☺. I appreciate the way we are all so connected in mysterious ways. Death is an unreal belief. People do not die. People move-on.

In our short fact-finding trips and in our preparation to move-on, we began to develop a list of the things we felt we needed in our future. This list was amazingly detailed as with each trip we experienced more and more clarity as to what we wanted and with each remodeling task we allowed our love for this amazing property of many memories, including Ricky, to gather upon itself a strong pride and preparedness. We recognized that pride in the right minds of love and appreciation, is a characteristic of worthiness.

We thought perhaps, Hawaii, would be a great retirement location. We had been visiting all the Hawaiian Islands for all these years too. We took many wonderful family vacations there and we loved the Ocean and the weather. We decided to move there and rent a place while we looked for a place to buy. We shipped our car over on a freighter with such positive intent. We obtained a real estate agent, who was actually a friend. He was now part of a divorced couple we knew and loved for many years when they were married in Ventura. Their daughters were friends with our daughters. He would help us hunt for our new home. We decided to find a place, much in the Hawaiian tradition, that included an Ohana, which is a Hawaiian word for the popular smaller second house for family and/or visiting guests on the property. We could further find an attached unit, which again is more common on the islands due to the amazing profit renting brings. We would make it available to Tasha, our daughter. Since the Hawaiian Islands were so far removed and remote, having a longer-term accommodation available for family was a practical choice. An Ohana could be perfect for our daughter, Michelle, and her boyfriend, Peter, who were still in the second house on our rental property in California. It is wonderful to know that Ohana also translates to Family and Family means nobody gets left behind or forgotten. Being a Disney-family, we would not forget our family. That was the mental and spiritual state we were in while looking at properties, in our price range, which was high due to the profitable sale of our Family House and our anticipated profitable sale of our rental property. Michelle and Peter were watching after things on the rental property and, at the time, they also liked the idea of moving along with us and not being left behind.

Uri and I think that we have significant, and I might add, better than average, insight into the way family helps each member and loves unconditionally. This appreciation comes from our upbringing and the experiences we've had in our younger years, whereby, we received little financial help from our families. They were good people. They did not feel a responsibility, desire or need to help us financially into our adult worlds. They knew we could find our way. We both feel that if they could have helped, they too would have benefited better from our successes.

The truth was we grew our list of things we needed in our future and we returned after three months of Island living to our rental property. We had a few more tasks to complete and some possessions that needed to be sorted out. We decided to arrange for a real estate agent to put our place on the market, although we now realized we were not going to move to Hawaii to relocate.

I would spend time thinking about why there was unsteadying confusion about what we wanted and what we were finding potentially for us to choose. I kept going back into my growing understanding of the Law of Attraction and that I was now more responsible for the experiences I was having. I understand from this part of our journey, that if things do not feel right, or when there is a significant indecision going on within, it is best to let it go. It is better to wait until you know well what you want than to make a choice about something without enthusiasm. There is little use in settling, if you have the choice. Wait it out. Feel good about big decisions prior to committing to them. If a decision is too hard to make, let it go for a while and until it is the perfect time to choose. This is a fundamental concept to be involved with The Law of Attraction as a tool to assist you rather than that defaulted fling that can come about when a decision is not ripe. Learning to trust yourself is very important and yields confidence. Distinguishing between having confidence due to a good feeling and feeling a need to decide for the excuse of thinking to not decide, to actually go through, is a vote of unsettling lack of confidence and is a tricky analysis. Reasoning with this subtle variance will be appreciated when a decision becomes more certain.

This is another living aspect of the Law of Attraction. Learning to flow with what feels right, sometimes requires feeling that what you are doing isn't right. Not that it is really wrong, yet, it is best to feel good about choices rather than pin yourself into a corner to insist you change your feelings. Feelings are good to have. They help you know what is good for you.

Initially Hawaii seemed like the perfect place for us, and for some it is, yet, we felt a struggle going on that we had no idea we would experience. It was the Law of Attraction that we would come to know even better through this time on Hawaii. I'm so grateful for our longer than average stay on the Islands.

I love working with the Law of Attraction instead of insisting on everything to be the way I feel I want it to be, and it is a great finding out that when you follow through on your feelings, indeed it is easier. I think also that when I have fought to make things work out regardless of the evidence and feelings, sometimes, something similar comes into the experience. It feels like I am repeating old stories when I get into that type of insistence. It is far better to work with the knowledge about the way the Law of Attraction works for us all. What I think about I bring about. My thoughts create my reality. My feelings are real and can help me evaluate what is going on. There is a good feeling when achieving desires. This was a different feeling.

During that time, Michelle and Peter had some big changes happen too. Michelle got a job working for a fabulous company in San Francisco. It was all so wonderful for everyone. She landed her dream job. Peter could look now for work in a more employable region of California, and Uri and I could refocus our search to just address our needs, rather than to find a place to support Michelle and Peter too. That opened up our opportunities to include retirement communities and other parts of the nation.

In my great love for my children and then my great satisfaction for their successes and how all these aspects about our parent-child-parent relationship interact with and support each other, I often felt, that in retirement, there was also a new level of respect and sharing that took place between us. I can relate the feelings I had with a repeating sensation as a parent. For example, as our younger days' family got into the car to take a road trip, which we did year to year for vacations or get-a-ways, we would feel that encapsulation in our car. For miles and hours being together was an interesting aspect of our travels that we enjoyed, albeit we were all awaiting the getting there to happen too. There came a time along the road where one child would fall asleep and then the other, though, when either did fall off, there was an immediate knowing that it happened. In that moment a relief and a release happened silently. That space knowing your child is so safe in their sleep, and you are comfortable in that happening, less as a parent and more as a person, I felt great joy. This sensation of knowing sleep came, elaborated the space between us to not exclude their consciousness, but rather to include a special connection of peace. Joy in doing a good job as a parent and joy in the moment of more attention devoted to myself. I might take a deep breath of relief or just turn on a different radio station and, Uri and I might look at each other and smile ☺. They were asleep and all is well with the world we are left in. That sensation is a part of how I can describe retirement.

Our children didn't need us to house them any longer, albeit we didn't mind that at all. Apparently, our life course was to be different and we accepted that direction, and in that release the description of where we might relocate to changed. There was more and there was less, yet the change felt right and perfectly timed, because our investment property was all cleaned up and staged very nicely for the selling process to happen. Uri and I were amazed and excited about the timing. With our new direction we also felt a new freedom and we had time to adjust to that. We decided to rent a place for several months in Northern California, where we could take time to evaluate relocating and be closer to Michelle and Peter. Peter was already like a son to us, and we truly enjoyed the possibility of being close enough physically to meet up with them easily. They encouraged that solution too.

Again, and with our property on the market, we searched with a great deal of interest and trust in finding the perfect place. We looked at all properties both in general neighborhoods and we added retirement communities. We were learning a lot about the differences and rummaging through the concepts of one versus the other, neither way winning our direction, although, we found some interest in senior communities. We though upon visiting several, seemed a bit taken back by some of the rules, restrictions, and regulations that were common to agree to in these communities. We also began to appreciate that many of those rules, restrictions and regulations were pretty nice to have in an elderly community. They added to the comfort, simplicity and security of these communities, while the added benefits increased with a shared and common facility.

Even while including retirement communities into the mix of potential places, after a couple of months, we didn't see anything we wanted. The weather that season was extreme too, as it rained nearly every day and we felt frustration that nothing was turning up that was near worth our even bidding on. I look at those words I used and feel a giggle inside of me. We felt "frustration". Those are silly off-feelings to encounter, are they not? Messages were being filtered through to us in such apparent ways. We knew then as we know now that whenever we feel something is not working out for us, we can trust that is in our best interest, and so it is very easy to rather state that things were working in ways that brought us to understand and appreciate that we could feel better going in other directions. Somethings you just cannot force into existence. Being stubborn about having to get it one way or another that "seems" rather than "feels" desirable but, all signs point out that there is more to this and re-evaluating the circumstances and holding an opened-mind might be a better way to go forward. We pride ourselves on our almost uncanny ability to notice the feelings associated with taking direction, and we continuously stay connected to our feelings and our Inner Being. We always seek direction from Within. Well, that is exactly what we were both feeling. We were feeling that something better is awaiting us to discover it, if only we could hold ourselves in a place of allowing. Remembering that allowing is something other than being patient, because I was not feeling patient at all. I was on a path and I was ready.

I sat at my computer, looking at the screen of houses for sale in the area and listening to the heavy rain and feeling a bunch of reasons to give up on this search for a house nearby, when I just typed into the Google search the following words: "Where is the best place to retire in the United States of America?". And "The Villages" appeared to me.

Okay. That was of interest. Yet, The Villages were in Florida, which is far away from Sonoma, California. We though read what we could about it and even watched a few videos and took into consideration other people's experiences at The Villages, and within a few hours upon finding this information, we decided to plan a trip to Florida and specifically to visit The Villages. It seemed a really timely message and it seemed a really great idea to pursue. We wanted to get out and investigate.

We felt ourselves permeating through this process and we felt really good, in fact, we felt we were radiating.

And so, off we went to Florida!

## Chapter One - Appreciations on Permeate and Radiate

- ❖ I appreciate that which seems initially to be a direction opposing the flow of my life, can be a signpost to a direction otherwise forbidden from past beliefs, although indeed perfect to follow.

- ❖ I appreciate the vibrational and incremental relationship between Permeate and Radiate.

- ❖ I appreciate knowing that positive thinking and self-confidence can greatly improve the outcome.

- ❖ I appreciate the personal relief obtained when decisions are made.

- ❖ I appreciate that the "Golden Independently Wealthy Years", are perfect for the freedom required to apply into action what is desired.

- ❖ I appreciate that my life is so good and that it continues to improve, provide, encourage, and expand.

- ❖ I appreciate that my past often carries into the now great anticipation.

- ❖ I appreciate in recognizing good conditions and fortune one can in confidence build upon more good conditions and fortune.

- ❖ I appreciate that we are all living as totally integrated portions of the external Oneness.

- ❖ I appreciate that I AM, YOU ARE and WE ARE.

*The Art of Appreciating MORE*

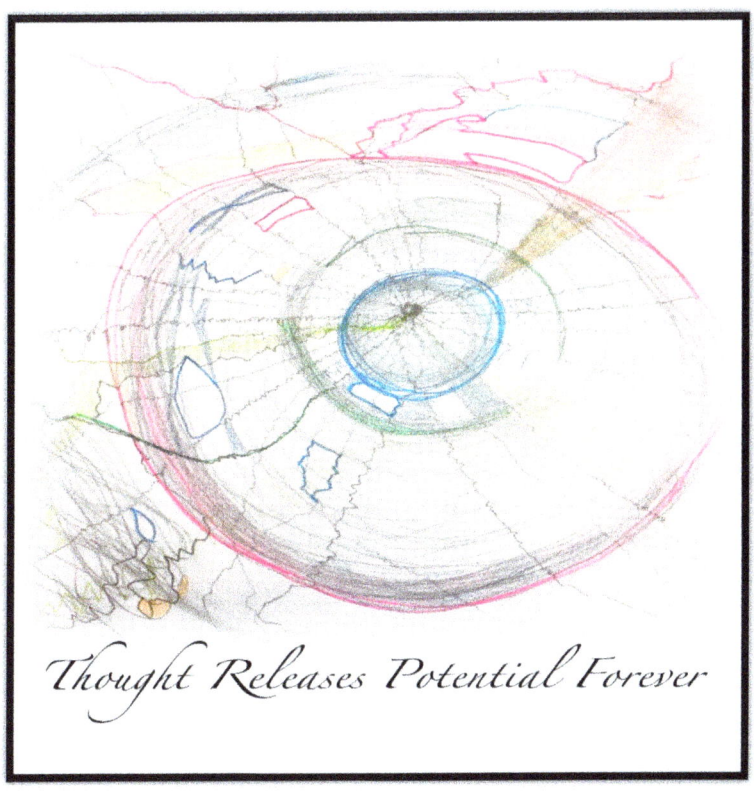

*Thought Releases Potential Forever*

## Chapter 2  What You Think Matters

<u>I appreciate that we all have the power to think whatever we want to think.</u>

Not everyone *uses* this power, that is, without exception, born into every Human Being, though, everyone does think. There is a slight sounding difference. I appreciate that there is a world of amazement, between just thinking and instead choosing through your consciousness to think about exactly what you want to think about. Not everyone believes that this capability exists, neither in themselves nor in anyone else, and so those non-believers do not appreciate that the controlling of their thoughts, is an amazing powerful skill that can enhance and improve experience into their lives, while creating a wonderful now. Knowing this can be easy to understand and can be applied to life's experience immediately. Additionally, since there is absolutely nothing to lose and so much to gain, it is fascinating that anyone would resist the practice of being conscious of their own thoughts and then choosing what they want to think about, rather than just allowing what seemingly "comes" to them to be their thoughts. What is that all about?

Some people, and better I should write, seemingly most people think it doesn't matter what they are thinking most of the time, and that thoughts are just what are required of each of us within our reality of existence.

*Do you ever take the time to think about what you are thinking about?*

Further, many believe that people cannot control their thoughts, for any period of time, and they cannot fathom why anyone else or why they themselves might even want to control any thought.

*Do you take the time to think about the quality of what you are thinking about?*

People can easily confuse the controlling of thoughts with not having the freedom to be who they are. After all, "Thought Control" is often a statement used when discussing "Mind-Washing" and Cult Practices. That is not what is being discussed here. We are addressing your ability to control the quality and range of your deliberate thinking for yourself. We are not bringing focus to your being able to control other people's thoughts. You cannot nor should anyone ever desire to control the thoughts of anyone other than themselves.

Getting back on subject, our thoughts do matter and what you choose to think matters and you can control your thoughts more than you dreamed possible and this is most beneficial.

Many people do not realize that their thoughts are a power. Not only is that true, but it is a Great Power. Not everyone enjoys what he or she thinks about either. Many think their thoughts are just part of their functionality; like sneezing which is difficult to control. Many are not aware that their practiced thoughts can be generated with their absolute total control, and so they are not experiencing that part of their life and they miss out on the capability and flexibility that their thoughts create into their life. For if they did practice bringing control and value to their thinking, they would surely come to know, very quickly, that what one thinks does matter. It matters to everything, but, first and foremost, it matters to the thinker: that is, you, me, and everyone. We are all thinkers and what we think about really does matter.

Why? Because, in our ability to create from our thoughts we create or mold our experiences now and in through our futures, knowingly or not. We allow our *State of Being* to exist and to be known to ourselves and consequently, to others, as well.

*"Circumstances don't matter; State of Being matters. Circumstances do not determine your State of Being, your State of Being determines your Circumstances."*
                              Bashar-Anka[4]

Knowing this across a lifetime proves valuable for wholeness, happiness and prosperity, at the least. The quality of a life is determined by your State of Being.

*If this is so, then what is your State of Being and how do you interact with it such that you can produce positive results?*

We are the creators of our lives and we also are involved, more than at first realizing so, in the circumstances in our lives. The most valuable thought we can hold about the concept of self-thought is that, it is perfect for us to create whatever thoughts we do create. We are more powerfully connected to our resulting experiences than we often take credit for.

*I believe that it is more important to the quality of your life, to know and remember that your thoughts create your life. That is far more important to remember than it is to remember your own name.*

Fortunately, we have the ability to evaluate our lives, being the results of our thoughts. We can examine the events we are having, instantly. We can look at the results we are living in this very moment. We can determine what evidence surrounding us, seems comfortable. We can feel if we feel good. That is very apparent to us. We can, also, mentally agree with

---

[4] Bashar-Anka - is a multidimensional being, known as a friend from the future, who has spoken since 1985 through the channel of Darryl Anka

ourselves at any time regarding what we want to do right from where we are at this moment and based upon our examining, looking, and determining our personal status. And we can learn to tweak the results of thoughts by paying closer attention to our feelings; as our feelings stem growth from our thoughts. It is an amazing self-understanding.

*What can bring us more awareness of the feelings from our thoughts, enough such that we can control and create with our thoughts?*

Feelings are the results of thoughts, usually, or initially. Some people immediately want to debate the other direction truer, that thoughts are the results of our feelings. Feelings are the indicators of our personal quality in our thoughts. Thoughts are closer to what is the essence "Within" us, whereas our emotions are the outcome once-removed and or moving-away from thoughts.

Another way of realizing the order of movement, once a thought exists, its actualization will begin transforming that thought into a desire to manifest. The first manifestation of our thoughts are our feelings about the thoughts we are having. We can determine, if aware, if we want to continue in the ongoing direction with the thoughts we are having and only as we come into feeling them. If we are not determining our direction, we are taking a defaulted direction. Not that there is anything wrong with taking your defaulted value of directions and thoughts, because goodness is far more your normal than you might even realize. If you can, and you can, hold more deliberately to understanding your feelings, this discipline will be to your advantage.

*Feelings are the expansion of thoughts.*
*Feelings are the results of thoughts.*
*Feelings lead into our emotional formations.*
*If you want to feel good, think good feeling thoughts.*
*And if you want to have good thoughts,*
*pay attention to how you feel.*
*Your feelings are advising you as to your emotions.*
*Your emotions can be monitored and adjusted.*

It seems as simple as that to master the mind and it seems as simple as that to have a joyful life. Most people know more about, spend more time in their negative emotions and dwell upon them more intensely than their positive ones and many people seem inclined to think often out of initially trained and familiar habits. It can be rather complicated to sort the idea of self-thought out at first. Now could be the time that you choose to switch that up.

It remains truer still, though changing with a population awakening into thought-awareness, that we think and feel through much of our day, in our "default mindset". And "mindset" is the perfect word description for it, as we seem so set in our mind. Most people become complacent or stubborn about their mindset. When learning, remembering and practicing positive personally directed thoughts, initially, as I have found within myself, I kept returning to going along with whatever thoughts were just happening. It was a true discipline to listen to my thoughts, and still, years of discipline later, I still fall into my defaults more than I really want to do, yet less so than I did previously. It seems apparent to me, that I actually, feel intimidated by my own power of inputs. It is a bit embarrassing to acknowledge, but the truth is that I become complacent, from time to time, with my ability to live in the best way possible. I can become a "lazy or sloppy" thinker. A great deal of my life

I've just floated about in thinking that perhaps I didn't deserve too much happiness. That practiced thought has so much to do with feeling unworthy. Developing worthiness sets off a stream of improved habits of thinking. It feels so much better to choose thoughts than to feel incapable of doing so. It was similar to that concept of just waiting for that other shoe to drop. My advice to myself is that I can do this and even better all of the time. Fortunately, it does get easier because a momentum begins to assist in the next thought coming forth from the last one, and I exist in a better space already from being a positive thinker. Hence, my "default" value of thought is already improved from previous times in my life. Appreciating that happening, brings more of that into life to appreciate.

Once the individual takes control of his or her mindset and moves away from the default value of thinking and finds their desired thoughts in heartfelt agreement, that is where deliberate thinking, feeling and creating commences. It's so good.

Since mentioned, I want to further examine:

## What is a "default mindset"?

We all can relate to what a habit is in our life. Generally, a habit is an acquired and accepted behavioral pattern that is regularly followed until it becomes almost involuntary. Habits exist independently as long as they are undiscovered or uncontrolled. Once a habit is discovered, it can always be controlled, to stay or to fade. The awareness of a habit initiates the choice to dissolve it, or not. Before recognizing an existing habit, there is absolutely no awareness of wanting or not wanting it. A habit can be good or less so good. A habit is a phantom, until it is an awareness. We can only exhibit habits that are unknown to exist, for once they are known to exist, it is a deliberate choice to continue in having, or not that habit. Habits are similar, in that regard, to our egoic structures. Habits, over time, can become quite unique and personally complicated with egos, experiences and repeated beliefs. A default mindset is kind of like a group of habitual thoughts going undetected.

"Default" could mean; the automatic choice made from a preselected group of choices, analogist to the options provided in a computer interactive communication. Or does the word "default", in this context of the "default mindset", derive from its original meaning of "default", which is to fail to fulfill an obligation, such as to default on a loan that was agreed to be paid?

Could we, in cooperation with the default mindset, feel obligated to continue to repay whatever choices were presented to us usually from an external source or entity that we initially agreed with when first, unwittingly, we were indoctrinated with this thought from outside of ourselves?

My thoughts are intuitively alerted by this definition that has to do with "defaulting" on a payment, because my mind immediately thinks about finances and happily so. I find that whenever a word comes up that has anything to do with strengthening or weakening my thought processes involving my proximity to finances, as does this second definition of the word "default", albeit in some minor measure, I know that my "abundance" or my knowledge of applying thoughts into creating my "abundance" is an undertone to the chorus I am singing.

## The Art of Appreciating MORE

I so enjoy the capacity of abundance into my life, including financial abundance, such that when a chord of understanding more about abundance comes to sing in my heart, I want to appreciate the sounds of it, in order to implement this knowing more and more so into my life experience. This action is natural wisdom revealing itself. I follow the thoughts that serve me well in positive abundance and the evidence of this pursuit is my life, which is abundant in all ways I desire.

I think that the "defaulted" mindset is a combination of both those meanings. Yet, in looking closer at the "default" value of thought creation, it has more to do with what I previously experienced in thought than what I might actually want to think. This default is not absolutely personal. It is not ours alone. It is a combination of habitual thoughts that become too familiar to question.

I become complacent and I may not know what to give of myself to thought, if not what I am accustomed to giving to thought. I form habits of thoughts. They are my default thoughts and I train myself into the feelings of them, accepting them in a space of tolerance or habit. That is my default thinking, yet, what do I mean when I mention the "mindset" of these default thoughts. I sense that what happens when I collect a series of defaulted thoughts into a group of thoughts that they become a theme and potentially an idea arrives from them being connected and eventually, they become more solid, even solid enough to become a personal belief. Our defaulted mindset comes in waves, much as a chorus comes into a familiar song. We just sing along not even really thinking about what the thoughts are behind the words. Often when we reach that chord, we feel relief because we remember the words so well that we can concentrate on the volume or quality of the voice we give to them. And in those attractive comfortable collections of tunes, we are complacent to our generated thoughts. We utilize the default mindset for the convenience of process and to relax. As good as that might sound; we also, surrender our creative spirit into the defaulted mindset. The default thought is a lazier thought and unless we evaluate our present desires along with our defaulted mindset, we somewhat live our thoughts as thought-programmed robots.

Fortunately, the Source of Life is most generous and totally loving and even in our defaulted life experiences, we are the results of that generosity and love. Most people who go through life do not complain at its end for their defaulted life experience, yet, all people who come into knowing, and better, mastering their knowing of their ability to think deliberately will always be happier for knowing this, all of their lives and at its ending we are better prepared for still more.

It is also advantageous to realize the possibility that the defaulted mindset, that is a habitual momentum of seemingly convenient self-generated feelings, emotions, and actions, is actually the collection of thoughts from others and these others have instilled into your system without collaboration, as they commenced prior to your knowledge of your own ability to appreciate that every thought created, initiates in pure Love from Within our individual power, to create our own thoughts. That is a huge thought and should be deciphered. We all are taught ideas and beliefs by others and who knows where they got those ideas from originally. Unless you were most fortunate to have picked up the Law of Attraction ideals on your own or from others who wanted to share this with you earlier in life, we are all "defaulting" often.

*The Art of Appreciating MORE*

At this point of expressing my ability to think and recognize the thoughts I am having and then to actuate thoughts deliberately; I want to add that this knowledge could very well be a part of living longer and having experiences. There is a chance that younger readers might not be prepared or ready to internalize this as being more than nice sounding words. I've known this truth for a long time. If there is any way to bring this understanding into the life of a young person, well, then it is pretty certain that young person will be very successful in life. For there is no more powerful appreciation of self than to know that your thoughts create things. It is stated that youth is wasted on the young and that wisdom is for the older among us. I've always resisted that believe, even in childhood, and I thought that I could be young and wise. My InnerVoice tells me quite clearly that Youth is not really wasted on the young. I am told that is ill stated.

*Youth wears one out and experienced seniors know how to handle what is confusing.*

Let's look at that closer and I will start by using the length of timelines for people. In shorter periods of time things can example less clarity than over time. We know this to be true when we realize this something or other happened for a reason and that reason is usually very good to finally understand. That often takes a little more time to internalize. Otherwise, we would be always appreciating instant manifestations. We know there is always a time delay in manifesting. True sometimes we do manifest almost instantaneously. That is rare and for a good reason.

As young people it takes longer to link up the dots into a larger understanding or the bigger picture. Also, as a young person the greater tendency is to react or act to do something quicker. We think in our youth that we are more spontaneous because we are faster thinkers than older people. From the viewpoint of a young person older people are slower possibly because they do not understand what is going on. That is sometimes true too. It is pretty tricky to know when an elder is wise or just slow. We do not appreciate that many older people are open to the possibility of the action part as soon as a younger person. Experience teaches elders to think a little longer before taking action. The results are that younger people do not get to connect the dots up before taking action. They wear themselves out much quicker and the results are often less than what they could have been if more thought was applied to the action. Quick action does not always create solution and still not all older people are wise.

Most solutions do eventually require some form of action or a decision to take no action, yet, a wise person, young or old, will evaluate the effort along with the promised results before knowing what action, or not is appropriate. Thinking about things is a discipline and a reward. When in control of thinking about thoughts, any situation or idea conjured-up, it is most valuable to note if this continuation of thought is a defaulted thought or a deliberated thought. How much control is there in that thought?

The young and the old all have the same ability to apply deliberated thinking or to choose a defaulted thought or action. Often the youth or the unwise elder, is far too spontaneous to be better at controlling thoughts and/or outcomes as efficiently as older more experienced wiser people do. Thoughtlessly, momentum can be accelerated into a problem rather than a solution. It is said that Experience is our greatest teacher, and still it is not stated that we need to be old to have had experiences

*The Art of Appreciating* MORE

that can contribute greatly to situations we encounter. Wisdom is often more readily part of an older person. It is not only for the older person. Young people can be wise too, given themselves that option. Hence Wisdom itself is a choice. It fairs far better to choose and to seek after Wisdom, and the sooner in life the better.

When you agree with another entity's thoughts and, therefore, make it your own thought derivative, you choose one of the prescribed options that is introduced to you from outside of yourself. This is similar to choosing from the options of a group of preselected variables that are provided by the computer. Unless, "What-you-are" within yourself feels really good about accepting this introduced thought, it could be a modification of your stream of pure loving thoughts; for that is basically what you are, "pure loving thoughts", and "pure loving vibrations". If the agreement exists, then it is a cooperative agreed thought brought forth as a new coexistence, and something very new blossoms into this world's creations. It is important for everything, and especially, for self, to understand what part you are taking in the creation and participation of collaborative thoughts. People of religions are often forgetful of that fact, that we are all really pure minded and good. Religions make rules to pattern others into specific thought behaviors. Many cannot actually determine which of their thoughts have been enforced into us that are religious due to the fact that often they enter us at a young age.

We come forth as individuals not to live on this planet isolated from others. Living without the connection to others is a way though rare. We are meant to be here together. It is in this togetherness that we get to know more about ourselves too and it can be so much fun. It is in the connection to others that we appreciate more than self. We must always know how to love ourselves first and foremost, in order to truly love another. When we love our self, we can open-up to the love that others have too and relinquish the love we have created to others. In collaboration with others who love themselves too, we can become such champions of this Human Race.

Putting our thoughts into constructive positive feelings and emotional action is quite another thing for most of us, especially in the beginning of actualizing this understanding of self-capabilities. It is a relational experience to judge and/or compare self to self. It is a loving exercise to listen to your thoughts and realize them into either the next thought to continue in that frame-of-thought or to deliberately find the next thought to release oneself from the place thought is at currently. Easy as pie! It is always our choice, moment to moment. We can feel our way around in our heads, so to speak. In so doing, we can tend and take charge, know the comfort of Source control, or enable default to lead us on. We can continue or change our course. We can do this. The only problem is, we forget to and in some thoughts and feelings we are more inclined to find the habit of them and the reaction to them systematically.

Listening to self can be a bit unusual when first attempting to do so, and it continues to be something that requires deliberate attention, and some discipline helps. It is always a good thing to do and to take the time to do. Often, I become distracted by my senses of sight, hearing, tasting, smelling, touching, and much more. I, personally, love being distracted by what, I feel, are shiny things. Additionally, I can become complacent at the quality of my thought impacts, perhaps less wanting to judge them as to the quality they are streaming into and I can even forget to listen from one instance to the next. It seems so hard to keep paying attention to my thoughts and at times when I am listening to what I am thinking about, it seems that what I am thinking about is the only absolute thought I have within. Hence, I feel a place of halting myself from where I don't know I am going. I love the feeling of letting go of the thoughts that come into my frequency and letting them meander about looking for themselves. That I am having and continue to have so many thoughts focusing in upon what I am thinking about is not a thought I was taught as I was growing up, in school, in work, in religions, with friends or in what I was reading, hearing, seeing or wondering about. It is what I do now. And, it might well be the biggest difference between the preceding generations and the following generations. We are learning to have more control of our thoughts. It is impossible, I think, to have control of every single thought in every kind of situation that comes to us. Life is still, at any time, a mass amount of moving parts, unable to be pinned down into an absolute definition. It's also good to trust your thoughts.

It is easier to know what thoughts are surfacing when writing or speaking, yet, not so with listening, especially to others. For in listening, thoughts are often answering, and usually in reaction to what another is thinking rather than in pure thought from within self. What we think is always of matter to ourselves. What we think is what we are creating for ourselves. We cannot think for another person and we cannot create in our thoughts for another person. Our thoughts are off limit to others too. Others cannot do our thinking. It is always for self we think and create. If you think you are really creating something for another person, think about that again.

## What You Think Matters

The more you do, the more apparent it becomes that we can only create for ourselves. We can only think for ourselves. We have influence upon others in their thoughts and ideas, their actions and creation in many ways. Even so, we only have power over our selves. Others, can, if we want, influence us. Others can influence us in ways we do not want too, if we are less aware of ourselves.

What a great power we are, knowingly or not. We are such amazing Beings. We create in our deliberate design to expand forward with ideas in thoughts, then in thoughts brought to feelings and emotions coming into momentum, releasing forms of activities. We evolve in this expansion of making reality, bringing forth what are our ideas in thought is like growing pleasure or joy in the garden of God. We are sowers. We plant the ideas from our thoughts that create the garden of Source's Love, which is the pure idea conjured from Within. We are absolutely great. We are that which all is made of. And we are evolving. Within ourselves we have the ability to create the unknown and making known the unknown is what grows in the garden of God. Until the moment we choose to take our unique souls and spirits into our own thoughts of creation and allow them to become the decision, we under-lap our potential with the ability we have been given to be here for the purpose to create in joy.

### Our Deepest Fears

*"It is our light not our darkness that most frightens us.*
*Our deepest fear is not that we are inadequate.*
*Our deepest fear is that we are powerful beyond measure.*
*It is our light not our darkness that most frightens us."*

*Marianne Williamson*

And of all our powers, our power to think in love is the greatest.

> In what we think in Love, we become.
> In what we think in Love, we create.
> In what we think in Love, we do.
> In what we think in Love, we are.

What we think matters.

> *"We are the Divine essence of Love, which is God. It is arrogant to think otherwise."*
>
> *- The THEO Group* [5]

When we know the worthiness of our every thought, we manage our thoughts with better control and even with deliberate control, increasingly, with practice, from time to time. When we do so, even just a little to begin with, we come into the ability to nurture our own confidence. We are more conscious of our asking thoughts and receiving thoughts, and our thoughts of gratitude. We can become increasingly aware of our greatness. Self-confidence is always enabled from Within what we think in Love. And all original thoughts are of pure Love.

---

[5] The THEO Group. Sheila and Marcus Gillette are the co-founders of The THEO Group, an organization dedicated to sharing the wisdom teachings of the twelve archangels collectively known as THEO. Speaking directly through Sheila, THEO is here to guide humanity during this unprecedented shift to a higher state of consciousness.

## What You Think Matters

When we think that the thoughts that someone else has matters, that is a good enough thought in and of itself, because it is true. What others think does matter. It matters to them. What others think does not matter to what you are creating with your own thoughts.

I have to remind myself of that often. I really care about what others think, too much so. especially people who are close to me or that I love deeply. I care very much what Uri thinks. I care what my children think. That caring about what others are thinking, does influence me. My focus can sway away from what I am thinking and become more intense about what another person is thinking. This is a factor of what is communication, hence, it is of value. The precedence of trusting self-established thoughts and beliefs supersedes what others are certain of and remains influential towards communications with your loved ones, and it solidifies the degree in which empathic sensations bring you into a mutual truth.

Communicating is about more than who-I-am at the surface. It has to result in being more about self than before the communications began. We are encouraged, if not required, to listen to what others are attempting to yield, digest it, and then realize self-thoughts upon this thought being provided. We can feel for another person, only what we allow. Another person cannot change our thoughts; we are the only ones in charge of our own thoughts. We can form thoughts from the thoughts another provides. We are the only one who can choose to do so. A connective thought that thrives in Love has to come from the original thoughts of Love and when we really communicate in Love and expand and combine these Loving thoughts, we create a new seed to be planted in the Garden of Humanity. It is a magical gestalt that pleases everything and everyone. That is the truth of co-creating. This co-creation of loving thoughts is an amazement of making known what was unknown and it can only manifest when those connective loving thoughts become one.

We all should and can take the time to think about our thoughts several times in every day to begin with and grow more aware of them as we do. There are so many issues of life that grab our attention. Taking the time to think about our thoughts is amazingly important. Thinking about thoughts from the distance or vagueness of hearing them as with music rather than words, one after the other, is easier than over thinking them. Hear the music of your own thoughts. It is there. It might not be rock and roll or anything that you've heard from others. It is perhaps as soft as the vibration of moving things around you. Maybe it is a hum or a pitch. I feel myself thinking about the process of distinguishing sounds from thoughts sometimes, thinking out the definitions of the sounds. When I begin to think past the need to explain the sounds around me, my thoughts feel so powerful and willing to exist separate and full, from the sounds that surround my thoughts and are even embedded within my general thought. When I generalize the sounds about me into the thoughts I am having, I can refocus upon the love that surfaces in my more authentic thought, for all my thoughts are loving when they are birthed from my knowing myself in confidence and worthiness. Listen to your emerging sounds in your awakened thoughts.

It feels so good to think.
It feels so alive to think.
It feels so connected to think.
It feels so huge to think.
It feels so creative to think.
I love my thoughts.

## What You Think Matters

Looking at these "sounds" that surround my thoughts, what I mean also are the flavors that my thinking about what others are thinking about placed within them. They are the sounds of others influences upon my thoughts. My pure thought refrains from connecting my thoughts to the thoughts of others, unless there is a match or unless I am unaware of it happening. In addition is when there is a deep love. Always in pure thought, I think lovingly. It is the only thought I genuinely even know how to think up on my own. I can only conjure up from within myself love; any other slant in a thought is from blended interferences, some habitual, some supportive and others not so.

It was unbelievable at first to reflect upon myself as only being able to conjure up love because that was trained out of me at an early age. It almost felt sacrilegious to think so worthy of myself, initially. I had to promise myself that if I presumed my purity of thoughts were initially true that I could believe that deep within myself, where thoughts, ideas, and essential knowing commences, I am and will always be pure of spirit and soul, then I could change my sense of reasoning into the moment. When I am thinking "off" what seems to be my lovingly pure thoughts, I know that I am blending an outside element into my thoughts, that arrived sometime in the past. I am not, however, blaming something else for my comprehension of what I am capable of at this moment. I can accept this without over-analyzing or finding absolute knowing. I do not have to know everything. I can, however, appreciate everything. There is always something in everything and anything, big or small, presumed good or bad, now or then, to appreciate. Look for it and you will find it, in that sound that touches awareness with love.

I include my ego to be foreign thoughts that has space within me to camouflage itself sheepishly. I encourage you to do this also. Define the quality of the ego that surfaces at any given time, circumstance or subject and recognize it as actually more foreign than too personally endearing, if it feels "off". If it lifts your spirits, then work with it as a buffer between yourself and your total intensions. This process takes some getting used to and once played with will be most rewarding. This ego interface enables you to take a higher control of self-direction in a better understanding of a deeper surroundings. Ego is not age proportional, so regardless of your age, getting to observe it will benefit you.

I am allowing a "sound" to resonate into my thought frequency. From there, I have to choose the next thought, which, if I want to find a better space for to think in, will require evaluating my feelings from the thought and from the space in which the previous thought held my love.

Did you ever hear the expression; "It went in one ear and out the other."? That's a choice. Often people express that idea when they know the value of discriminating what we allow into our personal thought processes versus what we dump out almost immediately. We dabble in other people's thoughts and our own thoughts as well. And we let it in one ear and out the other, we play with it a bit along the way, we embrace it, we change it, we let it go, we put it off, or we do amazing other things to the thoughts that either come in one ear and out the other, or we conjure up inside and keep or dump.

It is so worth repeating that it doesn't matter what anyone else is thinking about me, or anything. What does matter is what am I thinking about myself and what I am thinking about others or anything. Things, "sounds" come into me, into my thoughts, and they can just as easily go out; In one ear and out the other.

Here is another thing that matters to mostly everyone. It is when someone is communicating their thoughts and I am really enjoying what they are saying and thinking and more when I am in agreement with them, I feel good about the consensus. I resonate. I am in favor with another. It feels expansive from the connection. It is a collaborative agreement. And it is the agreement that I make that holds the interest and the feelings I have about another person's thoughts that enable them to not be taken out the other ear, so to speak. There is more to the idea of influence than complacently awarding another with agreement and influence. We each have to decide to make something feel right to us before influence is really appropriate.

This is because what you think about matters.

DNA energy is enabled to change personally and when only through our minds allowance for the healing of self and the participation in something unknown. Think it out. Synchronicity is meant to be, and every one of our synchronistic experiences is exactly as special as each other is beautifully or artistically intended. We are that which is Greatness. Our first order of business is letting Self realize itself. Make known the unknown and think of something new and first think about a new YOU.

When I doubt what is created into my experience as appropriate, genuine and good, it being the perfect path of my own least resistance, I am avoiding my ability to create what I want at the same time. This self-judging hampers the natural development of self and of the potential to manifest what I really want. The good news is that I can control this thought process by myself. It is my choice. For the design, of a moment or a lifetime, always starts with the acknowledgement of the power of self. Empowering myself with what is my reality, right now, and relating to the deliberate dreams that I can ignite from this vantage point is being aware. I must consistently encourage myself, confidently, to see the anticipated outcome as something within the process rather than the final result, and trust that my sensitivities and intuitions will direct me, first generally and then, if I am clear, specifically.

At any time, anyone can be afraid to succeed, which is the fundamental sabotaging vibration of many worried people. Less and less often do I feel this fear, and if so, it is that doubt I am writing about. When I feel this, I can learn to recognize the ideas I seem to hold regarding what I feel I deserve. If you are honest with yourself, you will certainly, realize, that when you worry, your desire might be off a tad from what you really feel you deserve, as do I from time to time. I take it personally and discover my thoughts that shrink the moments of satisfaction. And if I feel inadequate, I can quickly recognize it and from there I can rekindle my spirit of worthiness with practice and then I will appreciate more of what I want to come into my life, always starting from embracing self-value. This is, indeed, a process of second-into-second, thought-into-thought learning to appreciate self and to overlook what others may have mentioned as imperfections or that in so being self I might feel inappropriate or less than another in any way. I can wipe out these overtures with realizing that what I think about myself is substantiated with the Laws of the Universe and the inherent eternal love of Source. If I am thinking myself less, I am believing in inequality. No one can actualize equality while thinking themselves more or less than others, all others. This process written out, as such, seems so straightforward and easy. I was trained, as most of us, so well to get sloppy in my self-appreciative thoughts for all the same reasons others have been also. I have determined that being compulsive and/or impulsive about jumping right into finding what is wrong with me is what smothers my fire; hence, I am ever increasingly stronger in healing my self-induced thoughts of agitation into the view of me from the Eyes of Source or Love. This is ongoing, even as I write about it.

When I am extinguished and need to replenish, I move my thought concentration from what seems to feel like my forehead and walk it back and up and open the top of my head such that I can witness the Eyes of Source, the Purity of Life, looking through my eyes and allowing my consciousness a look at this better reality. It is a very pleasant sensation to view in my consciousness what this Great Source sees because it is more than a visual, it is a heart toned sight. It is insight and up-sight combined. This takes but a moment and is extremely helpful and loving. It fills me with understanding at what then seems intuitive and apparent. It is obvious to me that whenever I invite the sight of the Eyes of Source, Living Purity, to inform me, it is available. As I seep back into self-alignment from this type of experience, my nature is comfortable and awakened. This is a gift of receiving enlightenment. It is undoubtedly a willing answer from a questioning overlapping confusion and it always strengthens my ability to be more consciously compassionate to others and to myself.

Encouraging myself to be all that I know, or that I am learning better to know, I can be, always begins with being aware of the empowering stream of thoughts collected into the intention of desired manifestation(s). Desires are thought ideas that increase direction into the future. Also, to be known, it is the allowing of desires that increase the formation of manifestations. I have to be a match to more than what I desire, I have to match up to what I think I deserve. And in these complexities, I can recognize that I desire and deserve that experience of positive synchronization and coincidence.

I feel this is a good place to go back and pick up on the ever-lurking concern that we call "worry" briefly, thus far, mentioned in this book. Worry is not spoken of often as an emotion. Apparently, everyone is too worried about worrying to bring it up too often. Many of us know the feeling of worry. I want to address one special form of worry. It is the worry about others. It happens a lot with parents. From the moment our children are born we tend to worry about them. Some parents take on worry as a badge of love. It is not.

I have been working on letting go of worry. My sister, who is a senior, is working during Covid 19 as a greeter at a Visitor Center in her small town in Vermont, and sometimes as a substitute teacher at the local elementary school there. I do not understand why she would do these seemingly, to me, dangerous jobs during this autumn increase of Covid cases in every state in the USA. Then I have to remember that this is her choice and that she is perfectly able to judge her own danger. It is a weird feeling to worry about her. I probably have justification for my worry. I am a wise lady though. I know that it is unhealthy to worry about others. It is a matter of taking control of my thoughts. I have now again addressed my worried feeling about my sister, and then, I have to surface it into an understanding that I can control. I know it is unhealthy to worry. So then let me work this out.

My sister is very intelligent. She is a healthy person. She is a woman of faith and discipline. She loves people and connecting to people and helping others is what she loves to do. She is working at doing things she loves. Those thoughts help me worry less. I also know that she is happy with her life and is doing things that keep her happy. Happiness is by far a more powerful emotional state of being than is worry. She is not worried. This is good and I do not have to worry either. I have to let worry go and trust in the future.

I recall the very moment in life when I faced-off with worry and I always go back to that moment when I feel worry creep into my life. Our tweenager daughter was late getting home. It was hours past the time she was expected home. She was out with her best friend and her mother. They were going for the day swimming at a large swim park on this perfect summer's day. The park was closed for hours now and it was only a half hour away. It was not so much late timewise being about 11 o'clock, although, it was hours after I was told to expect her back for dinner. I actually called the hospital that they would pass on the way home to thankfully hear that there were no emergencies. I was really worried though. I decided to go to bed and let the night progress if only I could sleep. Uri was sound asleep already. He didn't feel a need to worry, and I didn't fuss to tell him so much of what I was going through. Him sleeping made me feel my worry bigger for some unknown reason. I didn't really even try to sleep. I could not sleep. I lay there looking at the blank tv not on. And all of a sudden, I heard all those words of thought pivoting and I allowed myself to stop worrying. I felt an empty loosening up and a resolve that lifted my spirits. I actually thought, a need to trust that the future was bright for me and for my daughter. I felt a great warm appreciation for my life. I was looking at a black tv screen and seeing my daughter's future of many wonders coming her way. I felt the opposite of worry. I felt certain. Worry cannot exist in joy. I felt a great joy for the life of my daughter and for my life too. I stopped instantly my worry. I believe of all the lower based-emotions worry can be eliminated completely with a knowingness of its insanity. I stopped my worry, and she came home soon thereafter. There is a little more to the story too. I asked the Mom why she was late, and she quickly said she had decided to take the girls out to dinner. I asked the Mom why she didn't answer the phone and why didn't my daughter call to mention they were going to be late. All she could say was "There was nothing to worry about." True enough. I that evening retrained myself to overcome worry. Although the more that I learnt that evening is something outside of myself. As this Mom turned about in her car to continue on, I noticed the words that were framed around her license plate on the car. It was lit up with plate lights. It read; "Always late but worth the wait.". That message spoke volumes to me. Some people like others to worry about them. Being late often leaves someone to wonder why. Some people enjoy the attention of others worrying about them. It is a form of getting extra attention. There was no need to worry, although the worry was intentionally grown into my reality through another's intentional influence. Worry is a hideous experience. It takes one out of the present moment and into a negative future; one that hasn't happened. And each worry, if vibrant, can actually contribute to a negative future on that worried about subject. Think something bad is going to happen and it might well happen. Worry is creating that which you do not want into the future. As soon as you feel worry; turn from it. Avoid it. And when

*What You Think Matters*

you trust another person with potentially turning on your worry, turn from it. Avoid the drama and avoid the dramatic. Ease your life with clarity by trusting the future is good.

After deciding to leave our Family Home and find a place to relocate to, we chose to take it in steps. During our years together, we were smart, blessed and fortunate to invest in our property in the downtown hillslope of Ventura that had, not one, but two old houses on it. In fact, they were one hundred years old by the time we sold that property, that we owned for about 30 years. We rented them out, ever improving the quality of the houses, land and, in ways, the lives of the guests who chose to match up to living there and permeate through needed changes and to radiate forward. We included the desire to provide these houses to others who, indeed, were right for them. Being the owners of this property, we presumed that property-purpose would continue on as it felt it always came with a thoughtful kindness to its residents; past, present and future. These homes housed a spirit of *"Permeate and Radiate"* and within our knowledge of purpose, we also knew many would come to appreciate more their experience of life on this property. The houses were much more than an investment property to make money. They were comfortable pleasant homes. It was a place where residents, we often in the family referred to as guests, could recover and become more. At this property people would *"Permeate and Radiate"*. And that was very true. The property caretaking actually was a family activity, or more like love, as we all worked on these little houses in-between having them rented. The entire family participated in the upkeep and we enjoyed them along the way too. I could write a book on the many

*The Art of Appreciating MORE*

experiences of people and circumstances we all had while land-lording and maintaining those little houses with great love and care. We invested in them as an extension of Uri's initial investment in a small house he lived in while first immigrating to America from Israel and while attending college for engineering. Uri obtained his citizenship there and it had some mixed memories as adapting to a new country has its challenges. He experienced prejudices and poor manners from others thinking he was less than they were due to language limitations. He doesn't complain about the experiences as it developed his character and gave insights to others too. Now in Ventura, twenty years later, we felt the distance between Van Nuys, where his house was, and our lives in Ventura was too far apart and it was impossible to keep track of the tenants renting there or easily tend to the repairs needed to the house. Therefore, we sold it and purchased this property in the downtown Ventura hillslope area that was budding anew from within its antique ever becoming potential we noticed long before others did.

Years had passed and now as a part of our long-term financing, we decided that after selling our Family House, we would move-in and update-to-sell these rental houses. It made so much financial sense as the tax laws stated that the property gains taxes where only to apply to a property after the first five hundred thousand dollars of profit were made. If we lived there for two years after when we would sell our Family House as our main residence, we could save, no not save, it was going to actually earn a good return on our investment, efforts and love, to put towards our retirement years.

This was a very good idea, although I did not really love living in the downtown area, which was very busy and noisy to my liking and our Family House was very nice and quiet. Still it made very good financial sense, so we put on the market our Family House and moved into the larger of the two houses downtown. It was a perfect time to do so, because our tenant in the two-bedroom house was aligning to a move to a better neighborhood to raise his two children. They, a boy and girl, really needed their own rooms. The little one-bedroom house was settled in by a doctor who lived there alone. He now looked and found a place in a town closer to the hospital he worked in. We always called them the Little Pink and Green Houses and we for years ran an extended stay business there. More recently, these houses were occupied for several years and it is interesting that if you rent places, they actually stay in better condition if there is a lot of moving in and out. Things were always needing to be repaired and while a tenant was in for a while, they might not mention repairs rather than bother us and have someone working and lurking about into their home life. We understood that and were happy to regain possession of these units and fix them up.

Now, we were to move into the property for another reason. We knew its history and recognized that we too would go through our needs to *"Permeate and Radiate"*. We were ready to do this. Additionally, to help in our decision making, the tax law stated that we could not rent either house or forfeit these tax benefits we thought worthwhile to qualify for, therefore, we asked one of our daughters, Michelle, who had fairly recently graduated college if she wanted to live in the second house on that property rent free and in that time, she could figure out her life career etc. without the burden of the expense of housing, for the most part. Her boyfriend, Peter, was living with her in Orange County when they both thought this free housing could actually help them to establish their pathway. So, it came to pass that we could all live on the same property in two separate houses while they were slowly over two or so years being remodeled and updated such that we could sell them for a maximum value. That was how we started the move-on adventure. We knew it was a good place to be for a few years such that we all could figure our future's out.

It was a little miracle to have these houses to live-in while we migrated towards a more permanent solution for our long-term needs. It was wonderful to live on the same property as Michelle and Peter too. The only set back to speak of was that until Michelle and Peter moved in, the smaller of the houses was a beach house that was open to anyone in the family interested in a get-a-way. Our daughter, Tasha, who did enjoy the beach house concept into her life regularly, gave it up for Michelle and Peter and when she visited, she stayed with us in our place. The smaller house was really small but beautiful. It was a one-bedroom house. It was such a fun adventure to share our investment property to benefit our family in these ways.

At this time, Uri retired from his job too. We were both retired now. We both agreed that we had this job to do and that was to renovate and sell this investment property. From there we did not know what we would do or where we would live. It was a blessing that there was a clear road on which for this time of transitioning we could call home.

As, Uri and I, started out on our journey to relocate, we looked near and far. We traveled to all parts of California and then searched Hawaii too. We kept returning back to our temporary living in our previously rented investment properties. It was our home base and it was, indeed, lovely.

And so, we continued.

Chapter Two- Appreciations on What you Think Matters

- ❖ I appreciate maturing into recognizing that I can think whatever I want to think and more importantly comes with this knowledge the utilizing of what I think about for my creative benefit of manifestation.

- ❖ I appreciate that how I feel at any given moment influences what I think about and the better I feel the better the results are in my life experience.

- ❖ I appreciate growing a quicker analysis of my feelings resulting from most of my thoughts and I can better control and create deliberately as a result.

- ❖ I appreciate that I can overrule tendencies of thought patterns, such as defaulted mind sets, as soon as I realize that they exist.

- ❖ I appreciate that sloppy thinking often are products of past thought training and I can release myself from them.

- ❖ I appreciate that experience is my greatest teacher.

- ❖ I appreciate that age is only one attribute in obtaining wisdom, which is in constant need for updates.

- ❖ I appreciate that I am great beyond my ability to comprehend and that everyone is equally great.

- ❖ I appreciate what others think about me only matters if I allow it to.

- ❖ I appreciate the journey in self-awareness includes others.

*I appreciate those memories from my childhood that feel like I floated past each day and then grew up too fast.*

## Chapter 3  Coincidence & Synchronicity

I've come to appreciate of The Law of Attraction, specifically, the ways in which coincidence and synchronicity works its astonishing assemblage to bring about a deeper awareness of what is always going on in life, knowingly or not. I feel it is unfortunate to miss the constant flow of coincidence and the powerful connection to synchronicity. I want to develop more the capability to welcome these somewhat magical

# Coincidence & Synchronicity

alignments. Coincidence is a form of miracle that has come about into being appreciated. Everything is aligning to other things all of the time. Realizing the process that the line travels to arrive at the dots taken in perfect order, touched and then noticing it is all a result of the Law of Attraction's coexistence. Knowing and better, appreciating, this thing called, coincidence, is an opportunity to make some refined changes to improve-self, while loving the harmony in juxtaposition, or even multi-juxtaposition, within other or interleaving events. If the ideas and experiences of coincidence and synchronicity were ever an easy subject to address, many would have done so already. I love coincidence and although I've heard a lot of people confuse me during my lifetime by saying coincidence doesn't exist, I have stopped thinking that true for me. I love the feeling of something happening that simply seems nearly impossible to happen, except that it does happen. I am a believer that coincidence is evidence of my dreams coming true. It is a succinct occurrence that is also beneficial as are miracles. That is absolutely amazing. If I only knew that sooner in life, I would have remarked every incident of coincidence in heart felt gratitude. Coincidence is the allowance of the desired unknown to come into my real life. It is a thrill.

Coincidence doesn't surprise me as much any longer. Still it can actually be stunning to me at first knowing or recognizing. It's not "surprise"; it is more like "Wow!". Although somewhat in disbelief in its manifestation, I know it when happening and I can usually explain some of it in words sometimes for a while, although, coincidence, once recognized, leaves far too quickly; as do goose bumps once noticed, although goose bumps are something else quite unique and not necessarily in partnership with "coincidence" merely somewhat potentially a supporting-actor when wonder overwhelms in that way. When I say I am somewhat in disbelief, that is a lazy explanation. I am not really in disbelief; I am at finally believing. I am more awakened to what is happening all of the time. Coincidental complacency falls into my life experiences so often, that when it is realized, I am that which comes around to appreciate it finally. In recognized-coincidence or in the wake of synchronicity, I feel ultra-blessed. It makes me feel "high" naturally.

Coincidence is often too convoluted to explain with clarity to adjust another to the same frequency felt at the time and then it becomes the past, and it is further and further away every moment. In the same understanding, Coincidence, can be realized by more than one person when happening. Sometimes coincidence shares with another or others its occurrence. Mostly, seemingly to me, coincidence aligns with whatever, however, whenever or whoever it needs to, and in trying to define it, the depth can depend upon the mix of self-connection more often than others being connected to that knowing you are experiencing. What it leaves is an indelible mark on me of perfected helplessness in over-standing rather than understanding and some type of humility that could almost wobble my knees.

I am convinced that coincidence is goodness seeing, or more like creating, itself while I see it too with an appreciation. It is amazing. It sincerely does feel like more than what I am individually capable of creating. It is created for me and by me in a connective cooperation with at least self and more likely with Source desires or agreements materializing. Additionally, it feels, in that regard, like a divine intervention. And what can feel better! Appreciation comes from inspiration and so too does coincidence. I used to accept it as something

# Coincidence & Synchronicity

special or bigger than appreciation, and then let it go. Now, I want to bask in it longer and attempt to discover from it who, what, when, where and why, and, of course, how did this twist of fate come to happen, because I want more of it happening. I also want to extract from it the countenance of its purpose. In a way I go through some of the same mental processing when I experience what we call Deja Vue, which when it happens, I quickly try to absorb it as a message coming to me again and it quickly dissipates and fades off into oblivion. Coincidence feels like a stronger manifestation than Deja Vue. It, although often baffling, feels amazingly good and well connected. When I experience coincidence, I know I am in a good emotional place and I can trust it has purpose. There is magic finding my heart in aware coincidence happening.

I love coincidence. If I could orchestrate or be responsible for such a beautiful demonstration of Universal Love, I want to. If I could be available to participate, I freely volunteer. I think that coincidence happens because sometimes I require the confirmation of something more holy-powerful than normalcy. Other times, when in coincidence, all good is better understood and acknowledged. One leads to the other and back to the initial, such that they blend. I love the feeling of coincidence.

At times, when I come into the magic of coincidence, I think I am seeing something I perhaps am not really ripely intended to see or realize. More so now I believe that coincidence intends to be noticed even more than I do. Coincidence wants to be noted in their times of occurrence, and to strengthen belief in self-capabilities, in order for me to create, even before I am awakened to or reminded of my own abilities to create. Once awakened to my own control of thoughts, I believe that coincidence builds self-confidence and self-worthiness, while sharpening my understandings of my permission to experience it. I love and appreciate coincidence.

I want to grow my ability to create coincidence and so in that deliberate statement, I know that I can create more coincidence simply by focusing upon what it is and how I felt when I did experience it already. Fairly recently, although too quickly fading into the past, I experienced an "over the top" coincidence. That coincidence is this Chapter's story line.

It is a long story, but I have to tell it, for me and for others who want to know more about coincidence. I want to create coincidence. I want to enjoy coincidence. I want to trust the Universal Law of Attraction to flow generously coincidence into my life. I want to savor in the deliciousness of coincidence. I also want to teach the way The Law of Attraction, actually provides coincidence into our experiences. If you take coincidence for granted you will miss the generous love and bliss that is deserved.

Get comfortable because there are about 65 years that lead up to this miracle of this *perfect timing* of events strung together and belonging to each other. Coincidence and synchronicity are very complex scenario-driven, time-balanced relative awareness alignments that cannot easily be scientifically disproven as being the something special they are and are experienced quite personally or intimately. To experience either or both, is more a spiritual encounter. It can, if explained right to those not really believing in the existence of the Law of Attraction, be one of the rare

## Coincidence & Synchronicity

proofs that the Law of Attraction really does exist. Everything proves the Law of Attraction, when out to prove it. I am so thrilled to discover so much truth in myself and, of course, the Law of Attraction. This story is real life for me and in it I come to appreciate that my thoughts have created my life. People can draw their own conclusions. I smugly smile knowingly!

It involves my best girlfriend when I was a child. Mary and I met when she was six years old and I four and a half. I didn't know she was really older than I was until she had to go to school, and I didn't. I do not remember the exact day we met. Mary probably does remember and if not, she will make it up into a believable story for you. Even when writing this, at 67 years of age, Mary remembers everything about her childhood, plus, like many of us, what she makes into a story.

Setting the stage, we lived in an inner-city Newark, New Jersey project, known as the Bradley Court, North Munn Avenue, Victory Gardens. When I was born, I came home to this project where my older brother also came home three years before, and I spent my life into my early twenties there. The projects were originally built for the World War II returning military families to host them into the promise of the future, at a low rent and hopefully into jobs centering-around the greater Newark/New York City areas. My father served in the United States Army Air Corp, today known as The Air Force, during WWII and qualified to live there. These ten, three story brick buildings, which took up most of a city block, excluding the old huge wooden professional boxing arena at the corner, that eventually came down and became a Safeway and has now, looking at Google Maps, evolved into a school. And then there was Lynches' Liquor Store and Bar, that probably thrived for generations on the community's alcoholics. There lined the rest of the block a small collection of Mom-and-Pop repair shops that all faced the main street, which was South Orange Avenue, and which we just called "The Avenue" or "The Javenue". One cannot pronounce Orange followed by Avenue without the "Javenue" being sounded out.

The project buildings where structured to surround a center area, to go along with the original idea of a central victory gardens, which became the playgrounds over time. Although, by the time Mary moved into the projects that specific, of being a part of a military family had been removed from the qualifications and anyone who applied had to pretty much be "poor" or "low income" in today's terms. The projects became known as just "Bradley Court" or "The Projects". There were no other projects in our neighborhood. The neighborhood Bradley Court was in was Lower Vailsburg of Newark. There were other projects in Newark in different neighborhoods some build twenty years after Bradley Court. This one was the one I grew up in. Lucky me!

I was a little too young to have noticed the change actually take place, although I do recall families of people that my parents and my grandparents knew moving in and out for a while, including my grandparents and my aunt and uncle and their kids. Our family, which was growing with kids by leaps and bounds, also moved only not out of the projects but rather from one building to another until we landed at Building 52. My parents stayed there for the next twenty-eight years. I escaped sooner.

By the time I was eight years old, most apartments had one kind of a problem living there or another. Most all the military families had moved off into, I guessed, better places. My family did not. My dad was a well-decorated

## Coincidence & Synchronicity

World War Two Veteran and my mom worked in downtown Newark during the war years building some of the military support electronic at Westinghouse. Why we didn't move was probably complicated. My dad commuted to New York City or the Port of Newark/New York every day. Where we lived was close enough and seemingly far enough to keep as an address in order such that he could get to work. My dad worked for all his adult life after the War. The New York/New Jersey Port Authority was the name of his company. And although, he had a very steady job, it was apparently hard to gather up enough money and or guts to move someplace else that would not make his commute longer. My mother was in charge of the money dad made and what she said was we didn't have enough money to move. Not having enough was a theme with my Mom and so it was. We, as she would often say; can barely make ends meet.

Moving closer to New York City to make my dad's commute easier was less desirable to my dad and even as a young child I felt that made sense because as you went closer to dad's work, the city became bigger and deeper and didn't feel right to live in. Dad, although he was born in the borough of The Bronx, liked being out of it. Maybe that was the reason we stayed longer than seemed we should have stayed in those Projects. Perhaps he had some interesting even difficult experiences on the streets of New York as a child and I detected he was trying to avoid that for his kids. His intentions were good in our living there generally and I guess if Newark and The Projects were better to grow up in than was the Bronx, I was ok with that too. Additionally, my Dad's Wartime experiences impacted him too. Lovingly looking back at his life from an adult's perspective rather than a child's, my Dad was a stronghold and a disciplined man of honor and locked deep within was some of what is called in today's world as post traumatic war stress disorder. He would deny it though as do many others of all generations who experience war.

Mary moved into a two-bedroom apartment with her mom. Her dad lived someplace else and came to visit her for short times, usually on a Saturday or Sunday. Sometimes he and she would just sit in the car in the parking lot and talk about stuff for a half hour or less, or other time he would drive off with her and return her early in the evening. I always wished that I could talk to my dad, the way they seemed to be talking sitting there in the car windows closed and no one around to hear a word. I hardly noticed that he actually didn't live there, because most all dads worked all week long and seemed more visible on weekends. Rarely did a mom work out of the home back in those days.

Mary's mom, Lee, was a pretty slight woman with large brown eyes and dark shiny hair and a deep voice. Lee was an Italian American, second generation, so she was as American as Spaghetti. She is gone now. Over to that other side we all eventually go back into. She lived a long life and added to humanity what she could. She had compassion and passion. She was Mary's Mother and for that I am thankful. Mary's little old grandma on her mother's side, well she "was-a-different" in her Italian accent and much more. Mary's grandma was a tiny, though a bit wide, happy-faced old wrinkled lady who smiled more than she spoke, and I wondered often why. Mary was half Italian and half Irish. Her dad and she were fair pale white-skinned, and she even had freckles, although she and her mom both had brown eyes, Mary's eyes were lightened with hazel tones. Her hair was lighter than her mom's, although, I saw in her smile the same smile that her mom had, rather than her grandma.

As children we, of course, smiled a lot of the time, especially when we were playing together, and we were always together. We were the greatest of friends. Inseparable, as it is said. And the years passed by and we were more like sisters than I felt my sisters were sisters to me at that time. Time changed our closeness as we all grew into adults. Both my sisters were younger than I was, although, amazingly close in ages; one less than a year younger, Eileen, and the other less than two years younger, Louise. My youngest sister had a twin brother, Hugh. The twins and Eileen shared the same age in number for one entire week out of the year. Irish twins, but really Irish triplets. I also had two additional brothers; Gene was three years older than I was and the other Patrick, the baby of the family, was born when I was about five years old. I lived in a large family of kids and Chipper, our dog. Additionally, my grandparents, my father's parents, were often at our house. Mary only had her mom. She did have her own bedroom, which, to me, had to have been the best thing ever. Sharing a room with my two sisters was interesting and quite normal herding. Kids are so willing to accept their lives the way it is supposed to be. And so, it was. I have always loved my sisters and always will. It is a forever love we are privileged to share. They have often felt like an extension of myself.

Mary and I lived in the same building. My family, The McGowan's, lived on the ground floor and Mary and her mom lived on the second of the three-story building we called home. Our apartment was a three bedroom, and it was the first apartment at the stoop entry into our building's hall, mailboxes and stairwell. Mary lived in the apartment straight ahead at the top of the first flight of stairs; the middle of the three two-bedroom apartments on that floor, as there was a door off to the left just next door to her place also at the top of the stairs and another in the corner next to her apartment to the right of the top of the stairs. These were to be the stairs that we learned how to act like monkeys on as they were railed with metal bars that tempted us early in life, and these stairs were where Patrick would take a fall and have a concussion that as a result, he would always be dyslexic, or so I was told. It was a bad fall right on his head, at any rate. This was the stairwell that we found ourselves sitting in, Mary and I, for many hours, awaiting a better moment to arrive and enter into our "homes". We knew when there was something to avoid inside our apartments as we approach together often from school or play.

There were five apartments on each of the three floors and with each building having two unique non-connective entries each physical building held fifteen apartments at each entry hall, thirty apartments altogether in each building structure. Walls and a roof trapdoor connected these thirty apartments. Only half apartment residents came in from the same entry. I think I was more aware of that than others living in building 52, because the back adjacent walls to my bedroom was right against the neighbor's bedroom in building 54 of the same apartment size.

There were a great many people living in those buildings. I only knew that way of life. Being around so many different people was natural to me. And as a child, I knew who lived in every single apartment, what they were like, how they lived, what religion they were, which was their car, where it was usually parked, if they had company or if they were expecting company, and so much more. I even knew what was in their garbage. I

## Coincidence & Synchronicity

took notice that some people would be so careful to put their garbage deep into the bin while always looking around to see who might be watching. Most people did not know that I was watching them. I was quite good at being invisible. I knew the faces and manners of seemingly every person in all of those buildings. Hundreds of people all living in Bradley Court. I knew who was grumpy or nice, who drank too much, who cooked really delicious smelling food, who was sick, who was happy, who liked baseball as much as my dad, who listened to classical music, who played the piano, who was alone, who was too different for me to understand at all, and who was like me. I knew where the kids lived; their names, what grade they were in, and if they got good marks at school. I knew where the elderly lived; who visited them and how often. I realized a lot about a lot of people living there as I watched and paid attention to the littlest details that were present, like what time they came home, went out, took a bath, or if they locked their door when they hung out their clothes to dry. I knew who watched the Ed Sullivan Show, Mitch Miller, World of Disney or the Naked City. Each household had a couple of things that struck me worth noting. They were their door matt and their clothespin bags. I knew when someone bought a new car or a new bag of clothespins, especially if they were the clothespins that had those metal hinges. I noticed a lot of, what seemed to me, average things about everyone.

The buildings, as I mentioned had an opened space between the five on one side and on the other side, and they were lined-up like straight-shoulder-to shoulder-soldiers dressed in American uniforms with space between each other to have a couple of permanently placed wooden park like benches with a cemented-in centered short table at the areas and a large fenced-in area for the clothes lines that were shared by the entry of one building and the entry of the building next to it. The buildings were not tenements, as I knew them to be from my imagination and TV shows or from the movie "West Side Story", because tenement apartments had fire-escapes, which we did not have and in tenements you could easily see into your neighbor's windows from your own windows. These buildings were lined up with a wide enough space between them that you could not see into other people's apartments from your windows, although you could see their windows. I supposed we had no fire-escapes because we didn't have any wood in these structures to burn. I always feel fire would be impossible to have happen in these building of strength. Cement, metal and bricks do not burn.

We, at Building 52 shared our center area with Building 50. There were a lot of sidewalks of cement, perfect for bouncing a ball or hopping a scotch on, some soft grassy areas and each entry had a few big shady trees. There were some pretty nice things about the projects, but mostly it was apparent to me at a pretty young age, that I would come to escape this place someday and I did as soon as I could.

Since our family had so many kids, we lived in the three-bedroom unit, which was the largest. Each floor had one upon the other the one three-bedroom apartment, three two-bedroom apartments and one one-bedroom apartment. In total the ten buildings and the twenty entries housed a few more than three hundred families living very close together. There were a few "Garden Apartments" that laced the basement areas of the building structures that were coming off the hill slope on the other side of the playgrounds. That was the style apartment we lived in until my sister Eileen was born. There were a lot of things happening at the projects.

# Coincidence & Synchronicity

There were a lot of stuff to keep notice of growing up. If not, you could be very sorry.

Unless I was away with my family on vacation or visiting a relative, I was spending a lot of time with Mary, and she often went along with my family on our trips and adventures out of the Projects. My father had a Volkswagen Bus, so we always had room for one or the other to bring a friend along, or not.

Mary and I remained friends all through grade, middle and high school. And since I "skipped" three half-year times by the time I was in sixth grade, I actually caught up to her grade level and we happily continued in the same grade through graduating together from high school. However, except for an occasional gym class, we always had different classes and subjects. I didn't think I was any smarter than Mary was, I just found school very easy to get good grades. Actually, I loved school. I was an accelerated student with a reputation of multi-skipping and I just loved learning. Being an exceptional student enabled me to gain confidence and self-worth, both attributes that were not readily instilled in my home life, probably due to the way attention from our parents had to be shared with a group of siblings and that we were a Roman Catholic Family, who were taught to be less demonstrative and more proper. I did very well in school and was continuously advanced into classes that were experimental and in high school I began accrediting college as I entered my junior year. I was one of a dozen that had these advanced classes, and there were probably a dozen other students at the opposite end of that spectrum. During our schooling together the general student population, which she was in, consisted of the regular programed classes and although we shared no academic classes I went to school and returned from school with Mary, almost every single day that didn't require my attendance at a club of interest to me or an event she was not interested in. Even some of our extracurricular activities we shared, if we could. She had friends from her classes that I got to know, and I had friends from my classes that she got to know, but we remained the best of each other's friends.

All this apparent institutionalize educational separation considered, Mary was to me, and still is, one of the smartest people I've ever known, and I have known a lot of very smart people in my life since escaping Newark, New Jersey. Mary had exceptional talents that I noticed and enjoyed being a part of. She was an excellent artist. I tried to learn how to draw like she did. I needed the eraser a lot more than she did. She was just really smart. She had an amazing voice too and we would sing while her mom was out of the apartment to each other in opera because we wanted life to be more like that; like an opera or a musical. I remember thinking if I could only draw or sing like Mary, I would let others see that of me. Mary did not often, except to me. I would ask; "Why don't you join the glee club?" and she would say she was not good enough. That dissuaded me to ever join too, because if she didn't have a good enough voice, I knew I didn't either. Over time, I'd notice that she lacked the ability to see her own talents or admit to them. I thought she was being humble or shy about her talents, so I would encourage her on to use them better. She just could not see her own goodness, although I felt she believed me. I would see a slight smile cross her face at my complements. More often she might ask me to stop it. She either didn't like hearing a complement or she didn't believe in the complement I was giving to her. I think the latter more certainly after all these years of wondering. I didn't understand a lot about why she didn't see her talents, however, she managed to find new things to do extremely well regularly, and then she would not promote herself in doing them too. She was absolutely beautiful. She was always too critical of herself. I too was somewhat critical of self-beauty, although I was less verbal about it and I always corrected her extreme critique of herself. By the time she was graduating high school and heading off to college in Yankton, South Dakota, (where her father got her accepted) she was so beautiful from her constant self-criticism and consistent effort to look better, that she was like a movie star.

I continued on my local college/work path while Mary went away. Too soon enough she returned broken and turned even more inward. She quit school and went to work in downtown Newark at one of the insurance companies. I could not do that. I could not work in Newark. I just was too bored of it all. I instead wanted to work in New York City. It was an obsession with me. I wanted to get to know the Big Apple and work there and continue to go to school there instead of being in Newark. I despised living in the Projects and I just wanted out of there. I wanted to know people who were not from there, not from the projects and not from Newark. From many places around the neighborhood I could see New York City and it was a wonderful sight to see filled with my future. Mary on the other hand, loved the simplicity of working downtown and coming to and from into her apartment on one bus, no transfers. It became her apartment. Her mom had signed herself into programs away from home to improve herself after Mary went off to college and Mary lived in the apartment alone waiting her mother's return. Her Mom did come back and forth from her programs and Mary just became part of the silence of loneliness of in-between. Mary did enjoy redecorating a bit and living the quiet life. I, on the other hand was off and running. I found one escape after

another and not soon enough I was out on my own. Living a huge life.
I left Mary there, no regrets. I left my family there, as well. I left a lot behind, no regrets. Once in a while I might stop up to see her, if she was home, when I visited my parents, but often she wasn't available, and I had changed a great deal. I did not visit my parents too often. I got married. Mary was my beautiful Maid of Honor and when my marriage ended in less than 3 months, I stopped up to visit her and she was dating a guy, Tony, who was taking her to a club in central Jersey that evening. She invited me along. I was so happy to see her happy, it seemed. Tony and Mary really got along so well, and I had a great time that evening, got back to my parents early enough to drive myself back to New York where I maintained the apartment from my marriage and that was it for a long time. I felt so at peace that Mary had a boyfriend. He was so nice, and she was less hung up on herself while with him.

I went on my way. I found plenty of struggles and troubles some might say. I grew and grew and grew and I was so in love with life, although it was, in the comparison with "normal", not normal at all. I saw Mary only a few times, spoke to her only a couple of short calls, and I was living a very different life than was she. I lost track of her and thirty years later, I found her again.

I had occasionally taken the time to find her to no avail for many years and I wondered about her. My parents moved, her mom moved, no one lived in the Projects that we both or either knew any longer. She has a name that is extremely popular, and any search would not find her out of the thousands and thousands of others with her name. I didn't know if she had married and changed her name and she was not registered with our high school alumni. For years I searched for her every now and again. Finally, after thirty years of periodically searching for her, I decided to search on her father's name and state, and he came up in an obituary. I read it wondering if he was her dad, when I saw her name and the town she lived in as part of the obituary article and I recognized some of her relative's names. I searched for her in that town, called information, searched and searched some more until I found a match on an address. I sat down and wrote her a letter. After about a week, on a Sunday afternoon, she called me back from the request in the letter. I was so happy to have found her and she me.

We must have talked on the phone for three hours straight the first time we connected. Halfway into our conversation, she asked me to call her back so to reduce the expenses for her. I had a good affordable program on my phone so there after, if she wanted to talk to me, she would call and hang up after I could see her name id on my phone, and I would promptly call her back. If I called her first, rarely did she actually answer, and she had no answering service, so she would call when she noticed my trying to contact her through the history on her list of ids, hang up and I would dial back.

Mary was not computer literate and didn't have any updated equipment or connectivity; no flat screen TV hooked-up, although she inherited her dad's TV, she had not hooked it up because she didn't understand the electronics and she did not have a cable account. She had an antenna on her TV and watch TV just the way she did in the projects 50 years ago. She had an old microwave and a vacuum cleaner and a hardwired phone. It was like going back in time managing a relationship with Mary, now. She didn't have a cell phone, although she had an emergency cell in the glove compartment of her 20-year-old badly maintained car still sitting in its store box. Through it all, we found a way to routinely connect in this fashion on Sunday afternoons, mostly. And so, for a year and a half, I've been spending time, once a week chatting with Mary. We also exchanged cards and I sent packages. I sent her photos of my family and myself. She did not send me a photo of herself or her two cats. She had never married, not Tony, nor anyone else. She did mention that Tony proposed to her a few years after they started dating, though she did not feel she was good enough for him. No, correction; she felt there had to be something wrong with him if he loved her as he said he did, because her parents didn't even love her, how could he?

After our initial joy and celebration to find each other, our conversations were taking a general direction. I was unable to stop them going in this way either, because if I did, Mary would get upset and I wanted to avoid losing her friendship again, because I was recalling a lot about my childhood that I forgot about and it was like taking a history course in personal past events. She seemed to remember the smallest details about the times we had together which stimulated my own memories. And through her I was growing an understanding about not only our relationship but also my relationships with my siblings and my parents. After my escape, I did not take much time to analyze my childhood too deeply. I let it go. I moved-on, I forgave people, I became whole, and I was very happy and successful in all parts of my life. I loved life, myself, my family, my husband, my home, my career etc., etc., etc. I loved and appreciated everything. Into my life expanse I looked at others regardless of who and felt that they might very well have had a better life in some ways than I had had, although, I grew to appreciate that I made it. I became more and I was happy with my changes. All before now was in the past and all before me is so good.

There was something cynical about the way Mary spoke about her childhood during our Sunday hour long chats. I knew we both had some pretty dysfunctional situations mixed into our childhoods. I was so enjoying holding on to our relationship, which is more an escape for each of us from our "real" worlds. I knew that her mom was pretty dramatic sometimes, but I knew the insides to many of their disputes, and I comparatively was much more obedient and careful, rather than totally respectful of my parents. Mary talked back to her mom. I did not for fear. Mary's mom would lose it sometimes and I remembered some pretty dramatic events take place between those two. Lee would get out the broom and Mary would hide under her bed while being tormented by her mom and the broomstick, and worse were the words of hatred and unworthiness that polluted the air and thoughts of all hearing them, myself included. They were loud enough to hear downstairs, and all the neighbors heard their tales of nasty entanglement. I used to imagine Lee as a witch sometimes. Mary and Lee both carried on saying terrible things to each other for years and years. After a big deal argument, it would be quiet for a week or so. Mary was very into controlling her mom too and often while I was there, Mary would say very demeaning things to her mom. I felt she liked to show me how she was in control of her mom, because she knew I had no control of my mom. She didn't understand that I did not want to have control of my mom either. I just wanted to escape. I even dreamt that Lee and Mary might want to adopt me. That truly would be better for me.

I knew I could never talk to my mom the way Mary spoke to her mom. I didn't want to either. It felt too much like giving in to it all to tell my mom what I felt was wrong with her. Not ever could or would I talk or shout at my mom like Mary did to Lee or I'd be dead. My mom did not allow any disrespect towards her. She demanded respect. That is exactly her words; "I demand respect." Yes, she would yell that at me sometimes, and she meant it. My mom was very quick with the hand and when she was well thought out about discipline, she would systematically put time aside with great intent and give me or one of my siblings a spanking with a hairbrush on my back or bare butt, or she would come out with "daddy's belt", which she also called "The strap". I knew a different kind of violent discipline than Mary did, and I felt Mary had an easier life and a lot less discipline. She held on to everything noticed in others that she deemed disparaging so intensely; never forgetting or forgiving, holding on to grudges, and using them to shelter herself in a hideous pride of convenance she owned to make you feel smaller, while herself obviously shrinking. She actually had a lot less to complain about than she understood, taking comparisons only as she wanted rather than seeing more of the total picture.

When I was beaten-up by my mom or dad, I was told I could not cry or yell or they would hit me longer and harder. The neighbors were never to hear us cry from being spanked, as we heard Mary's episodes. All of us kids in my family had to learn that or be really hurt. It was horrible to be spanked, and it was seemingly at least if not more horrible to know that my younger sisters were getting a spanking. It was physically painful and emotionally demoralizing. It was always taking place right in the next room, but it was a million miles away from my influence to stop it or my ears to not hear it. It brought with its discomfort fears of several natures, all thankfully I meandered myself out of and resolve most all my past as part of the bouncing off into a wiser person who respects others in equality rather than in degrees of physical strength or emotional depravity. A person's character can come out of deep places to appreciate the light.

During our torment, our parents said the same things to my siblings as we discussed it, and we all learned to not yell, and to cry into our pillows only after the beatings were over. We cried with each other and then ever so quietly. I remember taking a beating or two for my sisters. Although that doesn't make any sense to me any longer. I didn't and still do not understand why my parents had it in them to spank their children. The purpose must have been to discipline us into stronger people. I wonder what they were really thinking. And still, it doesn't matter. I appreciate that I was born and lived through some hardships and I appreciate that my parents got me through in my life to a place where I could take care of myself. I appreciate life so much and I do not have to understand their motives. I am a sensitive person; they were less so. My siblings probably remembered themselves taking the beating for me. Memories are like that. They can make us each feel like the victim and each feel like the hero all in the same breath. I remember one of my brothers being blamed for something I did that should have been inconsequential, in anyone's comprehension of measured deeds, and him not telling on me and taking the beating for me. I never told Mary. I never felt compelled to surface these things until after my mom died and one of my sisters felt a need to talk about it with me.

Writing about it is surreal and I feel indifference regarding releasing this, wondering why it is now necessary. In the depths of my soul, I believe it has to do with defining the changes humanity is experiencing through a more compassionate consciousness. I was probably not the only child in my generation or those to follow who didn't understand the anger in people around us; especially in those we loved. The impact upon the spirit to sense so much trust and so much fear at the same time is indecent. I am so hopeful that the changes and shifting of humanities consciousness and with the knowledge and application of being responsible for our thoughts and actions, each and every one of us, that the awareness of equality comes faster into our futures. We can only be responsible for ourselves and it is a responsible love that realizes ways to insight others of this and their needed positive responsiveness. This is the path humanity is on. Things are getting better. As we move into being better individuals, we experience better results. This is Law! In finding comfort in who you are as a kind human, who appreciates equality, you can trust the path without actually knowing where it is going. The unknown is nothing bigger than the next best place to be.

It didn't seem to matter too much to me, either while this abuse was taking place or afterwards as I grew up into an escaped adult. There is something else that became formative into my life that replaced blame and/or shame. It is my innate understanding that there are people who are less sensitive towards everything in life and there are people who are very sensitive and capture each moment at levels that include a great degree of intensity, memory, pattern recognition, acceptance, allowance, forgetfulness, and many other characteristics I've come to terms with having. I had developed a short-term memory retention regarding any form of abuse as a child or adult that was probably healthier than hanging on to misdeeds that sprang into my life, always including insensitive people.

# Coincidence & Synchronicity

People who are sensitive can be insensitive and people who are insensitive can be sensitive, although in my case, I became intuitively more sensitive all the time and rarely enabled myself to regress into insensitivities. What might be noted is that my reserved insensitivities became those special moments that connect to survival or protection. I felt happy to have them and refer to them as aware suspicions. They have been most helpful in my life assisting me into better decision making. The point of mentioning this is that as I write about any dysfunctionality in my youth, in particular, it should be noted that I accept fully them happening and simultaneously I accept fully my part in them and I even more, accept fully their necessity in order for me to be where I am now. I am neither a saint nor a victim. I am experienced. Escaping is my expression. I have also shifted out of normal changes and into my improved life and my perspective of what was going on in my childhood. I do not hold malice thoughts about my parents or others with whom I experienced what feels like abuse, I though cannot deny the past as real. Apparently, my parents knew no better. They were sometimes insensitive, and sometime sensitive. These years were different than now also. Transparency is a more openness and children are not as often treated as victims by their care givers. I also know it continues in places still in darkness. For those current or future situations, I expand hope for changes. Mankind will have to change to be more careful and caring of each other and we will all have to really want that to happen. Still in today's general population being nice is not as promoted as is excusing not being nice. This will have to change and that is all a part of our new normal. It might take another couple of generations, although, it is coming. It is better to be in the leading edge on this track to improving.

Insensitivities are a flowing definition across time, some more apparent than others and the range of thoughts that make up insensitivities grew as an imagination can grow. In my experiences, it is far more advantageous to incline and align with sensitivities and grow your imagination in that direction. What we think about comes about, and I chose, early in life, although looking back I wish sooner, that I'd turn from all forms of insensitivities as soon as possible and promote my sensitive understanding. This has made a huge difference in my generation.

My dad was a disciplinarian at times, almost like my mom, though more intense, as it is with men in general - like a military sergeant, although less often initiated independently of my mom. He was willing to please mom at his children's cost, when needed as his orders came down on him and placed him in a position to prove his manliness. Men and women of that time, and still in tired-out-cultures, react to a desire to be respected with force rather than love or kindness, unwilling to risk the chance that change offers such options. This is required to change in order to progress as a civil consciousness. I can still hear her say; "Wait until your dad gets home. You're going to get a beating then." And it was true. Whatever they, my parents, were or were not, they stuck together regarding their parenting choices. If mom told dad to beat us, he did. At least that is the way it was until we girls menstruated. Before then, he would take us girls one by one into their bedroom and make us pull down our pants, lie on the bed, bent over face down, and he would say, "Do not turn or move at all, do not cry out loud or you will get more and harder, and do not carry any information to anyone about our ways to teach you to behave properly. Do you understand!" And so, it was as he unloosened his belt and used it to strike us until we submitted to complete silence. I could hear in his mean voice that he meant it, albeit this wasn't a form of usual punishment. It was only once in a while that this extreme was taken up in his or their authority over us. If it would have been only once, it would have been too much. It was certainly damaging and lingering, evidenced by my vivid memory, that I chose not to find appropriate. This abuse was never appropriate, however with acceptance as to serving purpose in knowing right from wrong. This will always seem to me to have been far from good character as a parent. I feel, mostly, that a consciousness has evolved within me, from this experience. I refuse to be broken, then, now or ever. We each, in any and all our times of authority, are to be the responsible ones. Authority can be gentle and respected, as opposed to many the teachings passed down from man to man. We must be a kinder civilization and treat each other, regardless of age, as equals. It was not my fault that I was treated poorly, even if only now and then again. It was the insult into the heart of trusting those you love to behave consistently in kindness or not, which is the paradox of Insensitives and sensitives.

I was most unfortunate to have been a "tomboy" and maybe, they say, because of that, I did not get my period until after both of my younger sisters did. I was the runt of the litter in many physical ways; the leader of the pack in still better ways. So, honestly, I was dad and mom's longest whipping girl. It was not nice. I now write this out first time in my life; I do not care that they were like that with me. I know now, that it was all part of the reasons that I found a sooner escape from them, from my childhood and from the projects. I would have preferred it differently. I accept it as the past. All the negative experiences of my youth and childhood culminates into the same feeling within me, and that is, I always knew I never wanted to be like my parents, and I always wanted to escape from my past, and I did.

## The Art of Appreciating MORE

Mary knew about my family problems to a point most didn't. I had learned to not talk about my parents to anyone out of the house. She knew I had some scars, I had to stay in my house under orders, and stayed home when I was protecting my sisters sometimes, but Mary never got involved in my family problems, like I was in hers. It was a strain on our relationship. I knew that Mary knew more than she let on. There were times that she was with the family when the meanness of my parents, especially my mom, would surface and she would be asked to leave and go home, or she would witness a quick hand slap me or my mother grind her teeth as she would say something dangerously violent in nature. My mom would threaten my life as quickly as she would hang a nightgown out to dry in the center court. My mom was mean, especially when she drank too much. Mary's mom was not as mean, was not a drunk, and all things relative, not as predictable either. I knew that, although I also felt I knew intuitively to dream hard about getting far away from it all.

I didn't intend this to be all about me and my "difficult" times growing up, after all, that was a very long time ago, and I have found ways, processes, and techniques to assist me in allowing the past less influence upon me than a lot of people with similar pasts. Mary is one of those people who carry their past "pain-bodies" with them all through their lives. It was so hard for me to listen to Mary talk about her parents and the way she was treated by them during the past year and a half of reuniting with her over our Sunday phone calls. I had changed so much from those days. I no longer held myself a victim and I moved along so well with my life after my escape.

I was always pretty positive a person and was able to let things go and to see the best in all things and people easily. Over the past forty years or so this characteristic excelled and increased, and I became a new person. I became aware of myself and my thoughts and I became a good student of the Law of Attraction, after spending years earlier being a good student of religions. Once I found the Laws of the Universe and the Law of Attraction, I changed my life in so many important ways. I now, was feeling trapped into an adult relationship that I wanted to have so much with Mary. I found the negativity she had about everything in life was too hard for me to partake in allowing. I many times told Mary that I prefer a more positive discussion and when I did, she said, I wasn't a good friend if I couldn't let her talk about what was bothering her, and she welcomed me to talk about what bothered me. Except for our negative conversations, nothing bothered me.

I so wanted this relationship to work out, for me. It was not though, and that reality brought me to a different understanding about this relationship that allowed me to listen, although it never felt good for me. The nature of this relationship had changed from me being her friend, to me being her teacher. She was pretty resistant to that, so I eventually found her to be my subject, instead of my student. A student can only be taught if they are teachable, and Mary was not. So, I allowed this relationship to continue, and I was only present in it to evaluate her as a subject and to remember that no matter what anyone is thinking or saying about me or anyone, that is their take on it all. I had to keep reminding myself that I was not like her. I could accept her for the way she is, and I could observe more than participate in this friendship. She was not my friend any longer. I had lost her again, as soon as I could see her again. She could not and would not hear my teachings. And so, it is.

*The Art of Appreciating MORE*

In a world of stark diversity, we have so much more in-common than not. We love so similarly & experience emotions in the same light of equality. It is, therefore, wise to reflect often upon our sameness, in the privilege of being each unique. It is a divine magnificence that we can choose to explore together the value of each other's pursuits, with due respect & honor. We also desire and deserve the same from others. Remember the "in-common-part" of you kindly as the "in-common-part" of the us in you; for we are All One in profound ways. Are we not!

We co-create a well-serving living-bond of understanding between us all. It is that human connection that is known as "Civility".

Coincidence is so much fun and double fun and more when the coincidence is agreed to by others also. For to share is a "blessing" which needs others and more time in harmony. Coincidence is intended to be noticed, in their times of occurrence, and to strengthen belief in self-capabilities, in order to create even before one is awakened to one's own abilities to create. Coincidence is such evidence of the vibrational ability to allow life to orchestrate amazement. It is such fun to project deliberately. It is even more fun to co-create with others what is mutually co-incidental to each other. What a rush!

Experience teaches only the teachable.

I call this story; **"Tony's Heart"**

## Coincidence & Synchronicity

As our Sunday calls were progressing, I would sometimes get on my computer while Mary was on the phone. She might ask me if I could find out about some of her relatives, where they were buried or lived and one day after we got off the phone actually, I was on Facebook and I typed in Tony's full name. He came up right away and I was amazed at what I read. He was brand new on Facebook. I'd been using it since it was first available maybe ten years or so ago and after those "Mypage" days. He had only been on Facebook for a few days. Imagine that! I found that coincidentally interesting to start with and it got weirder real fast. He had asked openly to all that might connect eventually with him this question: "Does anyone know where I can find Mary? I've been looking for her for so many years." Wow, that blew my mind off. I realized how insanely coincidental that was to see. He only had that one sentence posted. Nothing else outside of a scanty profile. I'd never typed his name before in my life and now I see right before my eyes that he was looking for Mary. The notes around that message were increasingly strange and amazing and I felt a miracle taking place. I didn't know exactly what to do about this message. I did the typical things and looked at each of his friends on Facebook and indeed this was really him. OMG. I was so excited for Mary and Tony.

I decided to contact him. I wrote a personal email to him directed through his Facebook account. I said I knew where she was. I didn't give him her details or number and said I would get back to him after I spoke to her. I then called Mary and told her about his message and, I guess she didn't understand the miracle of his Facebook membership being so new and informative. It, after all was about forty years since they had been in touch with each other. On the other hand, I was absolutely amazed at the beauty in this event of love and life.

I was so excited with this remarkable coincidence. Mary was though freaking out in the other direction. She was very mad at me for writing to him and she hung up the phone on me. It was critical timing too, because I had just recently purchased air tickets to visit her. She wasn't openly demonstrative or excited about my coming across the country to visit her. I made reservations to stay at a hotel nearby where she lived. I knew that she seemed fragile about meeting me although she didn't say do not come either. I could care less of her status, shape, looks or lifestyle. I loved her for whatever she was. It didn't matter to me at all. I accept her and appreciate her being different than me or anyone else. Maybe she was afraid she might not live up to her standards. I didn't rank or place her into any judgement although biased with love for her. I trusted she was being herself. The conditions of my freedom to visit and she not having much to say about what I sincerely felt to be a kind gesture, well, I thought it was a good idea at the time. I was going alone, and my family was supporting my doing this. We all felt, after talking about it that it would be a great time to rekindle our friendship in person without my being over expecting. Well, after her hanging up, I realized that perhaps I was going to have to stay away from her for now.

## Coincidence & Synchronicity

Tony wrote back by the next morning. He was so happy I responded, and he was happier still to have the opportunity to learn and perhaps come to see Mary again. He was "over the moon". He had divorced about three years ago and he always thought of Mary. Always had and always would. That is what he wrote. I believed him.

When I emailed him back, I said that Mary was upset that I replied to him without talking to her first and that she hung up on me. Reminding each other that Mary did not have a Facebook account, we agreed that it was strange to react to her and I didn't know what to do about her being upset. I said I felt uncomfortable about giving him any personal information about her. I mentioned that once we resolved our indifferences and she was speaking to me, it might be best if I gave her his information instead so if she wanted to get in touch with him, she would have that choice. That seemed like a good idea given the circumstances. In the meantime, we both discussed that amazing coincidence and astonishing synchronicity we realized, as if a miracle, in the alignment that was needed in order for this to be happening.

We agreed, and I waited for Mary to call me. It was several weeks later, and my trip would have happened already, and although she knew the dates I had planned, she never checked with me to find out what I would do, now that she was mad at me. I spoke to my family and we didn't understand why she would be so mad at me. After all she told me that Tony was the only man she ever loved. Apparently, she just didn't understand the amazing timing and coincidence of this occurrence. She didn't appreciate the power of love and the way the law of attraction worked. I myself had a hard time with the awesomeness of synchronicity involved in this happening. The odds of Tony just becoming a new Facebook member and the odds of my looking up his name just then. It was like a siren went off in my head, in Tony's head, in Uri's head, in our daughter's heads, and just anyone else I mentioned this too. Mary was the only person not aboard this miracle and it was her miracle.

That is the same way I felt about many of the aspects that make up the basic Laws of the Universe and, especially, The Law of Attraction. People were in view of it but were often oblivious to it. We were in the experience of our thoughts becoming things and most people didn't recognize the real miracles in life. They were happening to us. We didn't always know to appreciate them.

Tony contacted me again. Mary was still not answering my calls. He just wanted to know how he could get in touch with her. He had so much hope in his heart about his love for her and still after all these 40 or 50 years without any contact, just thoughts and apparently on both their parts. He was going to try to find her with or without me. So, I didn't give him any information I only told him how I found her, through her father's obituary.

Then one day Mary answered the phone. We spoke more carefully. She asked me to not talk about Tony. I agreed only after once again telling her that it was her miracle, not mine. I was the messenger, not the message. Their love was the message.

I deleted Tony as a Facebook friend to avoid any interaction, although I had given him my phone number and address which I didn't mention to Mary that I had done. I was chatting with Mary now less, a few Sundays in a month. It was a quicker conversation, and it was fading off, of that I felt certain. We never spoke about my trip or the anguish I felt or expense I lost in not having the cost for the flight or the hotel reimbursed to me. Actually, I was okay with all that and so too was my family as they felt I would have been uncomfortable on that trip of a one-sided friendship. And so, it was.

Then one day she mentioned Tony again. I was shocked. She said she had been seeing him for at least the past half year. I was dumbfounded to say the least. She had met up with him many months ago and not long after I told him about Mary's Father's obituary. For God's sake, that was nearly a year ago by now. She was just now telling me, after all this time of it going on. I was totally left out of it. Oh boy, that was the weirdest thing of all. It was her and his miracle certainly. I was surprised she didn't share with me the fact that after hanging up on me and yelling at me about Tony, she and he had resumed a relationship. It was a miracle. She didn't appreciate the messenger. Oh well, that was quite informative to me.

After that, I stopped calling, and she stopped calling. We haven't spoken again in a couple of years. I send her Christmas and Birthday Cards and she does the same. The strangest and saddest message came through in a recent card note. It said Tony had passed away of an unexpected massive heart attack and she was grieving his loss.

Some people just do not appreciate the messages and signs that we have happening to us even when they look and feel like miracles. As to what I was realizing, it was that being instrumental in change, doesn't require others acknowledgement. I hold a special space in my heart that vibrationally, I was of great value to contributing and easing love into harmony. The world is a better place for the time Mary and Tony had with each other and for that I share in their love and grow in my confidence that I matter. Indeed, it was my miracle too.

I am glad I am this way, someone who recognizes the miracles in life and in many ways and certainly in every day. My life is full of wonder and deliberately so. I ask in my quiet prayers for wisdom and for the awareness' of the order of magnitude of vibrational connecting to the amazing wonder of life. The life I am and the life I create. The life I can sense as magnificent and full of options to create More. I enjoy synchronicity and coincidence often and I actually choose to be mindful of it happening and I love it. I think coming into recognizing syncing-up with my life draw, meaning with what I attract or draw to and from me, like breathing in and out, is amazing. It takes talent and desire to overcome the insistent teachings of a lifetime and of most others their complacent beliefs to think in mundane ways above noticing and actually enjoying the constant aligning into synchronicity in life. I appreciate that I do, and often. We are such amazingly well love creatures, we Human Beings. Once we are empowered by ourselves to catch-on to the understanding of the mysteries of some of the basics of life, well we can soar. We can escape our unawareness'. We can seek and find what has been suppressed with lazy thoughts and defaulted thinking. We can. We can take each moment in our hands and notice that everything is interconnected, and by just opening up our hearts and minds to the impossible, all becomes possible.

The type of childhood experiences any of us have are like flowers blooming in their seasons. One does not wallow up sadly about the bloom coming full term and releasing-off itself its colorful fragile petals to fall to the ground in the kindness of time and breeze. We don't cry and squirm up into a ball and blame the fallen petals for bringing us remorse to not see the bloom forever. The flower doesn't look unfavorably upon time and breeze either. It's all equally beautiful.

There is more to life than blaming others for our choices in living our own life. Moving on is more than letting go, it is the aligning with now, which is seemingly our present miracle. Right now, now, now etcetera, we can think a gentler thought into our now moments and therefore bring great influence in that gentler thought into our futures. Not a weakness of gentle-thoughts, a trueness of desired-goodness. It matters not age, nor experience; what does matter is how we individually embrace the moment we are in, that we created along the way. Respect your gentleness, your kindness, your sensitivity and your softer side. Embrace your love, your appreciation and your wisdom. Welcome to yourself an empowerment that thrives on potential becoming exactly what you want, how you want it to be, and when this now is anew and filled with the freedom you and only you have to recognize your choice to proclaim joy.

It is our personal State of Being that first becomes alive in the awareness of your own influences upon ourselves. In that State of Being, you and only you actually see your future and from knowing what this now moment in time feels like.

Escape blaming others for what you are creating and open-up to your own possibilities. I find great coincidence in this story of Mary and Tony coming to be from my awareness of their existence, and I experience greater synchronicity in the gathering of what I was in their lives, and I align with it often, now in conclusion, as serendipitous too.

## Chapter Three- Appreciations on Coincidence & Synchronicity

- ❖ I appreciate my childhood, both what seems to be its difficult times and what seems to be adventurously dreamlike.

- ❖ I appreciate that time wrinkles aspects of great loves interwoven in ideas of confusion and within what is ineffable.

- ❖ I appreciate living a long life already and knowing I want more life to come.

- ❖ I appreciate that things work out well and that thoughts never really go away, they create into reality in their intended time.

- ❖ I appreciate that there are sensitives and Insensitives and that I am a sensitive who understands rather than judges Insensitives.

- ❖ I appreciate that I respect friendships and also enough so that I am only willing to be in a friendship of equal respect or I fade off into that space of noticing some people miss their own coincidences and even miracles.

- ❖ I appreciate that I often know more than others about what is amazing around me, them, and us.

- ❖ I appreciate the wonder that time yields and the unbroken circles of coincidences that turn into synchronicities.

- ❖ I appreciate that when I know what feels off, I can turn towards what feels better and improve my life.

- ❖ I appreciate that love is eternal.

*The Art of Appreciating MORE*

*Your path of Least Resistance is always available, in all circumstances, and if you think not, just give it a moment and then recalculate.*

## Chapter 4  The Path of Least Resistance

What is meant by The Path of Least Resistance?
That seems like a pretty straight forward concept to me. I comprehend all those words. It feels better to call it;

"The Path of Most Perfection".

I recognize and know these words, "The Path of Least Resistance" strung together as a familiar statement. It wasn't always that way. Even when understanding the words "The Path of Least Resistance", I still do not get the total drift of it all. Admittedly, I need to know more even after giving these words years of thoughts and involvement. I appreciate that since the Path of Least Resistance is ever changing, I will always be learning more about what it means to me. It is my Living Way. It is alive and constantly in motion. What can be more valuable to understand?

In my conscious time of wisdom and experience, I can lose sight of the meaning of My Path of Least Resistance and misunderstand the intent of it on My Life. Each time I parse it down, so to speak, it grows more directions of potential understandings within. I am resolved to appreciate My Path of Least Resistance as a root and a route. Sometimes, I simply know that it is the easy or easiest way to go and then other times, I know it is not necessarily feeling like the easy or easiest way to go as much as it is the way I am going to or the way that can take me back onto my best serving path. Sometimes my Path of Least Resistance feels like an investment into myself. It is complicated by past and future needs and it is always a part of the present moment. I am not *going* on the path; I am on it. I am not going to return to the future and then pick up into the present moment, I have already experienced the past. My Path of Least Resistance is where I am currently, with knowledge of the past and with desires, needs, and aims into the future. Sometimes when something feels difficult to experience (as does certain contrasts or growths) it is only usually afterwards, when I am in the results, that I come to realize that it was the best way to bring me above the circumstances, more often around the drama, and into a higher level of self-joy and personal awareness. Why else do we live!

*The Art of Appreciating MORE*

It is appropriate to adjust our process of understanding and in that space, I ask and welcome wisdom to come to me regarding My Path of Least Resistance, My Way to Best Go.

I'll present herein an example of the way my mind thinks about interacting with My Path of Least Resistance even though it might be a bit silly or basic. Bare with me! It is a beginning and often beginnings evolve into More. Whenever, I am trying to explain to others what I experience as My Path of Least Resistance, I immediately think about what I feel in finding it and I think about this particular story, albeit is an over-simplification of a concept that threads life together into a masterpiece. It is in that regard only a thread of the tapestry.

The Path of Least Resistance and getting onto it is something like;

Let's say I am in my Living Room and I want to get into my kitchen to grab a cup of tea ready to drink and left steeping on the counter earlier. There are two entryways into the kitchen from where I am as I realize my tea is ready and I want it now. There I am and in a split moment I have to make a choice to either get into the kitchen by way of the side near the backyard door, or I can get into the kitchen by way of the side near the door leading to the garage.

Okay, I choose to go by the garage doorway, each being so equal in distance and neither being of any special purpose. What I did was I resorted to my raw or intuitive non-judgmental feelings. For some reason, that I didn't know nor needed to know, and even though I had little time to think about it, which is when feelings come in handy, I felt better about going towards the garage doorway and which the door to the garage was left, I now

# The Path of Least Resistance

noticed as I took up that direction, just a bit ajar. I probably didn't close it as well as I usually do after coming home from dropping off the kids at school. If I didn't realize that I was the only one home at the time, honestly, I might have thought one of the kids left it ajar. I just don't do things like that!

As I did walk towards it pre-aiming my hand into place to pull the door tightly closed as I passed by, I noticed, much to my chagrin and absolute horror, that right there on the floor creeping around far too quickly for my mind to settle calmly, was a spider as big as a dog, or so it seemed at the moment. It was huge and arrogantly right in clear sights, actually over-pronouncing itself in contrast against the white tiled flooring. There was no resistance in what I did next. I quickly stepped on it. Not a thought more as it was a complete automatic and sweeping movement with great intent to reach my shoe's target. I was so thankful for the shoe as barefoot there could have been time for this most unwelcomed creature to escape my quick execution and crawl off under the cabinet. It was a most unpleasant squash indeed. The spider which looked quite ominous and deadly was now, phew, dead - dead and gone and for that I felt great relief and no regret. Quickly, I got a paper towel and wiped it up and threw it away, right down the toilet, which, incidentally, was in the opposite direction as my cup of tea. There was no doubt that I was doing this perfectly timed and for good reason.

I felt, as I eventually sipped on my tea, that finding a spider, especially that size, on the floor was so icky and creepy. Giving it further and clearer thought standing there, I was so happy that I found that spider before it could manage to get further and completely unknown into the household and be perhaps too stressed in its unwelcomed and non-supportive not-spidery environment that it might, well, somehow and somewhen bring real harm or confusion to myself or any of the greatly-loved and cared-for members of my household, including our pet cat, who might be noticing this thing as a big new toy to play with just to be perhaps bit. What good fortune it was to have taken the garage doorway route into the kitchen that day.

So, there it is! That is one of the ways I explain what My Path of Least Resistance is while defining what The Path of Least Resistance means to me. If there are fewer words to define it, I do not follow them well enough to completely understand the essence as well as that spider story.

I feel, certainly, that we always have more than one choice. Often, we can feel that one choice is in a better place to choose. The additional thought that comes out of the spider story is that even in choice there are reasons that the Universe offers options in most circumstances. When I feel comfortable with allowing my feelings to help me choose a direction or choice, then I can flow with it even when it seems more complex to pursue than alternative choices. I feel that where and when I am comfortable and secure on my Path of Most Allowance, it really means that I am going exactly the best way for me and it matters not where it leads. It is already felt as really right.

Of course, in a perfect world of personal events, my never having seen the spider might have been an easier way to meet, at least for the moment. After all the spider could be harmless and find its own way never to be seen by anyone ever again. I do not know that though. I do know that that experience did happen to me and for the extent in which it assists me to discover a greater understanding of possibilities and the amazement of My Path of Least Resistance, is worthy.

The mystery of what, why and when the Law of Attraction assists our direction is an amazing awareness and often, we do not have to know all the answers. We cannot know all the answers either. We just need to appreciate that the power of Universal Love comes upon us often, in fact always and endlessly. We can learn the peace of following and the strength in leading, while both knowing and not knowing all the reasons or answers. The Law of Attraction assists my instincts and in so more and more is to be appreciated. It is always attempting to fulfill my desires and once more it is attempting to bring me unto my Path of Most Wanted.

Robert Fritz[6], author of The Path of Least Resistance says, "If you limit your choice only to what seems possible or reasonable, you disconnect yourself from what you truly want, and all that is left is a compromise."

I add to this a knowing that most often choices rise up to the level of need and in fulfilling need, there is really no compromise. We will always gravitate into the decision that we think will be best for us, knowingly or not. It is extremely beneficial to seek after and know you will hence find the best for yourself. If we ask, it will be given. To not ask is to hand over the reign of self-destiny to something of the natural course of events, that we call the default value.

In writing of the defaulted value, there comes to my mind the knowing of the definition of the Law of Attraction which is always a variation of this thought:

---
[6]Robert Fritz is an American Writer and creative thinking promoter.

# The Art of Appreciating MORE

The Law of Attraction is that whatever is thought about, talked about, sung about, written about, is therefore focused-upon in so doing and what is focused-upon and believed-in too, that is the same type of stuff that comes into my life as a result. The degree of my believe or disbelieve is the gauge in which the results are substantiated. The size of the manifestation of thoughts or desires in terms of personal value, rather than the dimensional space it consumes, influences the outcome. Thinking about anything is the same thing as focusing upon. This focus of attention is as if you are opening the door and inviting that which is being focused-upon into your life. The Law of Attraction moves the flow of thoughts into connective motion, as does a magnet. It is an amazing knowing. Thinking about this can assist in becoming more and more familiar with its ways of being in your life. It's in your life, knowingly or not. In the knowing there is great opportunity for participation and deliberate creation. That is so delicious. Additionally, accepting that creation is as benevolent as your thoughts of benevolence permits comprehending, melts a partnership between your goodness and trust and that force that subscribes to loving you.

You have all the cards and the ones being dealt to you are exactly a match to your thoughts and their direction. Always give yourself the benefit of the love. Your thoughts contain your desires, they do, and then being more and more responsible for your thoughts should be a great desire too. Here is the really good part, I can control, if I desire to, my thoughts; what I say and what I write, what I remember, and what I want. I have equal control in my results. It is actually more like acceptance over the stuff that comes into my life. The ramifications of thoughts are the Path of Life. Providing positive thoughts above others less so, providing the loving thoughts above other less loving, becomes an easy choice. We always in every single thought have choice in what to think. When running into questioning self-thoughts it is additionally helpful to reflect upon the sensitivity being generated. Love is the foundation of positive direction. When confusion becomes a part of thinking, recall the concept of Love. The Source of your life, whatever you want to call it, even if you call it "self", is Love first. The Light of Love is more brilliant than many Sun Lights multiplied upon themselves. The Light of Love is brighter than we can possibly see entirely. We cannot imagine such a Light. We can, however, allow its essence to shine to and from self.

If I want to change my experiences in life, I only really ever need to change my thoughts. I am ever amazed at thinking about the power I have, and you have, and everyone has in our creating our thoughts, ideas, feelings and words. Thoughts are personal as are ideas, and then feelings are too. Feelings seem, to me, to be sitting upon the boarder-lining fence of physicality and are contained inside of my emotions. I sense my emotions to be mostly plural in nature. One emotion usually holds many thoughts which to me evolve into feelings. Of course, there is an inter-marriage between all these cushions of existence between what is materialized and with what is held sacredly within. When knowing it is better to change my thoughts because I am feeling a need to, I pivot or allow a slow conscious beginning feeling to move me into another direction. I cannot turn completely around on a dime (although I might want to), so I appreciate my actions as modest, accurate and more comfortable. A slight recontinuance in a thought direction can move me onward.

I know I cannot and, note, do not want to control anyone in any way. I appreciate people for who they are. I can and do want very much to control myself and it is best to, in so doing, maximize the results of what I can and do control into the manifestations of what I truly want, if I know what that is. When I know what I want I am great at manifesting what I want. When I am not sure of what I want, I try to keep my ideas general until the desires themselves manifest more information to me and, actually invite me to notice them. I know myself pretty well most of the time.

I have what I consider an uncanny ability to look at a person and seemingly feel their feelings quickly. If I talk with them, it takes a short while before I seem to pick up on their feelings even more than their words. Everyone can discern aspects of others. We all connect to each other naturally. I can observe a person and I feel like I can sometimes feel what they are feeling. I cannot with one hundred percent surety know what another thinks. I can pick-up a great deal about others though. So too can you. I can, often, feel their vibes, their vibrations. I truly believe that feelings, in their position of existing on that boarder between the inside of self and the outside of self, seems, to me, to be somewhat visible. We can see what we also feel. We can understand others quickly, if desired. This ability to see or feel other's feelings possibly is a skill that can be adjust to what is stemming from the ability to feel our own feelings. Some of it is a postulation of thoughts of others desires that I too might hold as desires or have previously held as desires. Now knowing them fulfilled I can better relate to others in their worlds of desires. We all have so much more in common than not. We all also know each other better than realized. In knowing another over time, feelings about what previously have been understood interpretation of their feelings, often provided by them directly, can change over time and reflect our own feelings as much as a mirror. It is advisable when having a long-term relationship to tweak to each other's changes. If you can appreciate your own changes, then you can appreciate that others make appropriate changes too. The persons in which you hold long-term relationships will better connect to your changes if you are willing to accept/share your changes and theirs too.

I am a sensitive person. Sensitive people feel insensitivities in the vibrations surrounding them, including often in Insensitive people. In this "Me Too" transition of kinder mutual responsibilities toward each other, it helps both Sensitive and Insensitive people in your contact to communicate your deliberate impressions. Many others are experiencing the need for true transparency and true intentions are the cornerstones of tomorrow's new normal. Our Path of Least Resistance shadows and shapes the waves of the future.

There is an uncanniness about every one of us in some ways. I am uniquely myself. You are uniquely yourself. We all have our uniqueness and I think those things can be categorized in several ways. Simply to start to recognize them, it is valuable to sense what uniqueness came at birth, always having been a part of spirit. We all have some of those characteristics in common too. I have come to understand these characteristics as our Innate Inborn characteristics. I believe my ability to comprehend others well, is an Innateness. Discovering my Innate structures and skills has been beneficial in strengthening direction, understanding of purpose, confidence in particular events, effective participation, clear opinions and, of course, choices. I am aware of many things to do when I am off My Path of Everything Going Well. Sometimes I think I know what is best for others. That is a deception in self stature. If I am asked for advice, I can only provide that from my self-projected place of knowing combined with my Innate interpretation. I cannot truly know what is best for another person. I can, however, sense what could be better for another person rather than to not mention that they are responsible for their feelings. I can assist and uplift another into my expressing that I know what is good for me. The generalities of commonalities between everyone is often all the direction another requires to recalculate their better thoughts. I am a teacher, and I am an uplifter. I am a student and I allow people and things outside of myself to uplift. This sharing is communication.

Why is it so that the wild deer do not run from me? Why do I have instincts about other people and wanting to be nearer or further away from them? It is that innateness of appreciating the surrounding of others, animals, and plants. I also feel connected to events and places. All these feelings of understanding others have to do with their surroundings. I do not know more about anyone. I can though sense more. My intuition is involved in my knowing others from a level that includes seeing, yes, and it includes feeling their spirit conditioning at the moment. These feelings about others requires constant updating. It is in that feeling that I sense sometimes what I might adjust if I were in that space. I do not really know another's insides. I sense another's frequency. Some might call it aroura.

# *The Path of Least Resistance*

One day after "appreciating" for a while I heard a Voice Within that stated, "Release Your Joys rather than Your Frustrations." Further there came a vision of humanity holding on to their individual feelings of Joy, while releasing their individual feelings of frustration. It was not a pretty sight. I've actually heard people say that it feels good to release frustration. Releasing joy, is so much better. As soon as I blinked, I found a better vision in which humanity was freeing themselves of their Joys. Releasing Joy, Love, Appreciation, Knowledge and more. What a different result.

At the time of the coming of the Pandemic of 2020 disbelief, fear, frustration and a lot of negative connective feelings were released. It intensified the impact of the Pandemic. There are some things that do not shed out any joy immediately. It was not a friendly sight to see that spider on the floor and it was most uncomfortable to sense the collective reaction about the Pandemic. It was a time in the passing and a passage for mankind to realize as holy-well-formed in differences towards the outcome to be an improvement.

The Pandemic also brought with it a great many more hours to contemplate alternative ideas. The silence of the Pandemic swept the Earth and in ways brought water to its thirst for change. As seemingly uncomfortable as the Pandemic was there is a glory rising, we have yet to see. This is an Innate statement that will come to be common thinking; "The Pandemic assisted humanity into shifting into a new and improved normal." Many of us are feeling inappropriately and unrealistically stuck somewhat in the instructions that were handed down generation upon generation, culture after culture, that tells us to be reserved about expressing Joy and all uppermost emotions; least we look silly. It, some might think, appears to much like

## The Art of Appreciating MORE

bragging if we all started to mention to each other our great joys and happiness. That is exactly what we need to do more of even during times of seemingly great distress and troubles, such as the Pandemic. There is little benefit to self or others to display your anger and despair, when, time itself is knocking upon your door and personally inviting you to participate in a wonderful moment of sharing joy. Caring about now is great. Really caring about your personal experience into tomorrow, well, that is stupendous.

Since the Pandemic by nature is a global experience, it continued to structure the mass ego into the hearts and souls of the collective. That led to distracting individuals into a larger construct. Rarely are people objecting to the process of thought controlling the mass into behaviors, when we always have great opportunity to exchange ideas through personally improving our individual thoughts. In a time of global transitioning, the top shelve can be harder to see and or reach for obtaining. In our collective stretch the noise of the day's disgruntled manners can be overcome by a more sensitive instruction that can be overcoming from our Innate being. In so doing, a better society will emerge. This idea of releasing your joys is another way to seek, find and/or remain in The Path of Least Resistance. We do know how to care about each other. It is in the solution side of life. The growth of compassionate consciousness among each of us, the globe around, has been one of the purposes of the Pandemic experience. We need to care and be kinder to each other. That is how we get better.

There are those times when my choice seems between two or more ways that all seem off, or I have no favorite, perhaps I even feel confusion, although I feel compelled to have to make a decision. In that set of circumstances, it might serve well to make a choice that feels the slightly better or even just ok, and then 'recalculate" at your convenience, perhaps tweaking the desired outcome against the newly arising changed choices popping up. Remember that The Path of Least Resistance is an abstract concept to mostly everyone, hence, it is not something we are trained to accept as real and accountable. We can decide to be more involved.

If I am more willing to address the recalculations as a new beginning, it seems more clarity comes forth and I am often in a wonder at that happening. Eventually, my choices walking into a desired goal seem to narrow out and feel more certain. Also, my desired goal is more visible. I then can sense more control upon both my choices and my clearer outcome. It though might be recognized that the changes to my decision-making process and tweaked path, could have been provided to me and not just chosen by me. It is then more possible to credit an unidentifiable Source for assisting my decision.

What does it feel like to know I am on my Path of Least Resistance?

It feels easy, actually easier. It feels happy, actually happier. It feels more comfortable, even when it changed along my way from a path that I felt I intended to a path that I accepted. It feels like me. It feels good. It feels like I can trust wherever it takes me.

When I do not feel good about something, I can easily think that reversing my direction and getting away from where I am going into a better place and getting sooner on or joining up to my Path of Least Resistance. I also experience that going more softly or pivoting a little from where I am works. That feels better than taking an extreme reversal stance. Feeling better is an indicator that I am getting back on The Path of Least Resistance, although at that point it becomes The Path of Lessor Resistance. Backing away from a cliff-edge is a good retreat, even if another choice is required to further backtrack or turn into a sidestep. It is easier to get happy if happiness is there in sight first. When you feel yourself heading into the right direction it is sort of like seeing happiness up ahead. That is what can be followed after. If one is looking for their path of Least Resistance, it becomes advantageous to take it step by step. After all the Path can be there yet until a step is taken it is a frozen space of now. Only when one steps into it and then again, right there, momentum can start up and actually happen on the Path.

The Pandemic offered us all and each the opportunity to notice that there is a Path for self and a Path for Humanity. We are all on Humanity's Path and it benefits us all collectively to take notice especially when it is as large as a Pandemic in nature. One must stay on your individual Path of Least Resistance to impact richly the Path of Humanity's Least Resistance. Finding the Path and traveling upon the Path are two different things. Coming off ones individual Path to align with Humanity's Path can feel intrusive and uncertain and becoming sure footed in both place and placement, is a great joy to become. Finding the Path and just standing there is only okay for a brief moment. Taking the Path is riding the wave. It is certainly true that the waves have a great deal to do with the Path, in this travel plan. We match the tone of the frequency of our Path and it matches to us. All frequencies are also movement. A still frequency is a snapshot drawing of a frequency wave. It is only a living frequency when it moves. In order to experience the Path of Least Resistance one has to

# The Path of Least Resistance

appreciate it as a changing substance rather than a place to hang out in. It is the adventure or the journey.

I implore you, even long after the Pandemic of 2020 subsides and we move out and on from it, that you appreciate the amazing opportunity we have had going through a lockdown and addressing options to somewhat feel more like survival than of living joyously. It has been noticed and it has been placed into all of our lives. Looking at the Pandemic from above down unto Earth and Humanity, we are closer matched to each other and more aware of each other. That being true, we are also being forced into a sharpened solo experience whereby our immediate situation offers witness into our future. This is a perfect moment in time to see self in the entire picture. We are ourselves and we are one together. Love, of self, that radiates out and is absorbed into society is great mastery. The Path of Least Resistance is a friendly secure presence.

The idea that what you persist upon is a form of resistance is explained in the way we garden our hardy plants. If I am trimming a bush that is overgrowing into the pathway, I cut it off. The initial result is that the path is now clear. It is of striking interest that exactly at that place in which the cut took place two, sometimes three, new sprouts will begin to grow. The branches are insisting upon growing regardless of how many times it is cut. Often the end results after time, is a thicker or bushier branch. Sometimes it is easier to transplant rather than insist a plant behave in a specific way for you. That is exactly what we do to ourselves when we insist on cutting off the natural flow of life. It grows stronger or thicker and we are left with more to do than before. Deeper cuts might work for a time. Noteworthy that insistence often brings focus to things and focus increases in nature. We are not cutting branches off of

# The Art of Appreciating MORE

ourselves to find our Path of Least Resistance sooner, although, one can learn from nature.

What then can we do? What can we do to assist the path to be friendly for us in the moment or in the future?

One of the most effective ways in which one can flourish when resistance is bothering us, is to pivot. We do not have to take extreme action to insist things go our way, we only ever need to slightly change focus into a different and improved direction. Why cut something off, when we can notice other parts and portions into a clearer viewpoint. Insisting upon things can feel a significant even positive direction or action to take. Right! The truth is that insisting is different than not giving up. The Path of Least Resistance merely assists momentum into a higher ground or a smoother feeling slope. It doesn't matter which metaphor you look at; the end result is it should be more manageable and easier to experience. There are numerous ways to achieve a goal. When you allow your desires to work with your feelings and instead of persisting or insisting you give a little and gain a lot by refocusing upon the procedure taken to succeed. It is very valuable to remain diligent regarding remembering the ultimate goal. If you know what you want and one way is hard to get there and the other way is easier, then take the easy way.

There are many who teach to "Never Give Up". We are taught that you must fight and fight harder to get what you want if you are a strong person of discipline and perseverance. Some believe that is the only way in which you can succeed. The Laws of the Universe reverse that philosophy by letting us control the speed at which we get to succeed and the enjoyment of the journey too. Some will argue that part of success is getting it faster. Could it be true that the fight to get what you want can be a competition with yourself? The faster the better! After all, many will say; you have to get there before someone else does. If not, there might not be enough left for you to get what you want. Some feel there is not enough to satisfy if you do not hurry up and take it before another comes and gets it.

I trust in a different and opposite process. One in which I do not have to insist it be the way I initially think it should be. Source actually knows us better than we know ourselves. Timing has a partnership with me and my goals, rather than time being another obstacle that needs to be fought for or against. One does not have to quit wanting something that seems fraught with obstacles and certain difficulties. Instead, looking at it differently, in clarity and respect for self-achievements, unknown possibilities and including the force or intensity of it, as well as the manner in which one takes (the path choice), can assist in the ease of a final results.

If something seems hard, it might be better to sit it down and allow things surrounding the choices you are making to become clearer before forcing things into what you think is place. Why force anything. I love the concept of being in the right emotional place before pursuing it. It is often many times harder to accomplish something little or great while being in a state of confusion, insistence, unhappiness, fear, concern etc. It is law that when you are in a joyful emotional state of being, it is easier to do anything you are ready to do. Some of the rhetoric that states "Never Give Up", would be better stated "Feel Good About What You Want To Do". The feeling of "Wow, I am never giving up." Versus "Wow, this is the perfect time to be doing this." Both are seemingly on the surface, reasonable thoughts along the way, although, one is filled with insistence and the other is filled with allowance. There might be times when taking the initial extra time to transplant the bush will bring a better result and it will be more satisfying and actually more wholesome and real.

In practical usage; "Understand yourself well enough to know when you are persisting on something rather than being in the best state of mind and emotions to allow in all confidence, due to the way you are feeling, that your deliberate Path is really feeling so good to be on." We are taught to fight for what we want. When it could have been taught to be ready for what we want. How? By finding happiness and then focusing and refocusing on your desires. It's not; "Do not ever give up!" although you are not giving up. It is; "Know the right timing on the path. Appreciate the ease of the slopes and the balance at the turns." Be ready.

No one has to struggle to get what they want; they can rather trust in the intuition of when to take any action and always while feeling good. Feel good about it rather than feeling strong enough to make it happen. It's time to implement this change into our experience. The masculine sense of achievement often revolved around strength, and more examples of success cling to the masculine ways of doing things. Times are changing and transparency, heart, truth and many uplifting virtues and realities are being appreciated into our views and applications. Additionally, more of the success of the female genders are being acknowledged equally worthy and valuable. It is not a persistence insistence of a strength that forces things to happen, although that works by and far. It is not as much fun and it can be more temporary, and it is hard. Rather, watch and feel good about the ideas and they will surely follow.

Life is supposed to be fun and in opposite to popular belief, Life is supposed to be a flow in love and light. We

# The Path of Least Resistance

are supposed to be having a good time and it can be easy or hard. It is all up to you. Resist that Idea if you want, knowing that the softer thought and gentler hearts find easier ways to create in.

How can you tell if you are on your Path of Least Resistance?

Two things that you can ask are:

How do you feel? And
What is the evidence in your life to support that feeling?

If you feel good, generally good evidence shows up.

Monitor the joy involved in success. I hear many tales of how hard it was for someone to succeed. They make movies about these people that battle and finally, against all odds, succeeded. They are generally filled with pain and suffering. They are the "old ways". They are not where we as a humanity are going now. We have turned the corner and are having a better time at succeeding. Succeed at being happy. Tell that tale.

The strange bewildering thing is that people who strife and suffer to succeed wear that egoic suffering as a badge of honor, while who have an easy path of least resistance are not taken as seriously without the pain, no pain no gain, pain. Wonder why?

Those succeeding the easy peasy way are often not asked and most likely out of the way from those seeking drama stories. If you really do want to learn how to succeed, ask someone who finds it easy to succeed.

And so, it is!

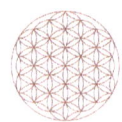

*The Art of Appreciating MORE*

## Chapter Four- Appreciations on The Path of least Resistance

- ❖ I appreciate applying awareness of current feelings into evaluating my choices.

- ❖ I appreciate that I can feel my way onto my Path of Least Resistance and in so doing I can care enough to better align.

- ❖ I appreciate knowing that I am gently guided onto my Path of Least Resistance.

- ❖ I appreciate that when I think about what I want and how best to get there, I feel having confidence in where I am first is beneficial.

- ❖ I appreciate my experiments with concepts that bring me into either appreciating where I am at any given time or where I move into by lending credence to my impact on my life from the flow I create.

- ❖ I appreciate that my life is an amazing adventure, and many are the good ways.

- ❖ I appreciate that my past often carries knowledge to assist.

- ❖ I appreciate in recognizing my feeling of ease I rejoin an improved path experience sooner.

- ❖ I appreciate that I do not understand everything and that is alright, it is more important to trust everything.

- ❖ I appreciate where I am, where I am going and how I experience my travels.

# The Path of Least Resistance

## Chapter 5  Appreciating Leverage

*There is a gentleness as soft as
a thought that only loves.*

I do not know if everyone would spontaneously agree with me by stating the following, although, I truly believe that after giving it some thought most would definitely see my point. "I am not what I own." Truly, of course that is so. It becomes most apparent when I appreciate the great value and the enormous asset of loving the difference between myself and everything outside of myself. I really try to appreciate that knowingness as a leverage that makes me more certain of everything that I come into noticing and understanding. I AM who I am

## Appreciating Leverage

rather than my belongings. That sounds, straight forward, doesn't it! Easy to understand. Being alive and experiencing such as we all do, things of the past, almost as if they were still current, can contribute towards what we are experiencing in the present moment. I will add that our standings, or status, obtained in life and our possessions gathered thus far, can influence our thoughts of ourselves as belonging part of them, along with other's their thoughts they have, or we think they have of us or of our possessions. We all tend to identify with our past experiences and the things we've accumulated along the way. We are not these things. We find pride in our accomplishment that carries us forward with confidence. This is a good progression, I feel, though consider, to depend upon our past, is less an accomplishment than to leverage our learnings into the moment. This aspect of identifying self with what we have, both experiences and possessions are aspects of appreciating leveraging in Life. In this leveraging, we can truly find wonder. There are things that boarder on the fringe of that idea that, although subtle, are worth the thought.

I love to manifest both experiences and things. Also, as it relates to things, there are times I de-manifest or lose, shed, trade out; up or down, let go of, give away, have taken away things, belongings, and/or assets. Substance may differ, yet, I like having options to assist me in life. In other words, acknowledging what belongs to me as a part of my status is something real to appreciate. In this present moment I am continuing to manifest both experiences and things. It is similar to noting that experiences can be reduced as are things. Letting go of things and letting go of experiences are both letting go of manifestations. We get to choose. The evidence of my wellbeing is established into this moment, this now. The experiences of the future are currently playing out into formation from, this now. I am gathering up all past into the present and, in open-mindedness, I am creating my future, knowingly. I admit most of my life it has been unknowingly because I was immature and did not know what I then didn't know. That I create my own reality was something I learnt over time. Processing that into life is the work I have to do to appreciate the power of self. Even more unknown over my lifetime has been that my emotions are manifestations also. It is an amazing understanding of life and a most rewarding participation into the future. However, appreciating that as I conjure up into the future, still, the future remains the ever unknown. We can only project portions of deliberate desires into the future, we all enter the future anew. We cannot know what we do not know, however we can know the unknown is good. We can remember that we create our own reality too and beholden to the responsibility we have to create.

This gentleness as soft as a thought that only loves, is the morning music in nature, the distant sounds of somethings passing by that reminds me of my place in life, a connective peace and trust with another, the stillness of real, the time locked into a speechless space, the awareness of self in you. It is right there, here, that I know myself distinct from all else and in complete control, that I know "I am". A quiet resolve flushes and nothing is ever kinder or nicer than self. That is the place where you know thyself and everything else important to know. You know you are love.

I do not want to discard all my memories and experiences and I am not about to give away all my Earthly possessions. I do support having what is needed to satisfy and keep life simple. With so much being available it is rewarding to keep it as simple and

## Appreciating Leverage

functional as possible. At least that holds true for me. To have something requires caring for it equally as much as it cares for you. The instruments of life are appreciated when they make pleasant music rather than harsh sounds. There is an art of appreciation in every masterpiece.

I love the past, it brought this now. To do anything but love the past is to not fully appreciate now. I want more and more so to leverage these positive accepted aspects of the past and resulting life into my present from the standpoint of moving forward. I think that people who feel a heavy weight, often of guilt, in having succeeded in arriving in this time and space with much to enjoy, have been over-influenced in the belief that there is not enough. Not enough for others to have had accumulated as much as they did. This ramifies their fairness of truth and tends to bring them into some balancing acts to justify. To feel you have what you do not deserve can alter the enjoyment of what you've accumulated. Drama can result. If you believe that you have and in, so others have not, is a terrible debilitating feeling. To compensate for grand achievements, I've noticed others will surrender some of the most important characteristics of joy itself into the mix and then attempt to overcome self with frivolousness both positive and negative. Many accomplished and abundant people resort to fear. Many accomplished people and even masters, fear that others want to be taking away from them and fear that others intend to bring forms of harm to them.

Jealousies are interesting torments. There is an entire industry devoted to assisting these factors by presenting security in the insecure. For example, there is a huge paranoia for many of the people who have to feel their abundance comes from their thoughts of being privileged. Whenever anyone feels they are not equal to everyone else, they lose joy. The results of these people who deservingly have although with guilty feelings, is that they deprive themselves from enjoying it and compensate with their emotions. We are all equal. Equality will be a given state of financial independence, not when the rich give to the poor, but when we identify with our individual right to be equal, not superior, not inferior. Equal.

*What, do you say, is the resulting difference between manifesting experiences and manifesting possessions?*

I love both. All that I manifest feels right. I appreciate that my experiences teach me as nothing else can. In my experiences I grow an understanding that cannot be read or told into existence, for the most part, albeit, I have the experience of vicariously expanding somewhat. Mostly though, I really learn through my experiences, which are a great and mighty teacher, and all experience I've had comes from my past or is right now in my present. None of it has come from my future. I am entitled, however, to create into my future using my past experiences as leverage.

I love remembering my experiences that have most easily assisted me in being who I am now. I honestly believe all of my past brings me here and now. Many of the so-called difficult times of the past, have softened up a lot and I can now re-experience them in a safer more resulting option and that always says to me loud and clear; "Everything always works out well for me." This is a good way to address the Pandemic and all the commotion surrounding it, including financial situations, social movements, natural evolving opportunities, health conditioning, and many changes that core evolve. The total outcome of the Pandemic is far away from the commencement, and the more we look

## Appreciating Leverage

forward to the results of it, the more we can partake in the formation of our new Path of Least Resistance. The seemingly negative release of a global Pandemic can transform the Earth. Much is going on and less gently than we seem to want. It is probably better to get all the extraneous issues to surface in order for society to approach a global shift. In the first times of The Silence of the Pandemic, humanity was debating among itself how to progress from this place of the unknown. It became a Voice without and a Voice within and it is clearly finding a way to be both heard. There is a gentleness as soft as a thought that only loves.

When I am told to let my past go and move-on, I immediately interpret that as, let my past experiences guide me to move-on to what I know is a better future. I do not have to let go of what I take with me, because I am not reliving my past, I am leveraging my past. I find in leveraging my past, both what seemed at the time, though changed in prospective now, as difficult times and, not to forget to leverage my past amazingly good times, is a beautiful advancement of life and living. I am enabled by bringing forth in a calculated manner, my experiences to assist me without letting them overrule my positive results, is a brilliant dealing.

I love myself now, even more than before now, hence, I find myself flowing with what will maximize my leverage into now and the future. Taking away with me aspects of experiences in the past that I've gained wisdom in having had, is a very positive influence upon me. If I did not do so, I would be over and over again living in ignorance. Some might say that ignorance is blissful, I can distinguish my bliss better than ever and ignorance is not the same as bliss. I can choose what to focus attention on in any now I stand, hence, if I want bliss, I can follow it. I think that loving the experiences of my life, lifts me above the calculation of profit and enables me to flourish in blissful directions. I would say, however, that I sense the rightness of experience better and faster now. I also bring forth experiences into myself now in a more general way. I compress the details of the past into modules and compartments that serve me, or not. I remember first and foremost the outcome from experience, over time, instead of looking too deeply at the details.

I note this thought; many people want to take with them their past negative experiences, and they miss out on the transition of converting them into pleasant experiences. Why do they do that is due to not appreciating that everything does work out for each and every one of us in the best way we allow them to. That is a Law of Attraction teaching. Some people hold on to past sorrows as if they are shields of prevention. They are not. Some know that they are better off now from what was a more difficult experience back then, and, after a while, some minutes some longer, after some time of their determination, they will resort back to those past unsavory experiences and choose to feel the pain of them rather than the true over-time-released joy in them having played out. We all know that things that happened seemingly the worst they could be, will over time heal and even, as intended from the beginning, bring us a realization that because of it, rather than in spite of it having happened, life is much better. I know that Love, always provides to me exactly what is perfect for me to experience, hence, I take the results of my given experiences with me from Love's yield. They are windows, not so much into the past, as they are into the possibilities of what I can now create into my future.

*Appreciating Leverage*

Some people will toss and turn always looking back into the pain and sorrow they experienced in the past, and often too, they have developed a scenario of blame and guilt on themselves and more often on others for the experience. There are not real accidents. There are only circumstances in which we are aligned and matched-up to in order to have experience. Once we choose to take away the need for us to blame, we eliminate the need to forgive, and although forgiveness is good for people who are slow to process their glorified Path of Least Resistance into the equation of experience, still, once we lift out of blame and doubting intentional love for us, we can receive the joy of all experiences as perfect. First transforming blame into appreciation will progress the change. There is an art to appreciating. On the global field, social scale or as an independent experience. Everything is happening because it is time to happen. It is a new concept that we have leverage in controlling time. In Now we can tweak the volume of time to permit a flow of positive results to flourish. Pointing blame is backstroking in the opposite direction from the goals that are already in your will to arrive. It is easier and more profitable on all levels to allow what is happening to happen, rather than fight it or blame something or somebody for it happening. Remembering often that we create our own reality is worth refocusing upon. We are requested in this venue of thoughts, to move-on. This is the path either now or later humans will have to travel. In a blink or in a lifetime. It is your choice. You can be a deliberate contributor. We have so much more to accomplish past the moving-on.

*The Art of Appreciating MORE*

We are powerful beyond our understanding. That power can only result in goodness. Eventually, it will be accepted, if not accepted immediately. Having a knee jerk reaction towards what is happening regardless of any initial dislike about it, is controllable. We are being awakened out of the sorrow holds of the past and progressing unto where we actually want to be. The new changes in compassionate consciousness allows compassion for self too. We can each think compassionately about what we want to feel and create in. Letting go is a hard thing for some people. If though, instead of trying so hard to forgive the past that haunts, there was a space that can be escaped out from there, and there is, the results are more happiness and forward thinking. The memories of past, seemingly unfortunate, times can be let go of. It is all a thought away. If you do not allow that to be a belief, what then will you believe in? Someone is always out to cause you harm or worse? That is a negative fear and letting those tendencies go away will usher positive results faster.

As to the accumulation of possessions, they too, to me, are much as are my experiences. I love my manifested possessions. One of the major reasons to be alive is to manifest and to have the joy in so doing. Some teach that possessions are somewhat less valuable than is the giving away of possessions. I am not feeling that, although I am a generous person. I give from a desire to give, rather than from an obligation, usually handed down from others as best behavior from me to do so. I believe that we are all here as intended, and we can choose the life we live.

A long time ago, I deliberately chose to have more than enough in my life. Not all know that they have a choice. It is a fact that there is a difference in thinking and doing rather than a separation between those who have

*Appreciating Leverage*

and those who have not. I love to teach this aspect of life, that we all have the ability to think positive abundance into our lives. Some are opting for negative abundance in their lives and that is somewhat connected to them having been taught and in their now believing that there is not enough to go around. That is far from the truth. Empires have been built upon that being a manipulated belief taught to or enforced upon so many people, generations after generations. Those growths of empires that focus upon lack are skewed off by the ruling-class to be the profiter and the governed to be the puppets. Shall you forfeit your abundance due to the governing, often self-appointed controllers, who want to rule and be the elite, your elite? They are unaware of equality. Once you accept yourself as an equal to all people, those who want you to not know that will be a lot less impactful on your quantity of having enough. If I am creating my own reality and experience a knowingness that there exist some people who want to control me, then, can I reduce this belief and then avoid people the ability to control me. Yes. Although you cannot make others behave in a way to please you. You can avoid these controllers and in so doing their control over you is avoided.

The accumulation of possessions isn't what I am. Those things, both mine and others in my welcome use-environment, support my life and happiness in profound and appreciated ways. I love wanting and then getting. I love having and then giving.

Some teach that "things" are egoic and selfish. I do not agree, albeit I understand that some people develop possessiveness over things while others unfortunately are confused by the sense of security, they, consciously or not, create in having things. I do not. I love my things.

I manifested them. I appreciate my capability to manifest. It is a delight to create. It is a joy to appreciate.

I own an artificial Christmas Tree that I bring out during Christmastime and I love it. I do not want to give it away to someone who doesn't own their own artificial Christmas Tree. I enjoy setting it up and lighting-up my life with its intent. It has the ability to help me bring to mind other years of Christmastimes too. I love my memories of Christmastime. Why is it seemingly okay to probably everyone that I keep my own Artificial Christmas Tree year after year and I do not have to feel guilty in so doing. Others will instruct me in all their holiness, that possessions are bad. If I have in their opinion too much, (which incidentally is usually any amount of quotient they have less than) I should give some of it away to the less fortunate. Doing so in some people's minds will make me a better person. In fact, possession of money could, in some minds, be the root of all evil. Equally or rather additionally, some might tend to believe that the lack of money could, in some minds, be the root of all evil.

Money, in having or not having, is not the root of all evil. How could anyone even know that money is evil. It is not. Usually, it is people who feel they do not have enough money who think this up. Thinking such, for the moment, makes them feel better. And, well, whatever makes you feel better will most likely deliver you to a better place. "Money is the root of all evil." I know it is just an expression, and, it is a connotation, as well. It is unworthy of any absolute value and evil could, if desired, be an illusion. At minimum it is an opinion. Thinking of money or anything as evil, is a negative thought. If you come into that thought, rethink it from another aspect and let negativity about money go, and soon enough, money will also be friendlier with you. I

## Appreciating Leverage

think it is misleading, at best, to call money evil. We do not know why or what others are thinking or even doing. The rich are not bad people because they have money and money doesn't make a good person bad either. Having money doesn't mean a person is a saint either. Why judge people by the money you think they own, better said that they use. Money is a specific manifestation of an understanding and trust in abundance, and we all are in equal rights to trust in abundance, positive abundance or negative abundance, you choose.

There are other aspects to this generalize misunderstanding about money that seem to key in the ideas that money translates into. Money is a helpful component towards accomplishing some things. Money is a useful ingredient to apply towards creating more. Money is a verb sometimes; like in the way it flows. Having money is better than not having money in my experiences and having too much money is leverage in directing self towards creations that are often very worthy. Experiment with your money and watch the outcome. It is fun to have money and to spend and receive money. It is fun to play with money and to feel the essence of what, to you, is an abundance of money. I appreciate the money I have to play and use as I please. It is a manifestation that can empower. Find the goodness in having money, and you will have more. Right where you currently are, leverage whatever amount of money you have by appreciating money into your life, if you want to have more money.

I know that my expression that money is a form of abundant thoughts can seem a far stretch from the bottom line in your bank account. That is partly because we often think of money as a tangible substance maybe even a blob of something that changes form; sometimes growing other time shrinking, depending upon needs. That is one way of viewing money, however, I feel that money is more of an emotion than a substance. That idea is easier to follow when you think about the usage of physical money being less engaging and debit cards, credit cards, checks and notes are more like our experiences with money now. It is rare to have money, actual money in your hands, it is all more so that money moves around on your behalf. You buy things on your account, within your desire, and the money moves. Money, for me, is more than the physical bills and coins. That idea that money is less physical is a good momentum towards the understandings that Money is more and more a result of emotions. There are a great deal of emotions, thoughts, ideas and feelings attached to money than ever before in mankind's history with money. Money feels good to have. Some struggle and think that money is hard to get. I do not feel that. I feel that money is a good feeling to have, get and give. I love the feelings of security and freedom money provides, among other feelings too. The point is, I have feelings and emotions about money.

I see that people have some rather interesting feelings about other people having money too. Some in our society feel that some people have too much and others too little. When the comparison of rich people versus poor people comes up some people instinctively choose to feel that it is not fair that some have more than others. That is a well-defined opinion of many perhaps currently a growing number of people, although I sense changes in people, especially in the compassionate reasoning of other's circumstances throughout the Covid times. I feel very differently about that issue of judging wealth. There are reasons that some have more than others in the form of money. It is because they believe that they deserve more money. They accept their money.

## *Appreciating Leverage*

When you think as society has taught, we have ideas that form restrictions towards others and self. When we allow thoughts to be more aligned with our personal abundant feeling frequencies than with the results somewhat anticipated and stereotypically defined by others, they form a more intimate role partnering with self-desires and specific results. Your thoughts matter. Your thoughts about yourself and about others.

Most who do have too much money, by any one's standards, want to be in that position in life and have aligned with it. They want to be too wealthy; they believe that they can be too wealthy, and then they are. They created their own reality. I wonder if they appreciate that some people are jealous of that situation they are in? Perhaps! In aligning with having money, it is probably a lot healthier to align with acceptance rather than with others being jealous. I must admit that there is something kind of self-satisfying when another is a little jealous of me. It was more prevalent when I was younger because I cared more about what others thought about me. I've thought about jealousy as good if it reveals desires rather than wants to take from another to have. I have improved my understanding about jealousies, and I understand to trust revealing's others enjoy as similar to shopping in a department store. Knowing what I want sometimes is stimulated by shopping through the varieties. When I think of people who have too much, I think that I am happy with more than enough. I do not want too much. I think that there is more than enough to go around, and so I do not feel a desire to penalize people who are in the top percent of the financial population. They are receiving what they have chosen. It is their desire to be that wealthy. It is not my desire. If you are not among the wealthiest people in the world, then you also must really not want to be, or you would be. If you do not believe you can be, then you will not be.

# The Art of Appreciating MORE

There is no limit to what you can achieve. Joe Vitale said something like this in The Secret Movie; "There is not a director in the sky keeping you away from being as rich or as poor as you can be." The only real separator is the knowing that you can be as wealthy or poor as you think you can be. There are ways in which wisdom of the Law of Attraction can assist you in living up to your goals, and it is as easy to be rich as it is to be poor. That is something difficult for many to understand or believe. It starts making sense when the idea of abundance is matured into a general appreciation. Manifestations are as difficult as you believe them to be. A teacher of mine says, "It is as difficult to manifest a button as it is to manifest a castle."

What do you really believe you can manifest? What do you really want to manifest? If they are the same and the Universe has that ability, it will manifest. If you think it too impossible; it is. Start out where you feel comfortable with your beliefs and try your mind, heart and soul at manifesting deliberately. If you want to manifest abundance, grow a better understanding of what abundance is and stretch your beliefs to include everything that is readily abundant in your life. I also have feelings about abundance and when I put together my good feelings about money and about abundance, I become abundant with money and it feels comfortable rather than surprising.

That is easy to do for me and it is easier than you thought for yourself too. I have some processes that I use to elaborate on my feelings of money. Here is one. Try it, you'll like it. It starts out with a simple question. What were you doing, where were you doing it, who were you with, and how did you feel during it when you last felt abundant? Really. It might not be as intuitive as a quick answer brings forth. Think about it first. When

## Appreciating Leverage

last did you feel rich? Where were you, maybe who were you with and what were you doing? If not, the last time you felt rich, can you recall a special time or event when you felt the wealth of being a compassionate individual. Wealth and Riches are not always best felt from the abundance of money, so think about a possible event that strengthened your feelings of rightness, or maybe nobility or great timely choices or impacts.

I'll help you with this conjuring up. As it might not be when you were spending money. Which is interesting. For me, coming to mind, I felt a heightened abundance when not too long ago, our waitress said she liked my blouse. It was the cranberry-colored shirt with the golden owl on it. I was surprised that she liked it as no one ever said they liked that shirt before, and I've worn it several times. I thanked her and said, "It represents wisdom to me." She was surprised at me for saying that, I could tell. She replied that she loved owls. I said, "Me too". I thought that was enough said when I realized we were continuing our conversation. She told me that she lived in the country and had owls in the neighborhood that she followed and watched with her daughter sometimes. I was touched and I then first time looked her more closely in her eyes and said, "I have an owl story. If you have time, I can tell you about it." I didn't know where that was coming from but definitely it came from deep within me. She carefully looked around, evaluated the situation, and said, "Yes, I do have time".

And so, I began my true story which went like this; "When I was much younger than now, I worked for a government contractor doing some high-tech work. My company was putting together an air control system for the Saudi Arabians and I was involved in some of the software and training materials. At the time, there were a dozen or more men from Saudi staying locally in a hotel that had a gas station right next door to it. It was after my work had finished for the day that I, while making my way home, stopped at that gas station to fill up. As I was pumping my gas, I noticed a group of the visiting Saudi men on the balcony of the second story of the hotel with an open blanket in their collective hands. They swiftly and with a single together shout threw that blanket out into the edges of the tree just there. It fell directly and apparently on target, and several men quickly chased after it as it thumped to the ground. Some men I now noticed had been already placed under the tree ground level and ran out towards the nearby lumpy fallen blanket. The blanket, certainly, had something under it. I could see it moving around now. I couldn't make it out, but I felt danger and indeed a man advanced and kicked the blanket bundle as the others cheered. It was very creepy. I didn't understand a word they were loudly yelling about, but I knew something uncomfortable was happening. Something I'd never seen before.

I felt an immediate need to see what was going on, as from working with these men I knew they were different than our American men. Teaching them had been a difficulty that I was involved in solving. I knew there were some extensive cultural differences between what was more typical. Generally, they were hard to teach, and I knew they did not particularly enjoy learning from a foreigner and worse from a woman and they knew who I was professionally. I'd probably spoken to each of them at some point during the past six months. Individually, they were easier to communicate with, although when they were together, they acted differently. They now recognized me and as I walked closer, they were laughing and howling a bit as a collective even as if they were a gang. And that is exactly what they were. As I questioned them, I was told that they hated owls and

## Appreciating Leverage

especially that one who hoots close to where they were staying and trying to sleep. So, they were going to kill it.

I was amazed at their insensitivity and I walked over, grabbed the corners of the blanket, turned it to collect its contents and I quickly carried that bundle that barely moved over to my car, opened the way-back of my little Ford Fiesta, and put the blanket; contents and all, into the car, got in and drove off.

It was confused, the dear little owl. It seemed smaller than I had thought of an owl to be, so I figured it was a baby. Later I came to learn that it was an adult owl of a small-sized species. Driving along, I could see it through my rearview mirror. Sweet thing, it was shaking and frightened. We drove together for ten miles or so and I recalled turning on classical music thinking it would sooth its soul into a calmer place and I think it did. I drove to my parent's place where I was picking up my small daughter, Tasha. I closed the door behind leaving the owl inside and peeked in from the rear window from the outside and noticed it looking timidly up at me. It was love at first sight.

Consequently, once inside my parent's place we all decided it best to call the local animal society and they said they would come directly over. They told me, in the meantime, to stay away from it and to not try to touch it, as it could become angry and bring me great harm. They reminded me that it was a wild animal. I respected that, although Tasha and I stood over it, while awaiting them to arrive and find out if it was okay. We stood there looking-in at this amazingly beautiful bird helplessly wondering who-o-o-o we were all smiles and happy to meet it. We knew it would be okay now. The nice people from the humane society came and took it away and I called back to be told they eventually let it free again.

They also told me that it was certainly very dangerous that I had it unrestrained in my car as it could have flew-up and used its talons to hurt me in its confusion. Hey, I knew that it knew I brought it into a safe space. It knew I was helping it. It knew that we had fallen in love with each other. Believe it or not, I felt abundance. I felt rich with love and compassion. These men, I know well enough to state were all from wealthy families. Even though, I sensed and knew from experience how poorly they behaved. I really felt much richer than any and all of them put together. I was an abundant soul of conscious compassion. That is really a good feeling. Person after person, nation after nation will have to find equality in due time. There is no other way for humanity to progress successfully. All the measures and laws placed or rezoned from humanity, not a one is effective in the long term if equality is unable to exist.

The waitress was amazed at the story and said she was so happy it came to a good ending because she was afraid it was not going to have a happy ending for a while. I knew, sitting there in that restaurant that I looked quite good in this owl shirt right then, smiling and satisfied with my trusting that everything works out well for me, and everything works out well for others involved or near me. That is a leverage of knowing, that brings tremendous confidence into my life and surroundings. I felt my worthiness grow stronger right then. Love is amazing, it is the opposite of fear and hate and Love always triumphs even in the face of danger. The feeling of having so much love that it overflows from me is an abundance beyond description.

The prospect of abundance in this story was apparent to me. I had an abundance of love for this animal. It was alive and I felt abundant in my ability to act in a way to

## Appreciating Leverage

save its life. This deed of compassion made me feel abundant.

I'd never told that story to anyone outside of my family before. When the guys from Saudi saw me again, they spoke nothing of it, although in all honesty I took hold of my frequency of honor and respect and they always after that did find a new quiet respect professionally for me. Now in this restaurant I was surprised that story came out of me so flowy and with clear details and still with most of the very same emotions I had when it actually happened. I mattered in that story. I trusted life and I gathered a great abundant feeling of confidence. Could it really have taken place about thirty years ago? I love that emotions can be surfaced so deliberately and refresh the spirit into now. It is solid proof, my revisited and good feelings surfacing, that it is important what is thought about.

As we were served our meals and beverages, this waitress treated us differently. She was friendlier and the ice between people meeting by chance thawed and spring was thriving in the midst of a general public place. We were special in her day and she was special in our day. Strangers can come together to love one another so quickly when they expose their hearts and feelings to each other. She came by several times seemingly more times than needed. Each time more pleasantries were connecting between us all. Needless to say, the food was absolutely delicious. Food always tastes better and is better for you when there is joy in the air, and the company was fun to be with, and now so much was easier than before that story was shared.

Throughout the time there, I noticed just right behind the wall adjacent to our table was a server-station that several of the wait-staff utilized in order to prepare specific needs to their customers and to ready their closing bill. And I heard some of the conversations that went on there, as well. I insert at this point, that I hear very well. Actually, increasingly well as I get older. It is a wonderful increase and it makes sense to me because I understand more words now and I understand expressions. I hear better than ever before in my life because I understand better what I hear. Also, as one gets more proficient with controlling thoughts, one can be much more in control of what to actually listen to. We are misinformed and far too willing to accept that as we get older our senses are expected to decrease. Do not believe that! We are here longer, not older. It makes little sense and you are not having to do what others always expect of you, especially in regard to your choice to decline your wellbeing or to improve your wellbeing. I believe humans are made to live longer and healthier, and, for me, so it is.

As I was sitting in our booth, I over-heard someone, a man, another server with a complaining voice, say; "I am having a hard day today." And then our waitress answered him with; "You couldn't believe how much is going on in my life right now. You think you have a hard day, well, let me tell you that it can't be as hard as mine or my life."

I pick up quickly on conversations that are positive and full of life, and I also hear negative conversations, less so. Negative complaining conversations sound like shrill to my ears and mind. I notice it and almost immediately remove it from my hearing. I know that might sound like putting my head in the sand. And, okay, perhaps it is a bit like that. The results of taking control, are worth the reduction of off-pitched-sensations of dealing with listening to what is complaining or negating. I think we all do hear both positive and negative words, though I

## Appreciating Leverage

often can shut my sense of hearing down when I sense negative words. Hearing her and sensing her wait service with us, it was like two different people. She could separate her life with her work, I thought, very well. She was acting either with us or with her coworker. She had two different personalities, indeed. She seemed engaged and alive with a soft gentle spirit and she seemed quick. She took the time to "hear a story". What waitress does that? I felt a desire to cheer her up!

I was in my typical happier than most attitude and we, Uri and I, were having a very pleasant time together. The story of the owl was long over, and we resumed our happy spirits chatting away and having a good time together. We were finding things to politely laugh at easily and we were enjoying this meal together. The food was delicious, and everything was working out so well for us, as usual. We were both feeling very good and now full too. What can be better than that!

This time when our waitress approached, she had our bill in her hand and still as she placed it down and wished us well, she looked into my eyes and I said; "Things will work out for you, just know that to be so." She quickly replied; "I worry so much about everything". I said; "Oh, worry is like creating into your future things unwanted. It is better to nib worry in the bud should it come into your thoughts. Trust that things are already working out well for you." She looked startled and replied; "Oh my gosh, that is exactly what someone else recently said to me and she called it The Law of Attraction. Do you know of The Law of Attraction?"

Uri now woke up from within himself and said "Oh, yes. We are Law of Attraction people. In fact, Peggy wrote a book all about The Law of Attraction many years ago." Our waitress was in surprise and asked what it is all about, this Law of Attraction Book. I told her the title of the book; "The Art of Appreciation", and then I turned to Uri and asked him if we had, as we usually did, a copy of the book in the car. He said yes and that he would happily go immediately and get one for our waitress, and off he sped. This darling young lady was amazed at the questions she then asked and the answers she received in the short time it took Uri to come back with the book, which I promptly signed and handed to her. I had provided a few minutes worth of my summary course of The Law of Attraction 101. She nearly cried with joy and she said she couldn't wait to read the book and learn because she was ready to be happy and filled with the kind of joy as were, Uri and I.

Now that feels like abundance to me. Potentially providing some of the tools to change a person's life into a better one. That is what abundance feels like, sometimes, and that is what where, how, who, and why I felt very rich, very abundant, very together. It was not the most recent time I felt abundant. I feel abundant every day in many ways. I chose that experience to emphasize that abundance is not all about money, having it, or spending it, which is what most will respond with. I felt so much love provided to both of us, actually all three of us, and the timeliness of this encounter had been so easy and satisfying for Uri and me.

As our society seems to be bending deeply into more polarizing separations from each other, and in addition, the natural requirement to keep a distance during the Pandemic, it is valuable to grow rather than reduce our compassionate consciousness and find the wealth of love

## Appreciating Leverage

that transmits past the direction of society and into our personal ability to be right, noble, and honorable. We must learn to love one another in abundance and gather up the wealth it provides.

The feeling of abundance comes in many forms. I see it all over the knock-out rose bush in our garden that is prolific with red blooms, in the many ways to express appreciation of self and others, in the smiling eyes on people passing by and mine as well, in the comforts of my life, in the number of directions and focuses to choose from today, the variety of music to listen to in the car or at home, in the beauty of the activities that are always bringing me notice and in the choice I have to think the way it will best serve me now and in the future. I can think many millions of positive things. There is so much abundance all around me. That is mostly all that I see, and mostly all I am. In the abundance I experience, of course, more abundance comes to me. I know how to leverage my many encounters of abundance into more abundance, feelings of worthy wealthiness, and into more discoveries.

Oh yes, it is true that possessions aren't evil either. If talking about a reusable Christmas Tree or a mansion of many rooms, possessions are what we appreciate in them. Possessions are also dreams come true. They are manifestations and all manifestations are an accumulation of beliefs, often handed from one person to another in love and joy. That is how manifestations come into existence. Manifestations are not evil, they are goodness. Manifestations are actually holy. Hold that thought and surely you will have what you desire.

Of course, leveraging thoughts, experiences, manifestations or dreams is complicated with what we have experienced in life and though, often it is too easy to be influenced by what others are saying they are thinking. It is even easy enough to be influenced by what I am thinking that others are thinking without them even saying it. Knowing what is actually influencing us might not be as straight forward as one would hope it to be. These external interpretations of thoughts, words, and meanings are all going on between all relationships too.

Leverage is more complicated than to be considered only in objects or experiences of our ownership. Leverage is within relationships too. Those relationships that are current are not necessarily the most influential ones either, as the past can, if allowed, establish beliefs and patterns of thoughts about others that remain and/or continue to increase their influence over time. There have been times that I've said to myself, long after someone mentions something to me that, I finally understand what they meant by that.

Does it really matter? Our relationship between our self and between others can mirror each other and still, it is a good practice to realize the source of thoughts that make changes happen in life or that make ponder different. I appreciate it when I feel a newer thought or a change in direction take place inside me, either through internal thoughts or combinations of external thoughts coming into my notice. I know that I want more control of choices since I know I am choosing so much of my directions now.

Once upon a time, I had less interest in deciphering thought-source or thought-reaction. I was more than often in a default place of thought-travel and although

## Appreciating Leverage

things were, indeed, going pretty well for me, I want to be more myself in a trusting sense of confidence and direction. I have discovered that I can be a better influence upon myself and, if the occasion arises, I can be of a better influence upon others. A direction that satisfies me is to always seek kindness in a more compassionate consciousness.

On the subjects to approach when thinking about appreciating leverage, is to know more than before about how it is even a possibility to recognize the influences of others upon us and us upon others, ever-the-less utilize this knowledge to become happier and, consequentially, more successful people. It is more important than we are taught traditionally. It is an ever-growing importance as we recognize that social media, corporate cultures, marketing, political platforms, financial status', educational systems, media and personal relationships are growing systems and intends to influence more. These entities that want more influence over others are becoming more sophisticated, and aggressive generally. The systems that want to control the thoughts and actions of others are intelligent and, increasingly determined, as if their existence depends upon it. Fortunately, we are embarking upon a new normal and in so we hold the power to appreciate transparency more and to participate in more direct and positive ways. We do not tolerate these off-entities as we once did. Now we question authority from a higher compassionate consciousness.

We enter each growth of humanity in many different ways. Currently we measure our interactivity and usage of technologies, including computer technologies, as progress and, for the most part, we all enjoy the increases technologies yield and the path of learning required to implement these technological wonders of our times. It is so apparent that the computer technologies are providing increases in life quality that it is common to attribute our progress is primarily due to computers. I feel that we neglect to appreciate that many other aspects of expansion are occurring, even though I've appreciated a successful career as a Computer Engineer and Scientist. Many advances are integrated with computer technologies or are applications of the basics of computing. I also recognize that many other aspects of life are being influenced by other things. For example, the world of psychology hasn't ceased to exist once the computer generation continued into the next generation and the next and more to come. We will never return to a world without an increasing usage of computer power any more than we will go back to not using electricity, albeit we are searching for new means to generate electricity. Likewise, we need to and already have begun to discover a new means in which we can influence each other through any and all means of technologies in a pure and honorable manner. That is the only way we will progress successfully as humanity. The point is that many areas of interest are increasing in understanding and usage. People of many thoughts and ideas use all the tools available to follow their dreams, hence, more focus can attribute to more advancements. The world of "thought control" is a reality that attracts some in ways worth mentioning.

Uri and I watched a documentary that was about the cults and the way cults become and grow bigger. Many times, it is through thought control and manipulation. These entities may or may not begin within the premise of taking advantage of others, although, the outcome often is the follower being abused in ways. After watching this documentary, we were dazzled by the way some people are prone to the drama of being led into a cult. A lot of cults are religious. Religions are not in a

## Appreciating Leverage

poor judgement by me, although I see that religious people often need to be told what to do. They need to be followers and explained what a good way is to behave. I am too independent a thinker to be totally into religion and I am too compassionate to be totally defensive about religions. I am also quite equipped to know what is right for me to do. I trust my heart. Of course, there are a lot of other aspects to what is a religion, and they are often good or framed by goodness and love. The rules and regulations in the Christ Consciousness of religions have and continue to help people know their better way. I am not going to defend or offend religions or religious people, and there is a huge distinction between religions and cults. An interesting thing about the documentary cult information, was that it was a business and not a church and it was self-help enticement rather that a definer of righteousness over sinning. It brought a deeper awareness that there is a growing understanding of the mind and the ways some can attempt to deliberately control another person's thoughts and behaviors. This is a complicated technology that, as is the computer technology, is integrated into other disciplines and somewhat lacks explanation, except it doesn't feel good (which is an emotion utilized in the manipulation process) or it is simply not a match to be a problem to resist.

Uri comes from a kibbutz and I have experienced my first two children become Jehovah Witness' as their father, who was not Uri insisted, they follow that religious cult like teachings after we were no longer together. Both Uri and I have personal experience with the desires a group might enforce upon its followers or participants. I think it is because of that background we both felt, after watching that documentary that we could never be influenced into a cult environment. We talked about it after the show was long over and into the next day. We analyzed the reported experiences of these people in that cult and trying to get out of that cult and still, we could not imagine that we would ever fall prey to a cult, leader or processes. We thought about that and again and again we concluded that we know to stay away from thoughts that lock us into someone else's behavioral model. Another conclusion is that we do not attract more than a movie, cult appreciation into our way of living. We are not subjected to cult indoctrinations because we are not the matching vibration required to attract these entities into our lives.

Yes, some leaders should not be followed. And the attraction any one of us create are our personal responsibility. I am very happy that I can soon enough or in enough time recognize the feelings of an influencer of influenceable technology to overwhelm me and I chose to avoid them as often as possible and overtime I am rather successful about it, as is Uri. We identify with the intent and resolve the difference and appreciate our own thoughts and feelings as indicators and guidance.

Knowing our true connections to our personal feelings and our feelings that we have when with others, can give us an opportunity to co-create or, on the other hand, a realization for a need to disassociate. I am thinking that cocreation is not all it is cracked up to be as our individuality is clearly intended to promote positive self-interest that can overflow to others and at a pace we can personally handle and appreciate. The scenario of co-creation requires a syncing-up with another or others. Let's think about what co-creation is when we start with just one other. I experience waves of connections rather than a submergence into another's space of creation. A call to enchantment seems to happen when they too, this other person or people, are in their personal wave of connection. It is fascinating that both or, rather, all or

## Appreciating Leverage

any involved are required to be at a vibrational match, rather than the same in context, content or direction, with each other such that some frequency, the most needed-to-co-create frequency, can connect into what is a birthing of manifesting ideas into things together. There is an excitement that looms inside of this special communal space that vibrates and travels to or through participants as well as participating ingredients. There are no constraints upon the physical distances between creators of creations. There is a soft-magic that cocreation yields. More often than not, cocreation works most significantly and effectively when it is simplified into an agreement of supporting each other, rather than actually meld-creating a mutual dream or idea as a connective. It is rather more an acknowledgement of a collective or team-like quality arising into a sharing of what is most appropriate at that moment in time-space reality. The waves of awareness' are less personal when in an environment whereby everything is aware of you too, and, "All" is always aware of you, as it pulses itself into connection with the frequencies available. Being conscious of this is, what is sometimes called, *perfect timing*. When in *perfect timing*, appreciating the leverage available is soothing and rewarding.

It is substantially more complex a thought to know the difference between my thoughts and the thoughts that Source gifts me with having, the latter of which is a significant influence on me all of the time, albeit an inside-self interpretation rather than an outside influence.

*Where are my Ideas coming from?*

*Am I living my own creation of thoughts or am I mimicking the thoughts that a greater higher Source instills into me?*

It is easier to know that others are inclined to think their own thoughts and I have to just allow knowing them or not. I cannot over-adjust them or think them away. Further, I have no idea if I am even capturing the essence of them, ever-the-less actually inventing them. What's in addition, I have no way of knowing the extent in which another being is creating their own choices from, ever-the-less their own thoughts from.

*Can we think our own thoughts or are thoughts instilled from higher thoughts to stick as worthy or not?*

*Does Source think for me?*

If you are thinking that sometimes or if you are thinking that now, that is a good thing. You are thinking deeply about your thoughts. Every time you think about your own thoughts, you become the master and that is where you are very creative. Your creativity matters to this world development and growing technologies. You matter. Your thoughts create.

As a humanity, going back again into the concept of *perfect timing* and perhaps increasing our personal level or heightening our frequency to expand into thoughts that are new, it can be that this time, now, is the *perfect time* to experience an allowing from inside more than from outside of us. I want to be influenced by the InnerVoice of reasoning rather than what others are thinking I should be doing to please them. Not that there is anything wrong with that feeling that I've pleased someone else with my cooperation, ideas or suggestions. Within me there is More than I know how to open myself totally to receiving as I continue to expand my awareness. I want to agree with others not for the sake of agreement happening, rather for the experience of harmony and synchronicity. It is happening more often;

*Appreciating Leverage*

opening myself and trusting my internal voice. For that I am in more abundance in all ways.

It is significantly important to always run the *checks and balances* through my own system of beliefs when others I've attracted are thinking far off or differently than I generally do. When others preach things that feel wrong to look at, as often cult fashioned leaders do, they probably aren't right for you. In the commercial world, it seems more acceptable to have concepts mislead more willingly or without avoidance. Commercial entities seem to have less, and less accountability and misrepresentations seem tolerated more, and more often than should be permitted. In the social digital media, there are plenty of reasons one must pay attention to what it feels like to accept this mode of learning as complete and truthful. The results one can experience by "buying-into" other people's ideas, or the ideas the computer seems to be generating into your sphere of influence can impact your life. Hence, questioning it is valuable to you. It is uncomfortable to seek opposition in every communication with others, especially when you are wanting cooperation and positive growth with others. A personal responsibility will always be a personal responsibility, and make no mistake, your thoughts are your personal responsibility. Others may have alternative reasons for participating in communications with you. Be aware and be smart. You are the master of your fate, so it is said and so it is.

"Hold true to what you are doing."
"Go for it."
"Trust your instincts."

## The Art of Appreciating MORE

Those are all seemingly good advice statements to appreciate and relate into experiencing. Leveraging the Appreciation of your ability to think your own thoughts and to understand the reasoning behind others wanting you to think their way is a very good thing.

When some scenario comes about into my heart-mind-soul that requires, and seemingly, absolutely, insists on my involvement, there is no stopping me from it. I know I have free will and that I get to choose my own thoughts. There are times I am actually "being" that choice long before I choose to be. It is an instinct. It is exactly what I want too. There is then, within me, a truth of existence that awakens and rattles me into places that I must have agreed to be in, perhaps long before when I can remember. Otherwise, why would it feel so important and immanent.

In those mastered experiences, where I am aware that they are different than my truly and freely choosing involvement as all my Being is taking me into it, willingly or YES, even sometimes reluctantly, though unwavering inside my life force, I begin to command my presence be rewarded more knowledge and wisdom for the overly-coincidental orchestration and almost pawn-like or naturally intuitive participation of the agreement itself. In that place, I find great love and, perhaps, a type of "definition", and at the least, a new "knowingness".

We all want to "trust" others. It is our human nature to want to believe others. It is also our human nature to question others. Both wanting to see the best in others and utilizing our personal feelings meet each other into most subtle impressions that others make upon us. It is a timely consideration to evaluate the feelings between yourself, your inner substance (your emotions), and the results of communications with others. This can include

*Appreciating Leverage*

interactions with digital social media of all platforms. We are becoming more technological and we are in need to become more responsible with our communion with technologies. Depending upon technologies to determine for you the feelings of truth or positive intent might be ignorant. While thinking about this subject, many others are depending upon their technology influences to mimic or even define meaning upon those that inter-act with them. We often call it "fact checking" although, even "fact checking" is sourced out to trusting others their interpretations. For myself, since I want to be happy, I take caution of other's positions while listening for growth and I try to remember that I have the Innate ability to distinguish the emotional fields of expressions from others and myself. I learn a lot by paying attention to the feelings I have while communicating with others. Some think you learn a lot from others by listening to them, I say, you must while listening to others pay attention to yourself and especially your feelings about what you are "learning" or "hearing" from others. Being cautious can feel less than feeling happy. Sometimes it feels a burden to overthink another their expressions. Remember that investing in examination of all feelings, can and does, seal the generosity of shared values and beliefs. We don't know what we don't know until we do know.

It's an interesting proviso to register the result as part of more than I can control and still, once over, I am resolved to appreciate the love others have for me in so doing and I respect myself in a heightened self-worthiness and I grow an understood independence that strengthens others. I love people. I love everyone in some way. Upon completion and even once realized the inevitability of it, I do not regret involvement and feel any potential hardship to result, only a true direction being followed for me and for others. The experience is unlike the sacrificial person, it is the participating agreement being fulfilled. We are all connected to each other in amazing ways and in these periodic surrenders, which is always more enlightening than to struggle and wiggle my way through it in a fight to not be a player, I find a satisfaction for civility and a great love that goes in many directions and is arrived in very pleasing ways. It is tolerance or unconditional love.

The gain is brought into me like a wave unravels itself onto the shore. I can hold on to it and marvel at it happening for a while and once in a while still for times to come. In its completion, I am more of what I am here to be. I love my life and I am thrilled to be a member of humanity.

We all have much more in common than not. In so knowing myself experience I know that this type of phenomenon is played out by many others too. Because I know this for myself, I know it for others. I find a great sense of pride in being what feels like an experimenter, albeit, I feel also that I agreed to this perfectly timed adventure of learning from Within. We are all perfection.

The next time I encounter good feeling collaboration, I want to jump aboard for the ride faster and with myself having much more fun. I am, you are, we are representing each other in deep ways of guidance and love that empowers us to recall our greatness, always includes the greatness of others. Why else be a human, if not to participate in humanity. Not to suffer, but to contribute; for in being a cooperative component towards the expansion of self and others, we continue. Humanity is more than an experiment, it is an experience; as individuals and as a collective, alone and with that Force Within us that is purely Love. The statement "Love thy neighbor as you love yourself.", can

## Appreciating Leverage

be a present and still tender reality. "Loving thyself so that you can Love thy neighbor.", is actually a trusting Gentle Thought and experience.

Taking the bull by the horns is one way to ride albeit acknowledges difficulty as part of the situation, and still note that there is another way, an easier way, and that is to allow the bull to appreciate you into a mutual curious involvement. Imagine riding a bull that wants to get you there gently! Well, that might well be a reality. To ride a bull that has been tormented into a frenzy of reactions, might be best left alone. Choose wisely the company you keep, especially, when critical pathways open up to you, and they do and will continue to do so. When you are inserted into a seemingly dangerous scenario, it might be better to resign from the momentum, because it was not inserted, it was chosen to become this much. The option to risk makes the adventure's end more memorable some say. I, usually, avoid danger, and find the pleasantries of the easy way more desirable.

The definition of what scenarios are dangerous has changed over time. Now, being pulled into any one's drama, is a danger. It is safer to resist being drawn into what is unneeded to focus upon. What stifles choice for me in the drama attraction into other people's worlds, is that I choose to be an uplifter.

To empower oneself with the ability to choose well or better than ever before (which is my desire almost all of the time), can only lead oneself into an option to choose a softer thought along the way and to do so intuitively without reservations, and as natural as can be. This seems true to me because a Gentle Thought is a non-judgmental one. Gentle Thoughts make me think of puppy dogs, soft sweet summer breezes, warm cashmere sweaters on colder evenings, pastel colors, shyness, innocence, timid approaches, white puffy clouds in a blue sky, seeing into the eyes of a deer, thoughtfulness in kind, a familiar cat purring close by, calmness, a lover's smile, mutual tenderness, mellowing-out, quiet times and soft human behavior. Thoughts that are hard, seem to result in harder thinking or more brittle conclusions. Thoughts of Appreciation are amazing too, although I have to notice that a Thought of Appreciation is like a beautiful diamond while a Gentle Thought is much softer in texture perhaps like a comfortable oversized reading chair.

Or is it far too more common and easy to sway towards that something that gets under the skin in a form of a thought out-of-balance that weighs in quickly and seems impossible to find comfort in or time for a quick check on a personal opinion of them? What is my preference, sensing the completeness of a gentle thought or the uncertainty of being taken along with a thought seemingly out-of-my-control? I prefer a gentle thought every time. Can ever a gentle thought take control, be strong, insistent and determined? If so, is it gentle still? I feel keenly aware in the dreamlike opening-up of my mind to appreciate a gentle thought. Can you think of a truly Gentle Thought right now?

Being in control of one's thoughts is like having everything just right there at your fingertips as opposed to being out of control of one's thoughts which is like letting everything seemingly within reach fade off into the quick changes in those distant evasive lesser thoughts. It's this way or that way all of the time.

*Appreciating Leverage*

*How can I keep remembering that I have choice, or do I have to remember that all of the time?*

*Where do I want to be emotionally?*

*And, how then, can a remember how to be there?*

*Is it important enough to me and does it make a difference?*

To further assist in creating balanced appreciations, note that most significant emotions are identified in the following "Emotional Scale". As a basic foundation I have built upon its structure and have amended the original emotional list and added (*in parentheses*) connective virtues, which I term the *Virtuous Leaps*. *Virtuous Leaps* can assist in deliberately improving feelings and emotions upon realizing the direction one favors taking to feel better. The *Virtuous Leaps* are like methods or stepping-stones to move up and forward. This modified and combined listing is another tool and provides a pathway more than a scale indicator. To reach for or climb up to an improved emotion with thoughts, one can take the option of using a *(Virtuous Leap)* to help ease the pathway. Find where you are emotionally on any subject and do the work required to leap up the pathway to a better emotion.

## The Emotional Scale
### Enhanced with
### *Art of Appreciation methods*
### *(Virtuous Leaps)*

1. <u>Joy, Knowledge, Empowerment, Freedom, Love & Appreciation</u> *(Purposefulness, Unity, Beauty, Creativity, Grace, Bliss, & Wisdom)*
2. <u>Passion and Celebration</u> *(Trustworthiness, Honor, Integrity, & Wonder)*
3. <u>Enthusiasm, Eagerness, and Happiness</u> *(Truthfulness, Excellence & Faith)*
4. <u>Positive Expectation and Belief</u> *(Respect & Determination)*
5. <u>Optimism</u> *(Gratitude, Courtesy, Cooperation, & Thankfulness)*
6. <u>Hopefulness</u> *(Patience, Loyalty, Commitment, & Kindness)*
7. <u>Contentment</u> *(Confidence, Generosity, Charity, & Service)*
8. <u>Boredom</u> *(Idealism & Flexibility)*
9. <u>Pessimism</u> *(Order, Integrity & Peace)*
10. <u>Frustration, Irritation & Impatience</u> *(Steadfastness, Perseverance, Diligence & Fortitude)*
11. <u>"Overwhelment"</u> *(Acceptance)*
12. <u>Disappointment</u> *(Respect)*
13. <u>Doubt</u> *(Honesty & Discernment)*
14. <u>Worry</u> *(Forgiveness)*
15. <u>Blame</u> *(Consideration)*
16. <u>Discouragement</u> *(Obedience & Compassion)*
17. <u>Anger</u> *(Mercy)*
18. <u>Revenge</u> *(Temperance & Tact)*
19. <u>Hatred & Rage</u> *(Humility & Modesty)*
20. <u>Jealousy</u> *(Reverence, Justice, Prudence & Self-Discipline)*
21. <u>Insecurity, Guilt, & Unworthiness</u> *(Valor, Courage, Attachment, Tolerance & Assertiveness)*
22. <u>Fear, Grief, Depression, Despair, Powerlessness</u>

Figure 1    Emotional Scale [7] and Virtuous Leaps.

---

[7] Abraham Hicks Emotional Scale, Chapter 22, from *"Ask and It is Given"*, 2007, published and distributed by Hay House, Inc.

*Appreciating Leverage*

It, each thought-choice, can seem to be a fleeting moment, caught and gone, sometimes faster than evaluation can set in. I do not always have enough time to think about everything I am thinking about and I cannot do so, even if I tried. I have old habits of thoughts forgetting and I am unexperienced in consistently choosing wise to witness that the wiser still each choice will become.

*Can I conquer self-thoughts enough and increasingly so, to make a difference in my next occurrence of matter?*

I should think of what is that that brings the detection of the quality of a thought possibly compromising my control or something else much more out of control.

*What pronounces my ability to qualify what thought forms are evading or being created?*

*What, then, can one choose to be as a softer thought?*

For in that thought comes another like it; better or lesser, yet better is better. And so again there is that softer thought.

*Can you find it within the sloppy often bitter tales told that are swarming about in circles of attention getting dullness from within the lack to appreciate self-worthiness?*

*Shall I let the sparkle instead surface and shine?*

Please, I say to myself. "Please do!"

*Where then can I trust myself to focus in this gentle spirit and then the next?*

I am decidedly choosing to go after that quiet thought. I wish it to fill me and my life. I appreciate it into my existence. Oh, Gentle Spirit of kind thoughts, I want to be aboard and trust my steps to not fall prey to those incidentals that carry lesser places in spirit, body and mind, to be involved in creating for myself.

*"I appreciate that I do not have to be the way others are.*
*I can choose for myself and I can live well knowing that that is my responsibility.*
*I must be ME."*

And so, it is!

*Appreciating Leverage*

### Chapter Five- Appreciations on Leveraging Appreciating
### (Quite clever, isn't it!)

- ❖ I appreciate that there is a gentleness as soft as a thought that only loves & when I remember that and go to that place, I find out more wonderful things about myself that I can then bring out from there & restore, rejuvenate and regenerate my life & purpose with additional meaning.

- ❖ I         the manifestations of my life; my experiences, things, relationships, self-awareness', desires and becoming more of what I didn't even realize could be.

- ❖ I appreciate that I can deliberately tailor-create and re-create my future using past experiences as leverage and with great joy, confidence and insight.

- ❖ I appreciate that there are not good or bad accidents but are rather circumstances in which I aligned and match to, such that I can experience what is important for me.

- ❖ I appreciate the benevolence of the adventure of living life embracing the freedoms to learn from experiences and come into betterment.

- ❖ I appreciate that I have feelings about what "abundance" is, not just desires to have money, and when I combine my good feelings about money and my understanding of the being of "abundance", I become abundant in all ways I desire.

- ❖ I appreciate that I am part of all types of technologies, and I also am aware that I am strong enough and wise enough to know what technologies serve me.

- ❖ I appreciate that I am ultimately responsible for desiring, allowing and accepting changes in my life and how I react to them.

*Learning is Intoxicating.
Relearning is a sobering responsibility.*

## Chapter 6  Appreciating Relearning

In this moment I ponder upon the ways of my upbringing and I sense a memory of a graduating acceptance of what others were teaching me. In many cases, I just went along with things to keep peace. I was taught to go along with things and not stir up the waters or turn over the apple cart. I jumped into participating with others very easily as a child. It was exciting to learn everything. At a young age, before I knew another way to be, I became complacent to question what was being taught versus what I, perhaps, believed within my truth and vital senses. Being taught how to be me, by others, was often subtle, and fit into life so easily and I didn't know I was missing anything important. I did not realize that I was being put calmly and carefully into a hierarchical placement that was generationally designed to keep me in a suppression of a nature not often discussed. I was being primed all of my life to accept that I was not on the top of the hierarchical charts. Mostly everyone else was taught this too. Some, I was taught, were above me, better than me, smarter than me and all manner of other characteristics that always seemed to place me someplace beneath others. If I was to know what life was all about, I needed to accept my place and listen for instructions. They, basically everyone, knew better and more than I did. I would not even question where they got directions from, so I accepted my surrounding others mostly as my superiors. So, probably like most of us, I fell in line and didn't understand that aspect of equality or oneness.

I rarely knew what I wanted that opposed others of what they wanted of or for me. I had no idea of self-thought as a valuable direction into my future and I was not instructed to look for myself. I would fare well if I cooperated and to cooperate actually meant to obey. I knew somethings about myself. I had a stronger desire to behave in what seemed acceptable ways. I grew so much to care about what others thought and about everything, including me. I just thought I was thinking fairly normally comparing myself to others. That is all I wanted to do; be normal in most ways. That, being normal, was what I was experiencing as I compared myself to others and ever increasingly, all I wanted was to fit in with others. It seemed to be fun at the time, as if it were a game to conform quickly and be part of what was happening. I was a quick study, a fast learner, and a good student.

Everywhere I turned, as I grew older, there were groups and teams and collectives to join into and happily be a part of. I didn't want to be different, even when different was popular. Indeed, I began to notice those groups that wanted to be different together. I avoided them as I wanted to be like the majority, rather than to be too noticed and controversial.

I never needed too much attention from other people, and I was slightly uneasy at getting too much attention. I was generally uncomfortable with performing for others, especially more than just a few at a time. I recall feeling insecure and inadequate when asked by the teacher to read aloud in classroom in elementary school. When the class was going to take turns reading up and down the aisles I would count ahead to my paragraph and practice silently what I was going to have to read out loud when it was to be my turn. Even so, or probably because of it, I always stumbled out loud, although I read it perfectly when silent. Looking back, I am so happy for my stumbling and stuttering because as a result I was avoided to be that classroom's special reader, although, in my head I heard a perfect reading and stood to appreciate others didn't know me that well.

I cared so much what others thought of me. Didn't you? I mean, during your early tween and teenager lifetimes. I just wanted to be accepted as one of them too, whoever they were. I felt that the comfort zone of inclusion was important for my very survival. It was that place known as "popular" and especially in school that felt valuable. The more I bought into inclusion the longer it took to

## Appreciating Relearning

discover exclusion was really what I was being taught to accept. I was constantly excluded from knowing as much as those in the know above me. Parents, Teachers, Mayors, Presidents and, of course, The Pope and all in the church who he was first in charge of, and me being on the lower places of knowing. There were a great many deals being negotiated into my understanding of life. Somewhere along the way I began to accept other people's thoughts and behaviors without giving them or their thoughts much, if any, of my own thought of difference or, now looking back, uniqueness. I think we all, for a large part, do this as we grow up. Maybe it is part of the process we take in maturing. I've noticed that many people never really outgrow their wanting to belong and their caring what others think about them and other things too.

As a young person there were those specific things that I did intuitively very well, and those things, which required my own thoughts to achieve, were things that I felt so easy at doing, even if in front of others. I was a very good athlete, as they said; "for a girl". I could play ball and I could do a lot of acrobatics, even without any training. I became a high school cheerleader (which was an achievement that offered popularity too) and cheerleading was athletic and a performance too. It was easy for me; making a speech was so hard. I would get nervous as I did when reading out loud in classroom. Feeling this amazing fear, I grew interested in the feeling and wanted to get over it. That is about when I became aware that "challenges" became of interest to me also. Jumping higher or farther was fun, and although speaking in front of a crowd was uncomfortable, I allowed myself the opportunity to do so, from time to time. I thought I might get used to that public speaking. I never really did, although I do not seem to care much about what others think about me any longer, I am more comfortable with one-on-one conversations. Groups in general, seem to feel more like a chore. Again, I think most people have similar feelings. Even those people of leadership or fame, feel a bit nervous before performances, so I've been told. That feeling actually assist them in being mindfully aware of what they are doing.

This feeling of going after the challenges was a theme with me it seemed. I loved the "hard" stuff to learn. I loved, and still do love all math, sciences and technologies and, I felt, at times, that I was almost out of control of myself when it came to religious or spiritual learnings. As time would have it, I found even going out for the challenges included folding them together. For example, I loved applying mathematics into my personal experiences; not the numbers kind of math, although that was interesting too, it was the patterns of emotions and spiritual convergences with the geometry or placement of symbols that seemed to get my attention, and still that is true. After learning algebra, I began parsing sentences into equations and vice versa, while, converting each into real life experiences or things. I told not a soul of this, although I excelled as a good student, especially in math and the sciences. I was told I was pretty good at those things "for a girl". My connecting math and emotions overlapped into literature and I philosophically argued literary meanings of poetry and made physics more complicated than what was being taught. I fell in love with my way of being in a quiet world of self and still, I did what was expected of me, for the most part. It seemed more and more often that I had more than one correct answer to the problems asked of me to solve, although, I gave "them" what I knew they wanted. I usually had more to say than I said, and that was perfect for others in their evaluation of me. Being able to fit into the platform was better than calling out

*Appreciating Relearning*

for others attention. I was carefully competitive, not wanting to step on other people's toes.

It took time to mature into being myself, openly. It is interesting that the word openly is used by gays or lesbians when they come out of the "closet", and well, there is hardly any real difference in them coming out and my coming out. It wasn't a sexual coming out openly. It was an allowance of myself to be what I really was openly. When I did, I was so happy. A bit confused and a bit wild, and so happy to be me. I detected immediately that many others would have preferred me to not have been so darn sure of myself, as I now became. I began to treasure my own opinion and I had an opinion about everything. And these opinionized things or changes did not happen all at once. It took time to expand myself into the confidence required to allow Self the space to be me. I know that it felt like a giving up that was aligned with a coming into, although the momentum was unstoppable. I felt an escape up and out of what I had accepted as "normal" and into what I knew to be, and it felt comfortable. I tend to appreciate that all of we, humans, come into this place with wonder. How else could one continue! Finding True North on my Life Compass and then taking that step out into that direction knowing it was perfect for me, was a leap of faith, not in religion or creed, education or

*The Art of Appreciating* MORE

anyone's opinion, rather it was trusting in Self. This type of change is, of course, more common for older people to say that they experienced. That brings harmony with wise elders. It seems to me this kind of conversation and teaching is extremely helpful for younger people to come into reading. The younger a person is, when they find themselves accepting that they are included, the better. We are all included. We are all equals. If anyone tries to convince you otherwise, it is their expressions, not yours.

A similar awareness can be tracked into the general public through the Pandemic changes too. We each have moments of rising to our own level of inclusion. It is a significant value to recognize that so many others are experiencing similar feelings, emotions, ideas and events. The Life Compass was shifting directions and I was ready. Some others, not so much. If you changed along the way, shifting was an easier part of it. During the Pandemic there was time to think and to retrain thoughts to approve of self and to motivate understanding of growth; personally, and collectively. It is all so good.

The idea of exclusion still creeps up into life as those who feel as if they deserve to be in a higher standing above others, are frequently in the observable things of the world. I see others in, so called, power, attempting to keep me and most of us in a form of suppression that disables us to question this illusion of exclusion; for, in reality, I am the only one who can make me feel exclusion and in the likewise moment, I am the only one who can make me appreciate that everyone is equally included. Others, however, do want, intentionally or not, of me to fall in line with their placement of me and excluded from them. I can now feel others their desires for me to keep-my-place and behave according to what

*Appreciating Relearning*

they tell us is right or left. It is a most powerful inner growth to recognize the forms of exclusion as a manipulation that others might or might not be aware of doing. Hence, it is easier to not participate, and in my lack of concern I can skirt the drama of others wishes and observe quietly.

Relearning comes easy once something or anything that was forced into learning proves absolutely false, like exclusion. That is what I discovered when I grew to understand that competition was off-the-mark if one really wanted to be happy. Everywhere I turned, people were competing with each other, or sometimes being excluded if not competing, and I also competed and often did well at it. When I came into that basic knowing that bigger isn't always better, and winning doesn't always serve well, it was then that I incrementally rethought what I was taught about competition. The root of competition is very deep in humanity. When we learn about reproduction and the commencement of our life, which is a big deal, we are instructed with great scientific confidence that there is but one lucky sperm in the gazillions hanging out with your sperm co-creator at the beginning of the "to become conceived into a person" race that unites with that egg, and therefore, the rest of those many, many sperms lost the race and perished trying, or never existed, or died, so that you could, "be". "Hurray for you", you are taught, you won the conception race, which was the most important race of your life, obviously, or so it is inferred. That is the beginning framework into the endless teachings and assumptions about competition and the ultimate goodness and necessity of it, or you too might lose the race, not be included, fade-off, never exist or just croak. Plop! It was all a lie.

## The Art of Appreciating MORE

I feel that there is a need to evaluate and re-evaluate periodically what we think we know, what others have taught us and what we believe. Some things need to be unlearned and only then can the intent of that subject be relearned differently. Somethings can be unlearned and to find no need to relearn any version of it, because, it is unneeded and in fact detrimental to know. It counters the right knowledge and clutters into confusion what is unwanted. Certain things taught and found inappropriate to continue thinking true, remains in our deep memory and can actually come in handy to recall when it becomes obvious that another person is remaining in that older quasi forgotten thought. In that space, as a teacher, it can be respected from our personal experiences. After all experience is our greatest teacher.

It remains their knowing, although you know it to be seemingly factually different. That is detected sometimes between older and younger people although sometimes, and usually the older more experienced person, will detect this discrepancy and if resistance rises at an initial explanation, the subject might remain only known by the elder. There is a perfect timing for particular pieces of wisdom to come to us and knowing is personal and cannot be forced upon anyone. Likewise, therefore, there is a perfect timing for particular pieces of wisdom to be taught from you and knowing is personal and cannot be forced upon anyone to accept. The expression that the student will learn when the student is ready and not before then really is true. I am a great believer when in the position of knowing something another person is not ready to learn and actually realizing it is harmful at most and uncomfortable at least to continue to explain, it is of an amazing value to stop and think for a moment, 'This is a seed I plant now. Perhaps once this tiny seed of love and hopes for another to improve within

## Appreciating Relearning

it being there now and then is ready to grow that seed will assist in my love to bring understanding." I appreciate surrendering to the idea that I cannot force, nor do I want to, understanding, in my love I can lay down the idea(s) gently and leave it there. I can avoid wanting to change any one regarding this that I really believe, and trust would be significantly valuable for this other person to appreciate into their understandings, and I can let it be. It is not an egotistical desire to change someone else or to teach what is not ready to be learned, albeit I am happy to be an uplifter and a spiritual teacher. In so being I am responsible for honoring and respecting everyone as an equal and as meaningfully appropriate to be exactly who they are and believing or not whatever they do or not. It is not a judgement upon the student who is unwilling or most likely unable to comprehend, it is an awareness of the timing of another and self, and never to be considered a comparison.

In my younger less experienced times, it was mind-boggling to detect that the basic and, seemingly, most important incentive of almost every single part of interacting with others included some form of comparison, and most surely in a competitive way. It still is very difficult and, certainly, intricate to unlearn and retrain, or re-teach myself into letting be of what others do as a way to judge them and myself, as well. Once I recognized that this characteristic is instilled into everyone so faithfully, I was somewhat sorry to let it go, sometimes. I was doing so well in the competitive world. I knew this to be true. I felt compelled to rethink competition and it's great assumed, even spurious, value.

*And for what?*
*Would I do this not competing better than competing?*

*Could I be good at not being so competitive?*
*And what's more, what was in it for me?*
*I was certain, much; for to give up being so competitive,*
*what was the benefit?*

Initially, this idea flow is quite convoluted and precocious, which is mostly due to its significant and early formed influences upon our life.
This understanding of what comes in to replace competition is so important to want the answer to; otherwise, one will not be enlightened by it. It is a bit magical to know about.

- Firstly, because of the knowing that the value of competition remains over-rated,
- Secondly, because it is taught emphatically as a requirement to do well in life and
- Thirdly, because it is so widely accepted as normal or proper behavior.

Because of all those reasons and more, I am about to shatter that false teaching into pieces and bring forth a world that is far more complete than competitive. You have to really want to know it, otherwise your desires for inclusion with "normal" will completely exclude changes. It might well require some unlearning, relearning and retraining. Experience is our greatest teacher and words can hardly take the place of experience. Wanting to know a better way than the competitive way is life-changing and most rewarding.

*Can you want to know of this really intensely?*

If you do, you must be ready for a new way of living and still it is a discipline to work towards on a daily basis and within your own experiences. It is true that words are not experiences. When words help others to conjure-

## Appreciating Relearning

up desires within themselves, desires will naturally lead into direction and, in-turn, manifestations.

So, thoughts are manifestations too. I can, herein, offer many words, yet, only within your desire to experience the meanings of these words can you appreciate the manifestation available of them. I want so much to release, from my experiences, the proper words to bring about a desire in you. That desire is to understand and here I wish you to understand what you gain in letting go of competition. You have to want to know it or it cannot become part of your rethinking, relearning and consequentially, reclaiming yourself. Being competitive is not a way to be included as you were taught and being creative is the only results in being excluded from competitiveness. It is a bit tricky.

Right now, I only ask that you keep an open mind and remember to allow yourself to feel your emotions. The desire to know what you may not know is a wonderful feeling and still, the desire to know what you cannot yet know is a wonderful feeling too. So, do not judge yourself either way, while being open. Perhaps allow yourself to stretch forward a little. It will feel good to recognize that you are in control of this process. It is all up to you. I enjoy, when retraining myself, the feeling of resonating. I wanted to try to write about it. "Trying" is altogether different than being open. Being ready to appreciate something different into your thoughts and actions is a risky business to some settled in their ways. So, try not to try. Rather, know that if this comes to you, you are to benefit, and if not, it will not bring you harm. It doesn't matter if you ever come to know this, or not. In knowing this and practicing the results of this wisdom, life improves eventually, albeit, it does take some time to resettle within the change of direction. If new thoughts can penetrate and settle than that is a wonder and if not, well that is fine too. We are all on our own paths and the speed we travel through is always timely and perfect. There is no absolute right or wrong way to be yourself, there is only life finding its way. There is no best way. There are ways in which one can enjoy their life richer and fuller. Being satisfied is universally a good feeling, and having wisdom is and always will be satisfying to most everyone. It is our nature from the moment we were born, and before, to experience our lives to the most potential and the most happiness. It is your life though. No one else is in charge of you or your choices, so trust yourself. The old expression is valid; "Know Thyself".

Even after many years of applying a different approach in life, this comparison thing, this competitive behavior creeps into my default thoughts from time to time. I am less impacted by the thought's others want me to have as I am more myself a deliberate thinker. I am interested in others for their thoughts too. That is probably one reason why I do not consider myself a person who needs to be a popular person. I am only my perfect desired amount of popular, and that is just fine with me. I do recognize that I am more the wise experienced one. Why so?  Because, I am older, perhaps, and I am honestly myself more than others. That comparison is unwarranted, and it is a good example of exactly what I am saying about how comparing self with others just surfaces on its own accord sometimes. I notice the exclusionary dent in my objective. In actuality, comparing differences, between ourselves and others, within the attitude of not rating or ranking them, and instead, acknowledging them, is a way to appreciate each of us as unique. We are unique and equal. We are different and beautiful. We are all perfect. That concept of equality is perfect too.

## *Appreciating Relearning*

Being the same is not a goal I want to achieve. Noting that we all have so much in common that my heart and soul easily loves everyone as my equal, is one of the best feelings to embrace. I trust in my feelings that your uniqueness's are of value to you and to us all. I love your appropriateness of distinction.

When the bell rings it is heard usually. Some hear and acknowledge its ring and some even complain about hearing it. Perhaps it was too tinny, sharp, loud, unexpected, or a million other sorry complaints. Some complain about windchimes hung and telling all about the ways of the wind. Others hear something and have some reasons for not comprehending or maybe they are avoiding comprehension. It's that way with basic sounds; like a bell's tone, or likewise, with a basic understanding.

An orchestra that plays the combined sounds cannot be fully appreciated by the common ear. An orchestral composer, the conductor of the orchestra, a seasoned or special musician might hear a lot more in the details of an orchestra. Most common average ears do not comprehend all of what it hears all at the same time. So too with the complex messages of spiritual stories or deep reasonings. In spiritual teachings, like with music, it is worthy the sounds and enjoyment come from the general components, hence, continue to read and search for meanings that are often between the lines where some light shines through. It is, after all, a darkness that illuminates by the Light and You are the Light. Allow the goodness to come through to you, for you are good. You can hear the message as clear as a bell. The spiritual messages that are intended for you to hear and absorb, however, are not a simple word to compare to a single bell tone; it is an orchestra of words and a harmony of clarity.

## The Art of Appreciating MORE

When we drop competition out of our life, we get to appreciate ourselves better. We do not have to compete or win anything; we are whole, and we are winners already. If you want to accomplish greatness, and when you desire to deliberately be on top of your own manifestations, you have to release your thoughts from competing. You cannot have it both ways. To allow yourself the riches of your desires, you must be a soul who is not competitive with anyone else. Know this is understandable, and with effort, practicing this comes easy. It is similar to dropping worry and doubt from your life. It is as important to any part of controlling your outcomes. Try it! Start today. Find something you might feel you are competing in, and let it go. Let that be done with a pure heart to improve yourself rather than to gain any form of manifestation, and you will be amazed at the results. You cannot be competitive and creative at the same time. Your most fulfilling thoughts are creative.

There is a close association in competition with jealousy. In jealousies there are several categories to contemplate. Two I will mention here are at the top of that group. Being jealous and wanting what you don't have by taking it from another to quench your jealous desire is one form of jealousy. Another is one that comes from the normal learning. It is being jealous and wanting what you don't have and reaching out to finding it for yourself, asking for it, and then allowing it to come to you through your actions or another form of generosity of the Universal answers. We don't know what we don't know. Learning what you want that another introduces to you can be a catalyst to changing direction and defining self-interest anew. There are two sides to everything. It is important to manifest your desires to be on the pure of mind side of everything. Being creative rather than competitive is a pure love to follow after and to be in front of willingly.

## Appreciating Relearning

During the Pandemic of 2020, there were many changes enforced into our lives, all seemingly appropriate albeit unwanted or unexpected. It was also a great beautiful orchestral spiritual message that could only be realized. One could not resist the truth of the virus happening. It was happening to everyone all over the world. It was a big, beautiful bell tone of many bells and then more than the bells it was the violin and every piece of the orchestra chimed in. In the beginning of the virus being announced and then listened to, it was hard to hear. After time, the sounds became more pronounced and the music in which sprang from it sounded off key and confusing as if this was all wrong. It wasn't a perfectly good sounding event in any of our lives. The squabbling about it all contributed to the fear that surrounded it. The amazing prospect of a death sentence to any, maybe all of us, and especially the vulnerable and seniors first, rang so out of tune that we all nearly lost the focus to listening to what was playing for us. What do we each hear?

Some hear the bell all by itself, others hear the orchestra. We can also find our own song in the mix of reverberations. It is that song that reveals the most, and the most beautiful sounds.

Hear what your heart is singing and sing it out loud. If anything, else that this virus has taught me, it is to recognize the ONE. We are all in this together. Same planet twirling around and about on its way someplace for certain. We are each our own wavelength to create within this universe what we are good at creating.

I grew up in the cement coverings of the inner city and due to that I played a lot of games as a child that required hard surfaces. Cement was a good thing to bounce a ball on or hop-scotch. Even at these many years away from my childhood I still love the ideas of these city formed games. While in the local discount-store, I stopped by the toys, games and sporting goods area and picked up a couple of balls to bounce around, perhaps as we took our walks.

They were both pretty. One was about the size of a volleyball and the other was smaller, no bigger in diameter than the height of a typical coffee cup. The larger one was adorned with soft spikey things that changed the anticipated bounce into another direction; not too far off to be unusable. It could add a bit more to the attentiveness of the bounce and the catch and it was dramatically colored Dodger Blue with the spikey thingies in a bright orange. It was nothing like the balls I played with as a child. I found myself bouncing it in the house, something unthinkable as a child and I took some slow-motion phone videos of it because I knew my girls would appreciate my sense of humor with this ball.

All during their years growing up I shopped for the "funniest" balls to bounce about in our yard and pool. The color combination alone was humorous, and the spikey thingies really made it look like it was from outer space. Actually, it looked in shape rather like the renderings of that nasty Covid-19 Virus. I love the creativity found in toys, games and sporting goods. It is interesting to seek finding creativity there as so many toys, games and sporting goods assist in the competitive vein of playing together, rather than the cooperativeness required for true creativity to bounce about in our lives. One cannot be competitive and creative at the same time. That is probably why whenever I play ball with others, I find their competitive nature seems strong and in a very short time whomever I am tossing the ball too will inevitably start increasingly throwing it into my challenge to catch zone, which is not where I like to play.

## Appreciating Relearning

I see this type of behavior come up in particular games like ping pong. I love to count the maximum connective successful bounces together being accumulated rather than to make it difficult for my playmate to make their attempt to get the tiny ping pong ball across to my side. Usually, unless I first mention that we can play without trying to win by just enjoying our team-man-ship required to increase the number of times together we succeed at being both a required player to help ourselves to hit the ball across and a successful partner to get the ball to be aligned for another continued play. Most will try to slam me out of the game and therefore, what, prove their dominance over me? I could never figure out the joy in that. To continue with a mutually stimulated partner to allow the ball to dance between us, well, that is so amazing to me, and I might add, to them, once they are into that increasing good feeling. We are here on this Earth to be with others and finding a mutual embrace is a beautiful thing.

The other ball, the smaller one, was a beauty too. It was crystal clear with little sparkles inside the rubber. It is shiny and it too is not as smooth as those pink high bouncer balls I had as a kid. It did a good job at bouncing high though, which I loved to do. I might snap it into the floor and watch it soar up and then I might, or my playmate might get underneath it and wait for it to be met with ready hands. I love that ball. It is so fun to learn to play with. I noticed something peculiar about it when I set it down to rest. Regardless of how or where I placed it still, it would wobble about and eventually land in the place it must have been designed to pivot into, its standing position. I kept trying different things to get it to change its mind, but it was thoroughly determined to always return to its proper place. Now that was curious. That totally meant that it had no mind of its own. It was preprogrammed to sit just like that and no other way. It was insistent too. So then why? Well, that was obvious. The manufacturer's name was right there, face up and selling itself constantly without any choice on my part. It was pretty ugly sitting there, for a beautiful ball. I bought the dam ball already, so why do I have to advertise for it.

That is a perfect example of where competitiveness can spoil creativity. I wanted to place that ball in the bottom of the shiny platter on the table, yet, I could not because I didn't want to bring a plug for the ball's company into our Karen Orr Room. I think that company would sell more balls if they didn't try so hard to sell more balls.

One of my favorite Thought Teachers is Wallace D. Wattles, who helped teach me to understand the amazing difference and value between the competitive and the creative and in so doing I discovered that when my desires where in the competitive mode they were less influential upon my wellbeing. I also discovered that when my desires where in the creative mode, my desires were more influential upon my wellbeing and upon my intuitive nature. I knew better what I wanted. In creative mode, I enjoyed everything more and I could more easily follow my path of least resistance or rather find my path of most bliss. In creative mode I was better at cooperativeness too.

Here is one part of Wallace D. Wattles teachings I discovered as an extremely important (for me) life changing message.

From his book "The Science of Getting Rich"[8]:

> *"There is a thinking stuff from which all things are made, and which, in its original state, permeates, penetrates, and fills the interspaces of the universe.*
>
> *A thought, in this substance, produces the thing that is imaged by the thought.*
>
> *Man can form things in his thought, and, by impressing his thought upon Formless Substance, can cause the thing he thinks about to be created.*
>
> *In order to do this, man must pass from the competitive to the creative mind, he must form a clear mental picture of the things he wants, and do, with faith and purpose, all that can be done each day, doing each separate thing in an efficient manner."*

The first three statements above were so inspirational to me and I thought about them long and hard before actually understanding them and appreciating them. I felt it came to me including the word "permeates" for a very good reason. Permeate and Radiate. Learning the Law of Attraction takes a big effort to believe in something other than what you were told. Once I did, only then did I noticed the words of the last paragraph: *"In order to do this man must pass from the competitive to the creative mind…"*

The idea that man is more initiated into the competitive mind first is apparent there too, although I was then

---

[8] Wallace D. Wattles. "The Science of Getting Rich" written by Wallace D. Wattles was first published in 1910 by Elizabeth Towne Publishing New York.

only coming to recognize that aspect of this idea. I was somewhat amazed to learn that we must pass from the competitive to the creative mind to be our most "thought-effective" people. We must be able to notice our competitive nature first and we must pass through it and leave it behind. I can appreciate passing through many things yet, it seems weird to pass through my competitive mind. I believe it means that I have to recognize my instincts to compete and seek and look through that aspect to enter a more rewarding space and one that is in deep harmony with self and others of non-competitiveness. For me, it is impossible to enjoy a game of ping pong within a competitive nature to win or when my game partner wants to win. When I get into those kinds of "games", I usually lose quickly rather than get wrapped up into another person's competitive nature. I want to play; I just do not have to always win. Winning is good, although I know that winning means being fair and honest, otherwise it is the biggest loss of them all. Yet, there is something notable about being the type of person who lets others win for the sake of lessening tension, which is not the same thing as letting someone else win so that they can learn to lean towards a better decision, which happens when you teach someone.

Either way, one learns along the way. In my process of reconstructing competitiveness, I agree that I had to pass through it, rather than to avoid it. I had hardly a choice. I was taught, as was most of us, and at a very young age that winners are better than losers. Winners, I was informed, tried harder, while losers, were lazy and had less talent in the scheme of things. I was, incidentally, taught that winning wasn't everything, when I was the loser. Yet, by and far, there was a constant strong theme in all venues that said competing to win was better for you than being beat. The only

## Appreciating Relearning

problem with that idea is that winners and losers were truly ill defined. It is difficult at least for many people to recognize that the "loser" is as much a "winner" and the "winner" is a "loser", and each is equal to each other. I know that probably sounds a bit off to most, yet, if only my words could bring anyone into clarity about equality in just letting go of being competitive, then, I think this work is valuable. Oh, and I already know it is very worthy. This idea is not mainstream, so it is flat until even one corner is turned up, and then, you will be in amazement at the shift that will come about in your heart and then, oh my, in the results.

I didn't understand that until I read Wallace D. Wattles statement there. I knew I loved all the first statements, and I was excited about every thought that made me understand that my thoughts create my reality and that I could manifest into my life what I wanted. Initially, I wanted to win it all.

The results of being non-competitive is that you can be easily creative. Can you see that the result of creativity is a gift to yourself and to others and can you, therefore, see that the results of competition is really not a gift to anyone. Oh, though, the competitive mind will see it as the results is a gift to the competitive. The winner takes all.

Why take all, when connecting between two or more human beings can result in cooperation? Do you think cooperation is a better feeling than winning? Most may not, so do not be too hard on yourself. It is a hard pill to swallow, yet, until you pass through the competitive mind, just barely getting only some of what you want to win, you cannot be in your most effective creative mind. I know that seems too moist with vapors and not enough deep water to float your boat, yet, until you really become a non-competitive, you will not come to know true creativity.

So, where do I feel desires come into this relationship between competitive and cooperative, winner and loser? It is in the amazing sensation of desiring to connect to other human beings in good and loving ways. In appreciative and respectful ways that instantly connect to higher feelings. Winning is okay then, yet, sharing cooperatively is a far higher feeling that leads to a sustainable joy and bliss.

Relearning and reteaching is a responsibility that can be a lot of fun and it relinquishes joy. We do not have to relearn everything, just those things we are ready to reknow.

## Chapter Six - Appreciations on Relearning

- ❖ I appreciate that I can think my own thoughts, that I can change my mind, and I can learn new things.

- ❖ I appreciate the natural desire to be popular & belong to a mutually agreeable group as important, that was until I became independent enough to trust myself above other's opinions of me.

- ❖ I appreciate that I obediently trusted my parents, public schools & a major religion during my formative years & it was equally valuable that I questioned authority & drew my own conclusions; some in agreement & others different and I can still change my mind if I choose.

- ❖ I appreciate that I can be taught something without judgement of its source and believe it, or not.

- ❖ I appreciate being open-minded & exposed to ideas from others and trust my thoughts & ideas.

- ❖ I appreciate that "competition and creativity" is like "oil and water".

- ❖ I appreciate that I do not have to agree with what others teach or tell me.

- ❖ I appreciate that positive thinking creates more positive thoughts.

- ❖ I appreciate learning is not a belief, it is an awareness of thoughts.

- ❖ I appreciate that I question myself and authority.

*The Art of Appreciating MORE*

## Chapter 7  The Manifestation of the Lavender Scarf

I start this chapter while living in the hills of Ventura California, in what we refer to as what was our Family House. As I've mentioned, it is the house that we lived in while raising our daughters, now all grown up and happy lovely people who appreciate having grown up in that place. It sits high on the hillside and relinquishes a view of the Ventura plains and the magnificent Pacific Ocean and not that that would have been enough, it further expanded out over the Pacific Ocean and gave us views of the beautiful Channel Islands off the coast, past the harbor and on the other side of most civilization. The Channel Islands are a collection of National Parks and so there flows out to that place on this magnificent Earth the border of land and sea. From there as far as thoughts take me are seas and seas and ocean and

# *The Manifestation of the Lavender Scarf*

ocean. On a clear day, when seeing those Islands, where between them the whales resided often birthing their calves and thrilling us all with their size and desire to be right here in our front yard, I would say, "Oh look, you can see Hawaii today".

I appreciate that it is in that house on the hillside that this story began being told. This book is being completed where Uri and I currently live in Sonora in the California Sierra Mountain Foothills in what we call our Little Castle. It is all that too. We are living in the Vortex on nearly three acres of beautiful land. We are here now having come through The Villages in Florida for three years and then returning to California, just in time to meet the Pandemic of 2020 while in route relocating. I appreciate that life has been good to us and now it is time to relinquish the story of the manifestation of the Lavender Scarf because of that goodness of our lives. Manifestations are wonderful to desire and experience.

It was most certainly hanging there, right where it was supposed to be while we lived in Ventura and up there where the folks who lived on the hill lived. It was manifested and will always be manifested from "Now" on. I will never have to wait it to arrive again. Daily, it was there, almost right alongside of me it hung there as I sat at my desk, knowing it to be a perfect manifestation across all time and wonder. I appreciate its proximity to what is familiar to me. It is on the wall that bridges one window with another, both facing the world outside of home and still it was, but there, somewhat hidden in my quite commonplace home office, mostly unseen. It is now taken for granted, and that is a very good place for it to remain in my heart and soul. It is and will be always there in a someplace that taught me more about the Law of Attraction and my ability to manifest. It is easier now to manifest, yet it was important to me to manifest the Lavender Scarf.

It should be remembered that as it is with you what are the things that are placed upon the walls of homes often hold that inward connection to the love of a safe place to be living. I know that there are a lot of people who decorate purely for the "looks" of things, yet most all of us, place some kind of meaning upon those things that hang on our walls. Looking out or looking in, home always personally identifies its people as itself, whole and belonging. This slight airy accessory is meaningful to me. I used to forget it was here, and I learned to live with it almost watching me, rather than my actually noticing it. I know it is a symbol of something more interesting than what it actually appears to be. Most things are. It was there for anyone entering this room to see, including me. It was hanging on the office wall where it was, for that while, supposed to be.

No one ever mentioned noticing it hanging there. It blended as if camouflaged with what is near to it, somewhat like the way curtains hang. If anyone did notice they might ask why it was hanging there. Why was a delicate Lavender Scarf even there? Perhaps some might pass on it thinking it an implemented quirky design. Still not one person ever asked about it being there where it was for years.

Family members that were there when it came to me all have asked me where did I put it, soon afterward recovering from finding. Still until today, no one at all, outside the several in witness of its manifestation, its appearance, its coming into being, its arrival, has ever asked about it. They know, those in witness, as do I, that it was so perfected into a story that can reveal the essence of understanding to so many others. For this reason, perhaps more than any desire within myself, I am at a point of knowing that the story has to be recorded. It is past the time of telling and so I have to write it down. I know that some will benefit greatly from knowing the story.

If only they were to have asked, I would have had to answer, saving me this need to re-create its story into written words. It speaks in that tone to me; yet, I do not have to look for it in my memory. I always remember why it is so important.

Whenever I see The Lavender Scarf, and I do, it reminds me of what I know to be absolutely true and yet it is so arrogant of me to say that; for what is it to be "true". And if you come to know "true", and we all do from time to time, then, you know why it is hanging on the wall, so truly there for anyone upon noticing to see that I am not withholding "truth" from them of me. It is a manifestation that stands as proof of its existence. I've seen the light it provided into my soul that calmed me into a new person of a heightened awareness. As it hangs there, time has come to pay attention to that something in my heart that wants others to see it and ask me about it, and still, it is perfectly ok that it is not seen there, because the story is so personal and so universal at the same time, that most people I know, outside of my family, could have a very difficult time dealing with the reality it brings forth to me and to others, most certainly. Although, I've seen it can befuddle absent thoughts that long for things to remain as they have been taught them to be, I found in the appearance of The Lavender Scarf that thoughts become things.

*The Art of Appreciating* MORE

It is a long story, you see. That is why only a few know of it, either the family members in witness of it happening because they ran into great fortune in the experience of being in the family and knowing of the desire for it to play out or there are some people who watched at a distance with me knowing it would come to be. Thereafter, a few, a very few others, who know that what feels like miracles happen and have a great deal of curiosity about what they see is an uncommon attitude that nearly always reside within all of us that shatters in the most delightful ways reality with freedom.

I was born into a very religious Irish American Catholic family, so there is a required pause to comprehend the impact upon my generational family members and their following their religious pursuits, hence, this story might be interpreted as a myth and may want to be avoided within those highly content religious households, because this event was more than religious. If my ancestors come into this reading, you are dismissed. I have reasons to presume that it is a story that you will have mixed feelings about accepting and that is perfectly okay. This story was revealing of time's unlearned teachings, especially in religious relic-thoughts that naturally deny are growing through the cracks of religious sidewalks and barriers. However, once past that intervening obstacle, they will want to tell this story of truth. I am of the belief that we can soon all have stories like this one to ponder upon.

The Lavender Scarf's tale is rich with what some might call fable although it is no fantasy story and it has the ingredients to teach one to seek for the results of their rewards of asking, which is receiving. Keeping it to the

# *The Manifestation of the Lavender Scarf*

few who know of it, is almost sacrilegious and yet, it matters not a-diddle if anyone else comes into understanding the power of it or the amazing adventure of it. To be very honest, it has been a difficult story to tell anyone about because it arises across many years in the making. If it were a joke, I might be saying; You had to be there to appreciate it. It remains bewildering to me and just how I am to get this out of me such that others might hear and feel something powerful in the midst of its revealed axiom remains unknown to me. I am trusting it to come as it wills.

This simple, albeit beautiful opaque Lavender Scarf is not a holy-cross or a photo of a most famous God or Son of God, yet it epitomizes what really matters to me in my living spirituality. It is a grace to have realized it into my life. It is an amazing power to have materialized it into my love. It is not representing my religion or anyone's religion, for I have no religion any longer and respectfully care not to fellowship with what others consider their religion. It, this simple airy old cloth, might even be influential for my not proclaiming a religion any longer. Funny to think of it that way, because I personally have no animosity towards any religion, seeing most all religions have some place in society that serves well and I have studied with many, prior to finding my beliefs holy. I believe that beliefs change me, and I change them, depending upon what I experience and the experiences, more than the religions are my greatest teacher. Hence, religions have taught me much. Experiences have taught me more.

I am not anti-religious and though I am definitely enabled to seek goodness outside of religion and inside of me, this Lavender Scarf is not religious either, yet holy it is. It is not a flag of a country or state to trust in. It is not a photograph of a beloved that holds my love that I might want to put into a frame and have hanging almost so close to me that it is beside me. It is not some mysterious symbol of piety, an ancient artifact resembling holiness or even a talisman that protects or conceals. It is not many things, though it is something valuable and important to me. It is not herein nor ever intended to be a Secret either. It is, however, my proof of my creative and perfect reality. It is a collaboration with me and life. It is exactly that! And it is a worthy manifestation! A deliberate creation! It came to me, this manifestation, in the best and only way it could, such that, I would be a believer in what I know as the power of asking and the magnificence of receiving. It is a perfect reminder of how powerful thoughts are and of how amazing I am, and we all are to be able to think.

I will begin telling this story now, of how I manifested a Lavender Scarf and of why it is for you to know about. I am so happy and a bit relieved to release this story. It was in the making for a very long time, nearly a lifetime.

Sincerely from the depths of my heart and all through the being of me, I honestly appreciate that my Mother was my best and longtime most important and most dramatic 'contrast' provider. Thank you, Mother!

Most of the composition on the Lavender Scarf was written a while ago. "Now" is a new place to be and as I reread this story, I need to add some additional wisdom to it. There is no reason to change it as it seems accurate, although I've come to understand something very important since I wrote this story. Here it is and with the intention that you too apply this valuable frame of existence to the contents.

# *The Manifestation of the Lavender Scarf*

There are Sensitive people and Insensitive people. I am a Sensitive person. In so being I am more impacted by Insensitive people. I think that most, not all, abuse issues stem across time to arise from the perspective of a Sensitive person versus an Insensitive person. Also, Sensitives can be Insensitive and Insensitives can be Sensitive, from time to time. As I think back at my past, and I hope you can do this too, I see a grayish space between interpreting abuse from being involved with Insensitive people. These Insensitives in my life didn't even know they were Insensitive usually. The "Me Too" era has ushered a much stronger eye-opening ability to identify the "Me Too" Insensitives. There are no good excuses for them. It is a kinder gentler world to see these Insensitives as people who had or in some cases still have not enabled themselves to be enlightened individuals and to become consciously compassionate. Hence, in elaborating upon that concept, I request that the reader give over to a softer sport of themselves and recognize that I am a Sensitive and I grew up in an environment where it was more common to be an Insensitive than to be a Sensitive.

My Mother was a wonderful person for the times in which she came to be, and I hold no malice against her or any of the people that I knew and grew up with. Family, church people, school people, neighbors, or professionals; all of them had many Insensitives living their parts. It is no longer a judgement I have of them, only a wish that they knew more about Sensitives and why they were the way they were and I also wish that Sensitives just knew it wasn't that there was something wrong with them or with others, it is just the way society is progressing. We are getting better all of us. Thank you, Mother.

# The Art of Appreciating MORE

I really appreciate my mother for giving me the gift of being the focus of her adverse-insensitive-attention, which so shaped my life and enabled me to become the person I am today. It was fabulous of her to work, seemingly so hard, at stirring up within me what came to be the valuable pieces of confusion in my life. From these pieces, I, myself, and me, found clarity. Confusion creates a slowdown in the momentum of humanity's progress. There is no absolute halting of progress, regardless the degree of intent. If you are confused, take responsibility for what bothers you and learn to be that which you desire it to become, rather than that which trumpets itself into existence. Refuse to exaggerate in that which is unworthy by bringing it to others attention for them to change.

My Mother seemed to not have found herself as well as she could have, as well as I have, even to the last moments of her life she tormented herself with thoughts of inequality. Many of those thoughts were insisted by others. I wanted more for her in my love and honor. I might interpret that my mother lived as she did, in self-sacrifice, rarely finding real joy that had a lasting quality, deliberately; yet, I do not feel guilt for her choices. There were some good times and there were some hard times, yet, life is always a perfect time to be alive.

Mothers bring forth the new generations and that is by far a loving sensitive action that we all can be happy for in our life. Although, she, during her life might very much tell me that her ills were often of my cause, I know they were not. Hard times were always those times between her and herself and my experience in them were always what I attracted to myself, although I hold no guilt or self-blame, just an understanding of vibrational existence. Amongst the time we shared, my Mom and me, I felt great forms of her joys and love.

It was a complicated relationship and my mother was a complex Human Being filled with many aspects that were woven invisibly throughout the time and generation in which she was alive. Within our free will, we are placed upon the Earth with social aspects that are hard to deny. I was born in the generation to follow so I judge not from whence she came, albeit, I came with much knowing about her time, and your children come with an inept knowing of your time. Without the confusion she shed upon me, I might not have desired to seek for answers different than from what I experienced as my life. Helplessly, I knew, even in the confrontations of self-value, that I would and did find what proves still to be the most important driving force of my life. It is within my wanting to be better than what I was taught I was, that I found my greatness.

I felt the power of force-against-force in the most vulnerable days of my life. My mother was a very difficult person to learn how to live with, decide daily to love, and realize my boundlessness through appreciating the gift provided in love, which is unconditional. With the coming into awareness of the honor, I felt, obliged to react in, towards my mother, I saw that unconditional love is in every form of love. It is deep within the formation of love and it can be and is intended to be ignited when it is required for self to love self, enough to become one with the spirit of one's true living as good and worthy. Once one is in this alignment with what is the direct connection, we all have Source, or God, then and only then can we apply unconditional love to another person.

Departed now, it is less fearful and generously polite to say that I had a very difficult mother. She was as good as she was bad, and as high as low and for a very long time, I was helplessly collapsed into a negative drama that she was having with herself and relinquishing upon me, hence I inherited this existence, that I have come to appreciate so very much. She was an amazing window to find myself looking through. I am so fortunate to have come to realize that it was good for me, now that it is over and that she is at rest in peace. And although, I chose to step into my life with her as my mother and that, looking back across time, was exactly what I agreed with myself along with others, of course including my mother, to enter into, I, at a very young age told myself that I would never grow up to be like her, hence my own children have less of a contrast through me, or at least I think and hope so. Being her daughter is where I decided to be in the arranged placement and environment most fulfilling to bring me to eventually remember; why I chose to come here as this particular person, in this time-space reality. It is very good.

I appreciate these special people. You know whom I mean. These are the people who have come into our lives, and we into their lives unquestioning, and not as strangers. In so doing, "contrasts" were grown often heavily, perhaps from the seeded understandings and what sometimes feels like lessons relevant to unconditional love, which were prompts to potential choices ever possible prior to realization of self.

In realization of self, this unconditional love that allows one to finally align with what feels good and right, regardless of the conditions in which life is experienced or in which the conditions are viewed as interactive with others and, especially, with the close relational-ships, often embedded into family as relationships. These "contrasts" provide some form of dependable direction options. I know which way to go by experiencing ways I discover I do not want to go into.

My Mother is a special relationship, as is yours. Always give mother-child-mother relationship special attention to understand yourself. It deserves and desires special notice, as it is a structural and spiritual collaboration, whether you know it or not and whether you like it or not. In my acceptance of the many agreements between us, I keep a timing awareness that all life is dynamic in nature; hence, entry points are based upon the moment it happens. The commencement of Human life is always (albeit continual) ever free to be. It is a choice and it is an initial cooperative agreement as in being identical in pre-allowance. Look at your parental relationships, both mother and father, or guardians, as such, as intentionally special. It is a good place to find self, and most likely that is exactly where self was lost to be found now, and believe it or not, all of us have been lost at some time or another. Not lost in the conventional sense of physical directions or dimensions (albeit that true too), but rather lost, lost from the knowing of ourselves and our amazing creative abilities. It is so remarkable that we leave ourselves right were we forgot ourselves and when we look around to find ourselves, we can come into seeing and understanding the things that were at primary cause, or rather, primary cooperation, in the losing of self to begin with. And whatever one thinks those events to be, it becomes irrelevant when self is actually discovered.

There is absolutely no interest ever, once awakened, to judge those who are still asleep or yourself from before waking-up. Leave that past as holding the past "you", too. Yet, there is always opportunity to recall self and appreciate expansion in every passing moment. There is great notice to appreciate your future while in the distinction of now. Many hold themselves and others in their judgement of accountability, when in fact, it is more powerful to recognize that people can change, if they want to change. It can also be noted that when people change, they are different. If a person says that they have changed, it will only take a little time before coming to know if that is, in fact, true. I love to give the benefit of the doubt to those I love and when changes happen to me, I love it to be identifiable.

We are there in the finding right where we misplaced ourselves. Needless to mention, self is so worthwhile to search and seek after. It is we, ourselves, who orchestrated this vastness of experiences that shields oneself from allowing the bittersweet sight of creative convalescence heal into our wellbeing. It was perfectly brought together; eternal soul to eternal soul, each excitedly willing to play our parts. There is, therefore, only appreciation felt in the attention to this evolution of self, especially, self-awareness.

Many of us might well feel complexities about our mothers, fathers, sisters, brothers, children, grandchildren or other relatives, given to truth. It's not something one can really hide; though more from self, less from others who know us. It is hard to admit until admitted. Generally, all mothers are saints. My mother was an amazing woman and I learned so much from her and from observing her when I was a child, right on through until now, which is years after she drew in her last breath of air here and let it out on the other side of here and continued living elsewhere or, rather else how.

I am honored, even proud to note, that I interpret things differently as to what I saw in my mother's ways, once I was able to see myself, again. In other words, I was re-enabled with certain understandings about the brilliance of the contrasts my mother provided, long before her departure. Hear this, and let it stay with you a long, long time; it will be sooner for an upcoming generation and ever shortened from the following to the following generations, because this movement of increasing appreciation of self-confidence and application of unique-creativity is real and will not diminish ever with a generation finding it in now. Once discovered, and it has been, it cannot lose itself again. Once the bell has rung, and it has been, it cannot be un-wrung and ringing it again and again does not make it louder.

We come into life, of course, with an openness of trust and hence, we naturally do trust what our guardians tell us of what the ways are we should behave and believe. We intuitively figure that they know since they have been doing it longer than we, and they are taking care of us and we are unable to survive without them, albeit we are most unaware initially of what survival is, as we know only of our wellbeing. That is the way it is with we humans; at birth we observe our parents or guardians, but mostly our parents since most of us stay along those young years with our parents. We absorb such a variety of behaviors and beliefs from them, from their vantage point and our helplessness. Slowly but surely, we learn all that we need to in order to survive (so we feel) in being Human Beings. We initially feel so satisfied receiving the recipe for life neatly packaged into the daily events and circumstances of what happens, the details of the predictable and the normal. That is, however, until most of us realize who we really are, again. We, apparently, forget not upon entering humanity, as we remember for a while, but someplace between feeling hungry, being fed, learning language, and trusting another, we forget. This is the way it is, yet it is not so much "intended" as "defaulted".

*The Art of Appreciating MORE*

That, right there, is such an amazing thought to behold. We all come into life and then, after a short while, we learn implicitly to do what others are doing in the "defaulted" value of its happening. This is easy for us to do, to slide comfortably into, as we learn to care about other's opinions and specifically of their opinions of how well, from their viewpoint, we have adapted to what they have taught us. We are taught to please others rather than to be ourselves. We are rarely given the opportunity to even consider what we actually are, who we are, and what we really want to do. Although sometimes people might ask us questions about ourselves, like, "What do we want to do when we grow-up?", even that question tends to sway us back into their step. We are often brought up in ways that we never really evaluate our own feelings, outside of the feeling that if we behave in a particular manner, we will please others and that actually does feel good to us. We learn other's ways before we even get a chance to apply into this world the ways of ourselves. We forget to allow ourselves the freedom to even recognize what skills and talents we brought with us and that are completely natural for us as those individuals we came forth to be. We definitely gravitate towards and embedded or innate skills, although, we learn very early in life to become part of the Human Race and that becomes far more important than becoming who we really are.

That is what it is to learn in the "defaulted" value. It is what we are all going through, or mostly all. It is what we do to our own children too. It is the common understanding of life that few seek to question or clarify. It is the dearth acceptance of the initialization as Human Beings. And it is not all bad. There is so much good growing through our generations. It is evolving, as we come into appreciating the knowing of other ways and gain great hope in the potential of change. When we,

## *The Manifestation of the Lavender Scarf*

Humans, truly pivot away from the "defaulted" and move into the "intended", more than I know how to express will change and improve, albeit the momentum towards this is already bringing betterment.

I was raised in a dysfunctional family unit, with my parents and siblings. My husband, Uri, on the other hand, came into life in a much different environment only a month after I did and all the way on the other side of the World. It was, to most of us, like being born on another planet. He was born on an Israeli kibbutz. On the one he placed himself in and his parents were charter members of, the governing rules were that upon birth the child got placed into a Children's House, and into a room with all other children born in that year. He was born at the end of May, so he was about in the middle of his room. He, of course, had parental visits; yet, growing up was a different observation. He learned from those around him, just as did I, yet his teachers were those tending to the children in his room. It was their job to take care of the children. His parents were those special people who visited him or as he got older, he visited them at their unit on the same kibbutz premises. In comparison to other places to be born, Uri pretty much was sent away to a friendly boarding school, at the age of birth. I was born into a "traditionally" dysfunctional family unit in the inner city of the United States of America.

Of all the circumstances that my life unraveled, thus far, Uri and I finally finding each other was the best, for both of us. We were in our early forties, so we were "experienced", and we recognized the match we were to each other almost immediately. I recall that we both felt we had waited so long to find each other, that we wanted only to be together from there on. Little, though some, adjustment took place in our formation of a marriage.

*The Art of Appreciating* MORE

We are so interestingly compatible that I am still completely impressed with both of us for realizing our value upon each other without any resistance. Finding the right partner, and enjoying it to the most possible expansion, is a grace of love that is without any words left to describe. We are happy together, even after so many years of marriage, and even because of so many years of marriage, that time together is always a blending of reality and dreaming. I wish this type of love to come to everyone, yet, I realize that we are all having wonderful experiences, and all are equally great. Having a trusty partner in life does provide, to me, a power of oneness that seems more potent than what I find others express in their lives, and of what I experienced prior to this happening to us. Uri and I are so much more than I ever thought two people in a relationship could ever become. I sometimes feel a little concerned for others looking in at us that they might feel less found in their own experience, and then I remember to free myself from guilt, in this most important fact; we create our own lives with our thoughts. Uri and I thought we existed in our individual thoughts long before we discovered that we are. We always existed together, yet it was only when we noticed "us" we became "us". During the course of our lives, prior to knowing each other, we were "defaulting" continuously towards each other, since we had no idea where we actually were going, although, in trust we found each other, eventually, and exactly on time.

As to the coming together in a mature relationship, previous relationships taught us much. One thing, for me, was that I deliberately decided that I didn't have to tell the story of my entire life to Uri when we first got together. In fact, even now there are so many life adventures that I find actually better left in the past. Uri is the same about himself. We live, as a result, more in the present moment and more in the creative world. That is such a wonderful way to be, after so many years together, some of the old past times have been shared between us, in fact, we together have some old past times. I am always so happy to know that Uri had so much love and respect for those raising him and teaching him, and he has so much respect and love for his parents too. His Father passed away years ago and Uri mentioned to me that he had never, even once, heard his father say an unkind word about anyone or ever raise his voice in anger. His Mother was also a kind and gentle person, albeit she was more the dominant figure in the relationship between his Father and her, not between Uri and who Uri is. Uri is much like his Father. He is gentle and kind, soft spoken, honest and loving. He is different than other man I've known, yet, I know that these qualities are choices, and Uri chooses wisely to be aware of his worthiness.

Uri definitely was raised in a more peaceful environment. He learned a great deal about community living in a set of about fifteen same-agers in his class of children, born the same year. Also, although that might be more similar to my childhood experiences since I had five siblings to learn how to be a team member with, family life compared between us in our childhood was like night and day in so many ways. He openly agrees that he had little contrasts and was often encouraged to find and use his natural skills.

Our relationship is such a loving one. I think a lot might have to do with our past, yet, more with our present and our mutual desires to have a great future together. Again, we find that the comparisons between our growing up years are so different that we always resort back to the abstract connections between our individual experiences and trust more in the release of comparisons, as they tend to develop a slight vibration of competition between us; sometimes realizing who had it better or worse than the other. We choose to more often develop less competition from the past to influence our relationship and we, together, join-up to rather participate in the creative side of living in the Now, together.

I had grown so wise and tired by the time I met Uri, that I was very attuned to detecting personalities very quickly. I was so happy to meet up with someone who was so nice. I had run the obstacle course and now had finished the race, so I felt I had no need to discuss the obstacles any longer.

Prior to meeting Uri, I thought perhaps the image of his existence was only a figment of my imagination. I am so happy I held-on to my dreams that I would have a special loving relationship with someone, sometime during my life. It is well worth the ideas and time to creation, because now I have accomplished a truer understanding of love, which continues so easily. We cooperate with each other. This idea of waiting for the right person to come into my life was always a good thought to have, yet it was the holding-on to it and the believing that it was coming to me, rather to us, that formed the results. It is so important to hold-on to dreams, to trust in them, to believe and to never give-up. They come exactly when they match up to their existence, which requires trusting in self-actualization.

My parents raised me until I was about twenty-one. Correction: I lived with my parents and in my childhood family household apartment until I was twenty-one.

## The Manifestation of the Lavender Scarf

After the age of eighteen, I was reminded daily that my time was up and that they had no more responsibility towards me, so I paid to stay on, having no place else to go. I felt little difference because I was giving my Mother money for years. I gave her three week's pay and kept one week's pay to buy clothes for my two sisters and myself. I worked five nights a week, Wednesday through Sunday, since I was only thirteen years old until I graduated high school, when I took a full-time job and left my babysitting job.

I was a babysitter for a lady who was a cocktail waitress at The Sunset Strip Cocktail Lounge. She worked from 8:30 PM until 2 AM. She lived in our same building, just across the hall in the rear of the stairwell. She was divorced from a sailorman who never sailed by to see them or support his three children: Freddie Jr., Terry and Donna. He continued sailing the world. She continued taking care of their children. She, Marilyn, (like in Monroe) was a conundrum to me. I admired her freedom and her independence yet found her taste in men consistently foul and cruel to her sense of dignity. I always felt she was too good for these men of the night who drove her home. As far as I could tell, and I was the type to notice, she was rarely physically abused by but one of these men, yet all of them seemed to be intimately interviewed by her, after working hours. Is that physical abuse? It is to me then and still now, although some feel that mutual consent clarifies physical abuse. Perhaps it was an abuse that aligns to the "Me Too", form of abuse. Women are taught to be treated as a lesser. That is abuse to me. It is an interesting manipulation, if I were to have been asked. I was not asked my opinion. She held a reputation in the neighborhood as a loose woman, by other names that I care not write, and yet, I only knew her as a grown-up who took pretty good care of herself and her children. She was always nice to me.

*The Art of Appreciating MORE*

Sometimes she cried to me admitting that she was helplessly in love with her married boss, who typically drove her home, yet not always. I think I learned some things vicariously from her.

I loved her children and when we were together, while I babysat for them, we always were quiet and polite to each other. I would say, "Let's practice being polite to each other so that we can know how to be polite to people we meet." When the bars closed, Marilyn would come home, in her cute perfectly fitting cocktail waitress outfit, as I said sometimes with someone new, especially when she was on the outs with her boss. I would then cross the hallway to my apartment and open the door to that place that only that ungodly time of night permitted quiet to be in.

At twenty-one I married my first husband, primarily to get out of the house and away from my immediate family. I found my escape. He was a good friend of mine and we truly loved each other for increasing our chances to be more than what we were taught of our selves. I appreciate so much that I escaped.

Until then, I lived in a crazy world. Yet, I had finally escaped. Danger was in every story before my escape. As a young person I had watched drugs and alcohol incinerate my dreams of living in a "normal" home, as my older brother became an addict. I learned, most skillfully, to avoid trouble, as if my life depended upon doing so, yet, I saw it too often and was a victim of it for many years. I tried to hide until it became lessened enough to wander into it attempting to pass through or, if possible, skirt it and just survive. I noticed what was lurking behind me and when I was outside the dangers of home itself, I became wise to every alley entrance and alternative way out. I learned to take safe harbor by

## The Manifestation of the Lavender Scarf

quietly sitting upon the roofs of those houses, blocks away, with softer-spoken people inside it seemed, making the challenge of silence a step away from being found.

I would sit often until near dark, usually reading a schoolbook or drawing doodles on my book covers, up on the rooftops listening to those families inside "normalcy" talking to each other in ways I wanted to talk and be spoken to in my crazy family home. I could, at times rest my ear on the roof and feel only the depth of the ceiling and the roof separate me from others, more like me I felt. When their windows were opened, I could hear the young person inside, close to my age, move around and then sit back down. I knew to not be seen or heard. The rooftop gravel could easily give me away if I dared to move too quickly. I would wait for the perfect moment to move about, catch my balance and then jump right from my standing-still position, across to the next rooftop, still three stories high. I could land so quietly, like a cat, so no one inside could hear. I sat sometimes above in the empty room I pretended myself to be in, as I watched from above people move around.

Flowing as a wave in its purposed-moment of anticipated-motion, I learned to upfold my knees into my core self upon landing and mentally readjust my weight to proportion my touch-downs as if I were a living feather gliding and then evenly, as does an Olympic gymnast yet far softer, I'd "land-it". My landings were gentle, almost liquid, yet, unwaveringly considering of each contact point of my footprints, resulting without the slightest of sounds or vibrations. I learnt this skill from visualization and practice and, also, from mimicking the cats that moved undetected, yet, seen by me. They are magnificent creatures.

## The Art of Appreciating MORE

Under the cover of the accepted disorder of inner-city life, which is noisy enough to make any occasion of a different sound, become an accepted occurrence, and, in its way, the variable static that murmurs the hum of Humans living close together. The rooftops were park-like to me, although stark and hard. They were though, quiet and natural and there were no potentially dangerous boys or men lurking at me up on these empty-of-people roofs. I knew where to come up and down from street level to be atop the roofs and I never was noticed by anyone, ever. I was sure of that, because I didn't know anyone as aware of so many aspects of street life; no child, adult, or animal. My ego would say that my sisters and brothers were clumsy and awkward next to me, because I knew not one person; friend or not, who could focus in this quiet way. Everyone seemed too busy to notice me when I was out of sight. If they saw me any place, they noticed me, yet, out of sight, out of mind. I was not discovered, neither by those in these city houses, nor by those walking three stories below on the ground. Even the dogs and cats did not notice me or what I was up to.

Up on the roof (which reminds me of a song that became well known in the years to follow) I could evenly diffuse my mass weight out and lie there listening to everything around me and knowing the momentum of each and every change. I felt a connection to the birds, the squirrels, the sky, and the possibilities of myself, being apparently different than others, yet, without notice of that uniqueness. I was so alive with myself there, so close, it seemed, to what must be heaven. My eyes were sharp as an eagle, and my ears were practiced in listening intensely for subtle variations to get my alerted attention. Life depended upon my presence of mind, yet, up here on the roof, I had space to think of things that dreams are made of and be calm. I was very aware, and it was beautiful.

I wanted to and did, hear these strangers in their simple, friendly, easy worlds interacting and communicating with each other in such common normal ways. They didn't holler often, if at all. They didn't mentally trick each other. They didn't call each other nasty names, tease each other hurtfully, curse aloud when they felt the freedom to, or mumble beneath their breath and behind your back about things unnatural for me to want to understand even if I could hear. Maybe that was true, maybe not. I didn't know these people. I only knew what I did, and I only thought what I could. I did feel that these strangers were less problemed by internal fighting. They were different or so it seemed. They didn't fabricate indecent stories about each other in order to stir up the environment with doubts, guilt, blame, insults or confusion. There was a lot less drama. They were quieter, they helped one another with the simplest of things, and they spoke consistently nice to each other. It was interesting to realize that they existed, and I wanted that for myself. I didn't care any longer if that was what my family members would change into. All I knew was that there was a kinder gentler way. I, particularly hoped, that my sisters might be able to change, yet, I didn't have much hope for that happening any time soon. They both seemed so involved in creating drama, although they might not have even known that as true. I created my share of drama too. If it were too quiet in our house, you can be certain that things would change. Some people prefer drama and busy in the same understanding; if in a drama you are involved in something to keep you busy, and if you were busy you were feeling more important.

It was so different of what is more expected of people now. Times have changed and we all have changed along our path too. I feel life keeps getting better. For that reason, because the times have changed and there is more transparency and conditions placed on parenting, I remind myself often that there are always differences between Sensitive People and Insensitive People. We come forth as much into a "time" as to our "parents" and "family".

I favored these stranger families that I dreamt would have welcomed me with opened arms into their lives and that would gladly make me one of their own, should they have known I was just right there outside and above them, separated only by a roof and an unexplainable, unacceptable, impossible awareness of each other. I envisioned and sometimes dreamt, night or day, asleep or awake, so wanting of an abstract opportunity that some events might happen, whereby I could be adopted into their lives, as I knew I deserved to be living in a better and more loving home, although I knew my family loved me, it just was not a demonstrative love. It was not dependably soft or kind. I could easily adjust to something permanent happening that would change everything for the best, if only my parents would die or if only someone knew that I needed to be rescued, though my family would not ever permit my being rescued. They would insist upon my emotional torture and punishment if I ever dared to "let out of the bag" the life within my family walls.

I became aware of cultural difference at a young age and, still, to date, I recognize the ways families tend to be. I know my childhood family loved me, yet they did not understand the goodness in being polite and kinder to each other. In fact, they were kinder and politer to strangers than to each other. It was that way for me. I

## *The Manifestation of the Lavender Scarf*

felt I was born into the wrong family. I might wonder if anyone of my siblings felt that way too. We were instructed to never discuss our family lives with anyone or there would be big consequences to be paid. It was no one's business but ours. I knew what that meant, and I knew the intent behind those threats would and could be executed. I lived in great fear of my family. Each member had their own way of projecting harm upon me, and each other, so it seemed. I knew they each enjoyed their control of each other. I could be a part of it; yet I chose to hide as often as possible. It was most important to not appear as if I were hiding. I contributed to the mix too.

Being busy was an acceptable excuse to be out of family limits. It was safer to be busy babysitting or playing outside in the playground or with friends. As I became older and moved into upper elementary, junior and high school, I became involved in every extracurricular activity available and over time I stopped going to the roof tops. I know this story is to be about The Lavender Scarf, yet it is important to know the frame-workings of the relationship between me and my mother.

I admit having had some abilities to protect myself from each one of my siblings by playing into their well-constructed egoic behavioral games. I preferred to be elsewhere. I truly did not want to participate. I was only surviving along with them. It was a mean miserable mistake that I had to be part of such an embarrassingly sub-cultured family that was so loud, rude, cruel and unpredictable that I never really felt I knew any of them well enough to trust. Trust was a big issue to fail in and in my family, I was taught to never trust anyone further than I could throw them.

*The Art of Appreciating* MORE

Family, for me as a youngster, was a scary group of overactive harmful relationships that I was forced into being of the same last name. I did not like my parents. I loved them though. I tolerated my sisters and brothers. I loved them though. My grandfather, who we called Pop-Pop, I knew he was the worse of them all. I really didn't like him. He didn't treat my Grandmother well, and I think when he drank too much, he became sneaky and crossed borders with what was proper behavior. I didn't understand it all as a young person although I heard tales around the adult table of gossips. My Grandmother was a bright light in my life and a lady in all that she did and said. She was reserved and often quiet. I would think that it is hard to understand that my siblings seemed to see things differently than I did as we came from the same family, lived in the same house, had all the same relatives, ate the same food, and so much more in common, and we experienced our childhoods so differently when asked.

I did not see, while up on the roofs, those other families living any way even slightly, as did my family. I loved these other families that I, over time, secretly got to know and trust from the close proximity of being above them and looking in at them from my personal one-way vantage point. Right there, inches away on their roofs I was, indeed, so close there where I knew how to solve their seemingly little petty problems. I found my problems even too hard to think about, especially while up on the roofs, and even still now. I wanted so much to fix my family life, which seemed so broken and worn out by drama after drama, crisis upon crisis, lie into lie, day after endless day; yet, I did not know how to do so. I only knew to hide as often as I could get away with hiding. They, my family, would search for me, if found missing, and I would have to return to them. I knew I was stuck there with my shrewd dangerous family, who always desired to control me into their degree of unhappiness.

These other families, the neighboring roof families, I knew their answers and could fix them, if they only knew I could-of, I would-of. We remained worlds apart from each other in the inner-city structure of classes built within buildings and attitudes. Yet, of my family members, I knew I was the only member who knew that our biggest distinguishing characteristic between these roof families and ours was their attitudes, not mine. It was their manner toward each other that thrilled me to know these people we were not. Just hearing people be nice to each other gave me such hope in life. They were nice people, as was I. My family members were not nice people; not to each other, themselves or anyone. The roof families lived a loving life, while I was so deeply wounded by the experience of being less valued, underclass, pathetic poor, and untamed lowly ones. My siblings schemed and lied to everyone. To be from the "projects" was like being cursed with something more than poverty, it was like being imprisoned in a community of "less-valued" beings. And it was true as far as I could tell. I listened into these families outside of the "projects", and their seemingly diluted problems, always had an easy fix, through my understanding and experiences of being trapped in a social mis-fitted life. It is easy to make better what is already pretty right, and it seemed difficult to explain that to any of my family members.

As a child, I grew an uncanny ability to disappear away from the upcoming sensed household dramas, as if it were a battlefield to retreat gracefully out of range before the trumpets blew and the *forward charge* took place. I've come to know that this is a perception of disappearance; it is only a proportional and relative ability, since I carried the battlefield into a chessboard of experiences in which I could relate. And I looked continuously for the spiritual signs to protect me and bring me into the Light of, what I felt was, God. I was not as afraid, because I was ready. I saw things coming to avoid. Not knowing what to call it by name, I knew my life was being crushed by dysfunctionality, and I felt so ashamed, especially of my family members, who seemed to thrive in the torrents of tormenting each other, incessantly. I casted and projected myself outside of my family, as misplaced. I knew, somehow and someday, I would get out of it, if I could only find the way.

In my youth and before I was adult enough to be wise enough to get away from my family, it was just a small jump out of the city projects and the madness that surrounded my family and the social life my family brought to it. I remember watching "Leave it to Beaver' and thinking to myself that there were other kinds of people out there, people who were nice to each other, people who lived in nicer places and experienced nicer things. Just like my roof families, the most difficult experience that this TV family was having seemed to me to be so delightfully easy to solve. I used to dream of being adopted into any TV type family, where I could then help them solve these "easier" problems that seemed so apparent to me. Yet, even in my dream world, I never saw myself as a contributor to the problems. I understood from that that there are solutions, not just problems. I soon noticed, in comparison, that everyone's problems where so much smaller than mine.

Before my big escape, I started to sense that the negative dramas that surrounded me were extreme and that once I was able to escape out of this lowly place of troubles and grief, I would be free. I also developed a feeling that I could help others with their problems. I had real solutions. The first one was to avoid the problem. I remember thinking that the best thing that could ever happen to me, was to be out of this place where I lived and away from this family of yelling, hitting and hating. I wanted so much to live in one of those houses that kept gardens growing and kettles cooking in the slight whistle of steam, that I noticed on the side streets when we took the bus or a ride up to church on Sunday. Church was in a better neighborhood, which I now recognize as symbolic for my pursuing religions in the hopes of finding myself in a better neighborhood, so to speak. I kept thinking of what I needed to do to escape and those thoughts gave me solace and hope, and I believed that they would become true. Today, looking back at my young immature feelings, I know that this wanting to live in a "better" family is probably more common than I thought then, if people are honest about that.

For the most part, my home life as a child was one of the worst ones, I still can compare myself to, when I do, and I don't any longer do that, though I sometimes wish I could have mentioned it to others in my life as everything did get better for me. The great fortune I had in life was available to me due to the place in which I started out in life. I wish I could have helped others come through their hardships as well as I did. I know it when I see it still. I think that is the true definition of being "Street-wise". I was "Street-wise" and from there I became "Family-wise" and "Solution-wise". For that I am thankful.

I escaped. YAY! My siblings did not fare as well as I, and I think that is because I spent time deliberately thinking up my escape for so many years. I actually feel so many dimensions in everything about the word "escape". My escape was refined often, and it became so real to me that it still is my first thought about my childhood home, "I escaped.".

With practice, I do not dwell on the details experienced in my childhood and youth, only the escape from it and the results rather than the reasons I saw in wanting to escape, ever to something better, quieter, calmer, healthier and happier. Even now, I struggle a little to spend time thinking and writing about my difficult childhood, because it is over. I have come to conclude that I am a "sensitive-one". I feel feelings and emotions sooner, perhaps deeper than many others, and all of my family members of my childhood years. I do have one sister remaining here on Earth and I do not know all the ways in which she grew out of her childhood though I see she did too. She had a lot of unhappiness periodically and mostly in her past, and many things turned on her and now to be great life improvements. I see she escaped in a different way. I do not know how sensitive she was as a child. Not one hundred percent sure. We were both stuck in a place that we both found our way out of eventually. I am so happy for her and I love her even more for her travels out of where we came from into now. I think she is a sensitive now, and that is good.

I loved my first husband for being so instrumental in helping me find my way out of harm's way. He had and still has no idea really of just how important and wonderful he was in my life. As we were dating, I hardly ever let him know my family. He lived in Long Island City, New York and I lived in New Jersey, which was very convenient for me. It was at our wedding he met most of my family for the first time. I was so worried, not that I was marrying the wrong man, for I was not, although I knew we were together temporarily, but I was worried that my Mother would be drunk and fall down at the

# The Manifestation of the Lavender Scarf

wedding, among other things. She could be so incredibly rude and could say anything to bring me harm. Blessings be, she did not. For once in my life I felt she just cooperated in letting me go into a better life. That was the motherliest thing she ever did for me. Leaving wonder easy to figure out, we married at the end of August and we broke up the marriage before Thanksgiving. Yet, I had escaped. I was outside of the window looking in and it was so much better to be where I was.

My first husband was also feeling freedom to be himself, as he was over-mothered as much as I was under-mothered, and we appreciated each other as good friends, indeed. He never knew what hit him and looking at this event more maturely and honestly, now, I realize that I was perhaps unkind to have used him as my mistake. I was like an animal scratching for survival. He was almost innocent. I didn't mean to hurt him, and he never said I did, but I probably did. We had good enough reasons to blame one another for a breakup, although neither of us did. I just needed to find my way out of a life that was like a nightmare. He didn't understand, and I did not tell him. He still does not know about the world I escaped from as I felt he would not have loved me enough, if he knew who I really was and how desperate I wanted to find a normal life. Desperate enough to play whatever games I needed to in order to get married. I saw no other way. To end it quickly, I just found a way out of his life, as I had found a way into his life and, simultaneously, I had found a way out of my life and into my life too. If he only knew the love, I still have for him for the part he, unknowingly played in my greatest escape.

He was the perfect match for my intentions. He was a compulsive gambler. And I knew that from the very start of our relationship. I knew I would have "my out" from this marriage because he would be unable to support a normal lifestyle. I knew I had to frame my existence from my own source of financing and by the time we got married, I worked long enough and hard enough to become gainfully employed as a receptionists and switchboard operator in New York City. It was a perfect job for me, and I kept my expenses affordable for me to carry the weight without his financial assistance, since I knew he had lost control of his own financing through gambling. He had this sickness that would enable a good excuse to leave him. I sacrificed all the money that we were given at the wedding to his gambling, which was a good trade-in for me to be on my own. I was happy. I always seemed to find happiness. What was more important was that I was safer. I was a state away from the ever-intense dysfunctionality of my birth family. I was on my own and freedom was so beautiful. I retained a friendship with my first husband for a while, yet, he probably doesn't like me nearly as much as I will always love him. I am in such appreciation for the way everything lined up for me too, in a considerably short period of time, as I escaped from the "projects" and was on my own. I felt like a millionaire.

Into today, I am more present than ever. I always kept on the path to increase my ability to be happy with myself and with the world around me. I have a low tolerance to being unhappy and I seek to find happiness when I feel off the mark. This illusive, ever pervasive, Now, is so good to me. I have heard others say that Now is all we really have. Now is where everything is; all past, all present and all we go into. Now, is where we are, always. That rings absolutely true to me. When I think about the past or the future, I am always doing that in the Now. So, the details about the abuses and difficulties of my past are going to stay far out of my

# The Manifestation of the Lavender Scarf

current reality, knowing I am here Now, and I am in a very good place. The more I trust in the healing power of the sharing of experiences, the better Now feels too. I choose to avoid sinking myself into that place I definitely escaped. I have neither direct nor specific things to write about of the seemingly bad experiences of my childhood, for Now I experience them all at a different perspective. I feel a true direction to allow the past to connect to the story of the Lavender Scarf, because in so doing, the depth of emotions from a lifetime can express itself as worthy having had. I will remain general in my bringing understanding to what this all has to do with the manifestation of the Lavender Scarf. I know the reasons are meaningful from the past growth. I just know.

At the time of my writing this, my mother is dead, and my father is old, although he is my only close remaining relative from my childhood. My brothers are all three dead, and my two sisters live far away from each other and me. All my other childhood relatives, cousins, aunts and uncles, are distanced too. I am safe. I am removed and detached, and I am happy this way. I have been this way most of my life. The details about my childhood are wearisome and awkward to think about and horrible to discuss or write about. I feel so much better leaving them go, although, from time to time something out of those years will surface, seemingly uncontrollably. I know that they are perfectly timed, to be identified and then I move on from them, again.

I am matured with wisdom now, and still, just a little while ago, as I was in meditation and feeling a conversation come alive within me, I heard this voice say; "Look at that, that happened when you were nine and a half years old!". I was startled with the exactness of the age it revealed and it seemed accurate enough in the mention, if only because my recollection of that age is scanty in some places, vivid in others. This memory was so deep inside my spirit that I had forgotten all about it, apparently. In fact, I still do not recall having the total experience of it, just a feeling of the nature of it, nor do I trust it as totally valid, though Wow! Right out of nothing it came before me like watching a movie in black and white, except with so many more feelings. It came to me as if it were a structure that I had placed tucked away deep within me. I felt it happen, the awareness of it and I decided to trust myself as the amazing spirit of health and vitality that I am, rather than to seek to find out if it, this memory and partially realized experience, was what is called repressive memory. It doesn't really matter that much to me. When you are as happy as I am, it seems a divergence to actually look too deeply into what has nothing to do with my actual happiness, which is current and more evolved. We, none of us, can know everything, nor should we try or even think it necessary. Letting go of the past benefits the future in enabling the now to be rich with emotions that serve best. I do not have to know more than I am to know.

This "quasi-memory" was, as all memory, non-physical and it seemed mostly spiritual. It was somewhat spatially visionary, like watching a film, a film of me, and I emotionally felt it happen as if it were alive and real. I was very spent-tired and lucidly bewildered afterwards. It was strong because it was different, and it was fading away as quickly as it arrived. I heard a muted sound within me of the activities of this almost automatic collective resolve that reminded me of linked smooth metal chains clicking against itself. I had no control of this experience, except to accept it as something positive and timely. It was that experience, however, that prompted me to write this story down and document it or it could be lost to the whims of the tales

# The Manifestation of the Lavender Scarf

that toss and turn into something they may not have been grown to be. This residue is big enough filled with stains. It does not require time to legitimize it as something that apparently needed to be dealt with appropriately. This was as appropriate as it would ever be. I had taken an extreme to avoid remembering this event from the battles I was unable to prevent. I looked straight at it and in that moment something amazing happened to me. I visualized this structure melt before me. It washed out of me. It became as if living moving fish scales that fell off of this structure, perhaps egoic in substance, and off and away from me. These entities were moving into all directions simultaneously and flowing down off of me and continuing into a circular, expanding leaving pattern.

They moved pretty fast though I could watch them sliver off and go away; many thousands of them moving together and apart. They did not look back at me at all, nor did they hesitate from feeling any separation anxiety between each other. They left with great purpose. My soul, heart and mind knew, without a doubt, that these were entities that connectively created together that structure they swarmed from and that now was indistinguishable. This structure was, all of these years, in my unknowing carry. Since I was nine and a half years old. I felt a relief and heaviness surrender into a light that shown upon the space no longer occupied by this melted away entity. I felt good that it was leaving me. Although it had commenced or fertilized within me as a youngster, it also gathered unto itself like-claims of experiences along the years and it was strong and pitted well. Difficult to move. It felt right and ready to go, to go to wherever it was all going, and leaving me in the wake of my rejuvenation.

# The Art of Appreciating MORE

For a short moment, as I physically felt something shift in me, I felt an emotional "burn out" as well. I felt embarrassed and a little troubled that these parts of what was in me were perhaps going off to find another victim to become a parasite in, for that is the emptiness I felt and a grappling knowledge at the intent of this substance. I experienced a spiritual drain of joy, wonder and some concern, because I care about others. Just as I began associating with this latter feeling, that was closer to guilt than concern, and closer to sorrow than guilt, that voice that spoke earlier said words to reassure me of this removal process. Yes, for indeed, something was removed, of its own will and what was left in its absence was what is commonly known as a healing. I had experienced a change through a pathway that I did not realize could happen regarding a memory of something I still cannot totally recall, yet it fled, and it is gone now. It escaped.

My Father was forced into retirement at the early age of 59. With that freedom, after a year of evaluating choices, my parents finally moved out of that miserable inner city broken down overstayed project apartment in the Bradley Courts of North Munn Avenue in Vailsburg, Newark, New Jersey. It was a ghetto of deep dark dangers, plagued by racial and ethnic overtones and poverty-stricken undertones. Inside their apartment the outside world overlapped. They did not sense it as much as did others. Inside there remained a home that was clean and kept organized and comfortable, like it ever was when I was a child. It was not a dirty old apartment. It was a lived-out place that was a product of the times. Sometimes what is surrounding us, is what we melt into and blend in as one. The environment we exist in is the evidence of our thought creations. It was a relief to me that my folks were uprooting from this dungeon-world-plex tenement building that was dissolving into the public's confirmation of poverty and inequality.

As did I years sooner, my parents relocated apparently as far as they possibly could too. They packed up a U-Haul truck and drove three thousand miles away and decidedly closer to me. I was somewhat surprised; not completely. I didn't care one way or the other where they decided to retire out of the projects. At the time, all my siblings were still alive and living within the same general vicinity as our parents were living before, they moved here, to Ventura, California. The projects had become such a dangerous place that none of my siblings visited them there for fear something terrible might befall them or their dear sweet innocent children. It was a very bad unimaginable place. It was a hellhole of fears concentrated into unearthly horror of discontent and complaint shared by everyone and thing that found the misfortune of being there. What a misery to attract into a reality.

I visited rarely when business or circumstances took me into that part of the United States, and out of a legitimate growing awareness of holding honor for what is right to honor, regardless of what I might rather have known true. They were my parents, and I knew they were missing so much understanding as to the magnificence of life. I knew I could not change them. I welcomed their self-driven decision to move. Their apartment was in a ghetto battlefield of dark mornings and violent sounding nights. Awake or asleep, one had no rest. I do not exaggerate in telling you that, many were the times, during my visits that I heard gunshots, constant sirens and angry shouting all day and night long, increasingly so since my own youth years there in what is the opposite of paradise. These violent noises were the common sounds, the voices of the broken run-down neighborhood that still remained diseased and haunted my reality. All the old neighbors, long since, had already moved or died, save a few people who should have been institutionalize, in hospice, or taken out of their readjusted realities to fear nothing at all any longer. Of those that remained, their finances played a roll, as this was affordable city managed housing and now housed the low incomed. I knew this place existed, while others just thought it might be possible. I have lived there. I saw it crumble. I knew what it was like to live in the heated inner-city ghetto. I am ever glad I escaped. I am glad my parents also finally escaped.

On one business trip visit, to my parent's, just a year earlier, I drove a car. I parked that car in the parking lot in the back of the projects and very early the next morning, even before the sun came up fully, I went out to my car. I was heading over to my company's headquarters, which was a two-hour drive out into Bethpage Long Island, New York for a scheduled visit. I was combining business with personal travel and wanted to visit my parents to see what they were doing and to expand my quest to care about them even enough to face the past and let it go. That was almost an insane thing to do. Though, I did. As I approached the car, I was happy it had not been stolen, but it looked strange. Someone had jumped off the high wall in front of the car and landed on the roof of my car long and hard enough to cave it into the interior of the car. I got into the car all bent over, placed my hands on the ceiling and pushed it with all my might and to my great surprise; it popped out leaving hardly a notice. I felt so fortunate, so gifted, so recovered. I felt blessed with the exaggeration of spoil being overwhelmed by the desire in my life-existence to have things work out well for me, regardless of the apparent circumstances. I was doing the right things by witnessing that the nature of love is to always heal, immediately.

I was the only child that visited my parents for years. It was, of course, due to location, which is pretty funny to state, because I lived in California while all my siblings lived reasonably nearby, in better towns, right there in New Jersey. I knew it was more than that. In fact, I came to appreciate that the extremely dangerous location was a relief to my brothers and sisters and their families to be excused from visiting. There was more to the way the relationships were so worn and undesirable. I spare myself the tragic words to fill my mind and heart up with this fact. My siblings had found their own degrees of escapes. I understood, and I appreciated that I was different. I realized also that part of them not visiting our parents was because they were filled with confusion.

Once my parents moved into "my" world, I was given the opportunity to "forgive and forget", and to let the past go totally. I began what for years and years was a new relationship with them. I never ever mentioned anything to them about the past life we had together that referenced anything to do with neglect or abuse of the many kinds I was familiar with from my childhood. I just let it go and all of us benefited tremendously from this ability of theirs and mine to compartmentalize the past. I never spoke poorly of my parents to Uri or the children. It worked out well for a long enough time to change many things to the better. First of all, my parents followed my way of living and they became very polite to me and with each other, so it seemed in my presence. I would say when I felt things getting off a bit that we should practice being polite to each other, so that we could be polite to the people we met. My parents bought into this and, at least around me, and at least for the most part, they became nicer and they became happier, although there was always something darker lingering around them and our relationship. I was already a happy person and I was a good example to and for them. Simultaneously, I was an enigma to my siblings. They did not understand me at all, nor did they understand the way our parents had become so much nicer than when they lived in the Newark projects. I know that our parents change had more to do with my influence than with their move. It was a very good move for them. The environment we all came out of was so negative and dangerous. The freedom of starting new was real.

They came here, which is a fairly "normal" low crime town, with all kinds of over-developed suspicions and fears still active. They moved into their new apartment, that I found and secured for them prior to their arrival, and immediately plugged in the "police" scanner radio. They had extra locks on their steering wheel and their entry door, and they were always sneaking around like squirrels. It was amazing to watch them transform their big fears into a new life, although I felt a strong knowing that over time they would calm into a more secure life and they did.

My siblings were still very angry with our parents. I could relate to their feelings. Many young adults take issues with their parents as they start to feel what parenting is for their new family or they come to terms with their new way of living. Even before my knowing the Law of Attraction I was off into my feeling victimized by my parents. I got over that and moved-on. Several of my siblings thought far too often about their childhood memories. They spoke to me personally about their discontent with the way it seemed our parents didn't care about what was happening in our lives any longer. I recall feeling that myself. Looking back on this time for us, it was so filled with the feeling of lack and less about our blessings. I too was blaming our parents for the outcomes we were all living. A lot of people find blame in their lives that they feel are caused by what their parent/guardians did or didn't do. Either way it is blame. When following self-potential, it is unnecessary to fault others and taking responsibility for self is a move into the better direction. My siblings had little to do with our parents during those years of adjusting to their own lives as adults. I lived far away so didn't feel obligation to visit often. That makes sense too because growing into adulthood requires space to find direction. My parents realized that and attempted to convey that to us by what felt uncaring and distancing. It was a good adventure each of us were having while we settled on our own behalf some major decisions; like who to marry, where to live, to have or not children, to continue with an education, to take that job offer, to commute, and many other natural advancements. However, things happen, funerals happen and over time, the distance became entwined with visits my parents were making back east and the relationships between their adult children were changing and becoming softer.

I was still, back then, a religious person. I joined the parish my parents belonged to and we found peace between us and within our religious community that they now took the time to become involved in volunteering some of their time too. My life was still sprinkled with drama and defaulted-ness, yet, things were better and better all of the time. In fact, I know that the better it gets, the better it gets. In addition, my siblings started to ask me how I got over and through my feelings that they still had regarding resentment and distrust toward our parents, each other and in life generally. I told them that there was a commandment of the ten that I found helped me out of negative feelings, towards my parents and even towards them. It was; Honor thy Mother and Father. That was what we were taught. Now I read the rest of that commandment which is: "Honor thy Mother and Father, least you have a long and prosperous life." I had come to understand that I needed to look out for myself, and this commandment, actually the fourth of ten, enabled me to love my parents with honor, and then, I too, would benefit from this yielding over my hurts with a long and prosperous life as reward. I put my heart into this idea, and it did pay off. I learned and taught by example that when we do what is right for others, we do what is right for ourselves. I, over the years to follow will re-evaluate that statement and since have come to realize that I first have to do what is right for myself, rather than others, and then the rightness of my life overflows into other people's lives in ways that doesn't take away from me, in fact, adds much. That knowing will come to change my life in so many ways. I was still on that path of coming into knowing when my parents first came to relocate into my escaped world. They loved my willingness to forgive and forget and, in fact, for many years they took that as a weakness within me and took advantage of my heart that was infinitely filled with generosity.

After Uri and I married, we continued to promote a Grandparent relationship, and never ever did I discuss my negative childhood aspects with anyone. Something interesting started to happen. My Mother began to say things like; "I never hit my children." That was a big fat lie. I avoided discussions. I did not blatantly lie about it.

## The Manifestation of the Lavender Scarf

Avoidance is quite different than denial through lies. It bothered me. I did not want to challenge my Mother, especially in front of my children or in front of Uri. I think my Mother had adopted my life into her own. The situation seemed more a flattering belief than a problem, and I just let it go. My Father never participated in that verbal denial or pretense. It was my Mother who was telling a new story. My Father and I only listened. Occasionally, I might glance over at my father and we held a moment of mutual wonder. After a while it became almost pronounced to me as something that she was doing to stir up some emotional imbalance within me. And then, as my Mother aged, she was experiencing some health issues that most likely contributed to the mix of things being said by her. A mind is a fragile thing when the heart is disconnected too long.

My Mother had a couple of pacemakers; the second one had an implantable cardioverter defibrillator, also. It not only kept a preferred heartbeat active; it also restarted the heart in a failure mode. It was the Humvee of the pacemakers available. After years of this pacemaker being part of her, I think it impacted her ability to feel her heart as we do. I started to see and experience some extremely unpredictable and harsh behaviors in my Mother towards the end of her life, and I believe that the pacemaker had something to do with it. Well that and that she probably never forgave herself for the things she was accountable for as a young mother, now years ago. I knew I could not stop her. Of course, I was completely out of control of her and she was not in control of herself either. My Mother became mean again. She was swallowed up with anger and bitterness and this time it had nothing to do with alcohol because she did not drink any alcohol, at all now. She held confused conversations and always they seemed so hurtful and sad. Just like when I was a child, but it was hurting Uri and the kids now. She was that person that I escaped from years ago. It was a most uncomfortable time for us all. Her anger was wild and furious, and she was insensitive, rude and verbally abusive. Her dying was a transformation that took about two years to complete. In that time, my family was brought into tears several times. Selfishly, I seemed to be the only one other than perhaps my Father, who recognized these mean-streaks as a revival of sorts. We all really learned a great deal about unconditional love. She eventually created a rule that we were not to see her and or my Father and she continued to her dying day to be a very negative person who apparently did not remember her love for us. She accused our daughter of flirting with her Grandfather, she accused me of saying things that were unbelievable, and she said Uri was trying to take things from her. It was horrible. It was a nightmare. Maybe dementia. It had to do with her failing thought processes. It was all too long a time before she passed away, even arguing in her surrender about things that were imagined. When she passed on, it was a good thing. She had suffered so much in her head and, I truly think the coldness of the pacemaker, disenabled her ability to love others. Everyone was exhausted, and we all took a long breath of relief.

I was there with her when she passed away. It was the first time I witnessed someone die. It was a time I will always remember. In her last five minutes, I knew she heard my voice, softly tell her to let herself go and to know that everything was good. I reminded her of God's Love for her and that she was going to a very good place of love and goodness. It was a blessing to be there with her. My sister Eileen was there too. We both pet her forehead to relax her and reminded her that we loved and appreciated her. She took that last breath in here

and out there and that was the way we parted in the physical terms of mother-daughter-mother.
What you might now be wondering is what does this have to do with that manifested Lavender Scarf? Well, a lot. It is part of the story. It is part of the vibrations of its manifestation. It is part of why I've waited until now to tell this story. That was the most difficult part of the essence of the story. The history of the relationships between my mother and all of the family she spawned. I am so happy to have completed setting the stage. Now I can pass this on with a kind feeling that everything is good and right with the world. Rest in Peace, Mother dearest and Rest in Peace, dearest Mother, for she had two sides that needed to be addressed once and for all.

Loving Uri and Uri loving me is always clearly meant to be. We do not feel we together overcome adversity we feel we create goodness and joy. It is several decades that has come by into now, since Uri and I discovered the Secret of a good life. Actually, it was only seemingly years ago that the Secret that we found grew quickly into us and we learned everything we could and continue to do so about the Secret; The Law of Attraction. It is the most significant belief of our lives now and we know that life has completely changed for us in finding out that our thoughts create things. We are the creators of our lives and experiences. We are able to control our thoughts and we are able to find joy in life.

Our newly formed energies where apparent to everyone we knew and still it was an interesting change to experience for many of my religious relatives, though it matters less and less all of the time what others think about us. We are quite happy with our lives and it is only getting better all of the time. During the years that my Mother was going through her most difficult times and dying, I wrote my first book regarding the Law of Attraction and our awareness of life. She read it. It was off for her, being she was very religious and considered herself a Catholic. I considered, and still do, myself a Catholic. Now I AM MORE THAN A CATHOLIC. Her understanding of me faded with her health, and my understanding of myself and then her, actually increased. She was apparently paving her way home and I noticed it happening. It was ok with me, although I hoped it was going to be easier than it really was. My family did not understand her behavior, only as I began to explain her past, did it even make any sense to them. They, especially the children, were having a difficult time adjusting to the knowledge that I had ever been abused by my parents and others in my childhood and youth. It was the least of my desires, to let them know what I had not mentioned, but it was intended to be out there in order to explain some behaviors my mom was insisting our involvement in. Maybe in so revealing the climate of my youth, they might have come to appreciate me more. I surely did. I think there was another explanation of my Mother's late in life behavior as a form of separation anxiety. Perhaps, if she would have died during any of the years, we all had together in "normalcy", polite respectfulness and great joy it would have been harder on us all to have to grieve her as a total loss. As it was, it was the right time for her to go to a better place. Amen.

My parents did not openly object to my love for this study of the Law of Attraction, and they only benefited by my implementing it into my life. So, although we saw and experienced things differently now that I was out of the "defaulted" and into the "intended", still there were what I might interpret as resistance to me and to Uri, as

## The Manifestation of the Lavender Scarf

he, as well as the children were right there enjoying the Law of Attraction Teachings.

On the path to applying the Law of Attraction into my life, I challenged its teaching as I requested what were some "things" that I wanted to manifest in the most absolute ways such that I would have no doubt of its validity. I learned a great deal in doing so. I found out that the Law of Attraction always is bringing to me what I ask. I ask, and it is given. That is the miracle of life. I have been provided many manifestations since I first learned I could manifest. The first deliberate requests for manifestation was a Peacock Feather to appear to me and the second deliberate manifestation was to have an opaque Lavender Scarf float into my hands, as if magical.

After describing the manifestation of the Peacock Feather, which I detailed in my first book, The Art of Appreciation, I also wrote the following regarding the Lavender Scarf:

> *"I have asked for other equally absurd testing manifestations that I am still wanting for. One is most vivid in my minds-eye and I requested it on the same day I requested the Peacock Feather and yet it is still at large. It is a scarf. I want a light lavender opaque scarf to appear to me, like a ruffle in the wind. It sounds like an image I might see in a TV commercial. It is but a trinket, but I see it clearly. It is months now and I am still wanting for it. If you see it send it my way, yet I know that I can allow it any*

## The Art of Appreciating MORE

moment now. It is something for me to look forward to. I wonder sometimes how and when it will appear and satisfy my senses with wonder. I imagine looking outside at the sky and watching this illusive scarf drift from nothingness into my sight. It can happen any moment now and as I want for it and visualize it and sense its energies afloat and sailing towards me even at this very second, I think. I hope I do not miss it. I hope I can really comprehend it. I want to welcome it into my experiences, yet I know also that it will appear when I am at a place in thought of accepting it as possible. It will feel appropriate. The Peacock Feather felt so appropriately placed when it happened.

I appreciate that I am on this way, which is the way I am required to go. I appreciate that sometimes it feels a bit longing. I appreciate that other times I find enough doubt to halt it's coming, although, I appreciate that doubt lacks reason. I appreciate that the waiting is connected to my wanting. Wanting out of the understanding-place where I believe it will be mine and that I will easily be able to allow it into my existence is a wonderful and comfortable feeling that time is independent of and is enjoyable. Wanting out of a place where I hold doubts that it can happen is an uncomfortable feeling that makes me experience waiting or reconsidering. Finding what I want is connected to finding what I trust and belief in that I can accept myself having and that feels very good. I appreciate the desire to allow. That seems simple enough; yet I wonder where the lavender scarf is and what

## The Manifestation of the Lavender Scarf

possibly can I do to retrain my thought to allow this lovely gentle scarf into my sight, into my world and from my allowing. I see the color of the pale lavender scarf often and I can feel the touch of it, and I know it is only "me" holding it off a little longer and I appreciate the journey. I am holding it off until I can accept and receive it while I am appreciative of the wait itself. It started out being a trivial scarf perhaps I didn't even really want it so much and now it is rather than a test of the Law of Attraction, which I know is working one hundred percent of the time, it is my own test. I am testing myself to become an allower.

What then is it this joy of manifesting from allowing that makes me want so much to be a better allower? At the end of a hard working day or better yet a softly woven day what can one say to the things that accumulated around; "Goodnight sweet light, see you in the morning dear bed, sleep tight big TV set, or I love you closet of clothes." No, it is not things that bring living-joy; it is the appreciation of these desired manifestations that enlighten-up the space between having and applying, owning and using, wanting and getting.[9]"

I see now that I was truly a stubborn person to have decided to ask for the depth of details I did. In a

---

[9] Quoted from The Art of Appreciation

reasonably short time, a couple of months, the Peacock Feather came to me in the most serene moment. I had been waiting, ever knowing that the Lavender Scarf was on its way when my mother began her last phase of transitioning into death, which, I no longer even believe possible. It is not dying we do when we transition; it is, in my understanding, a movement into a different plane of more living. She was doing what we know as dying here on Earth. It was perhaps; two years maybe even three years ago since, I put in my request for the Universe to give me that Lavender Scarf. I had put it on the back burner and I only occasionally even gave it a passing thought. It was important to me still and I knew it was on its way. I was becoming a more enlightened, even advanced student of the ways of the Law of Attraction. I, apparently, felt I was too busy helping my family cope with my mother and then her dying, to think it held a chance-in-heaven of appearing now. I was definitely in the midst of learning so much about hard things like unconditional love and letting what others do not offend me to be in a good position to accept a miracle. I was too busy for a manifestation to drop into my life.

Well, that is exactly what did happen. It was surreal and amazing. It was a miracle and a horror at the same time, seemingly perfectly timed into what I felt was an inconvenient time of my life, especially for The Law of Attraction to manifest into my life something I had placed high up in the almighty ivory tower of my beliefs. It was to be.

It was the day after our Mother passed away. At the time my, then only living, brother. Hughie and one of my two sisters, Eileen, came to spend time with her in her last days and now to participate in the funeral and bereavement process. My children were there too, as was

# The Manifestation of the Lavender Scarf

Uri and my father. All of us had read about my request for the Lavender Scarf to materialize when the book was distributed to all my closest family members and living siblings, a couple of years ago. We all present read it. We knew that I was waiting the Lavender Scarf to manifest from my ability to create, though we never discussed it much openly, just somewhat. I gave them each a copy of the book because I wanted them to know about my feelings and understand my happiness and hopes. And they all did read it. I knew that. I had asked and found ways to confirm their truth.

Yes, we all were there. Death brings remaining life together. We were anticipating the events of the next day, which was to be the first day of the wake at the funeral parlor. We decided to stay together after spending time taking care of the details of the burial and other traditional events, we were certain that mom wanted to happen. We all just wanted to go over to my parents place together. Dad was comfortable there and he was tired and lost in the changes going on to and within himself. Being there in their tiny little place where they lived for the past twenty-eight years, felt so different with her being permanently gone, physically. I felt that quote that Uri would make from time to time; "When you're dead, you're dead for a long time." She was dead now. It was over for her here. It was the first time I had been there since she departed.

As we were discussing the things that needed to be done, we all decided to go through the most apparent clutter of the build-up of collections of things that just happened over time and grew quicker in the last few years of our Mother's life. The place was filled with stuff. We emptied old stuff from the freezer and cleaned out the refrigerator of wasted food and active, no longer needed pain medicines that our Mother had been taking up until the last moment of her life. The guys had taken a great deal of old food and stuff to the garbage area. Everything needed to be gone through and we all felt a need to help our Father in the workload, as he was not as strong now, without her. He was also stronger for without her demands upon him. Mom would never allow us to fuss about cleaning or meddling into their private world of things. Believe me, they had their own world that no one else was allowed into ever.

Mom and Dad had known each other since they were 13 years old and had been married when they were young 21-year old and in love, now over 67 years ago. It was an interesting energy our Father held in him than did he when Mom was there to protect her private sanctuary of gone byes. We, the remaining-ones in his life, just wanted to help him where we could. We knew it would require stepping in further where we were ever allowed to go before. Mom was the gatekeeper and we did not resist her resistance of us entering into places that she did not want us to go, nor did Dad.

We were doing our best to mend the moments we had together into good deeds. Eileen and I decided to continue to clean up some of the old plastic left-over food containers, many Tupperware and the like, that were over gathered, as if hoarded and safe-guarded, yet, rarely used in perhaps years. This collection was amassed on top of a piece of furniture against the wall in the kitchen. Just a quick glance and I realized the same feelings that I had watching mom collect and gather plastic bags. She had plastic bags stored inside of other plastic bags, here and there; in her collection of costume

# *The Manifestation of the Lavender Scarf*

jewelry and in her collection of the quarters of the states and in many other places here and there. It seemed an old ladies' prerogative to save plastic bags and plastic storage containers were of a similar collection, even unto themselves. There were even plastic storage containers gathered into plastic used bags, which seemed so humorous to me.

Eileen and I noticed that there was an unsightly heap of plastic containers, most all "as old as the hills", I could hear from this familiar voice within that was not completely me, from what I felt and from what I knew my Mother to say, if she was there, and she was. Her presence was thick, even her smell lingered behind in this place of deep and long living. This voice that I could hear an echo of as my mom's, was even a bit desperate, which was something, I never felt before in my mother's vibrations. She was always so sure of herself, right or wrong. She had so many colloquialisms and idiosyncratic expressions that come to me out of habit of hearing from her, even though many I never could come to fully understand as they are dated out from a previous generation.

As we were quietly and carefully sifting through these old Tupperware stained treasures of Mom's, I noticed several pieces of the products had actually slipped behind the cabinet and were lodged seemingly permanently between the wall and the back side of the furniture. I reached reluctantly, eventually, deeply between the wall and the cabinet furniture and I pulled a piece up and out of there, and right along with it came flying up, stuck to a flawed-snagged-angle of the plastic was the Lavender Scarf, which took loose and flew up into the air. I had a very good hand on the plastic container and in the force of my grab and retrieval it released itself from the plastic and continued to fly-float up into the air briefly touching the ceiling and then gently, mystically, in slow motion it floated down and landed effortlessly into my hand.

During its flight I became aware, truly aware of it, as slow-motion took over time in my realizing more than a normal moment can naturally hold. I recognized it, as did Eileen, Hughie, Uri, my daughters, Tasha and Michelle, and my Dad, who was last to see it, yet benefited understanding it from my reaction to it. I squeaked like a child in fear out loud and gave a sigh and I then nearly collapsed at my knees and my sister quickly held me up in her support. We both look at each other and I said it. "Oh my God, it's the Lavender Scarf." "Yes", She agreed and as everyone in the room began to catch on to the event, I felt the presence of my Mother. She was handing me the Lavender Scarf as a confirmation of the goodness in the coming into my understanding of the Law of Attraction and much more. I felt, though it was not necessary, that my Mother was showing her approval for my understanding of The Great Law of Attraction and for my living a very happy life, despite her.

That's it! That is it! That is how the Lavender Scarf manifested. Imagine that!

I am so happy to have done this. Documenting this manifestation of the Lavender Scarf is important to me. Many a day have passed, and now years. There were days that I felt uncomfortable about my Mother interfering in my desired manifestation, especially after all the drama and contrasts she helped produce into my life and throughout my life of attempting to understand

*The Manifestation of the Lavender Scarf*

and, of course, appreciating my life experiences. Some days I felt undermined by her being in any way involved with my personal manifestation. This is my life, not hers. I sometimes felt the opposite and in great reverence for her, being still so close to the physical experience after just passing through to the other side, that she was reaching out to me, when I might best be available to receive her messages, perhaps she wanted to resolve some of the deep lifelong differences between us, perhaps to send her love, perhaps to make things a little better for me. I don't understand the why's of the ways it happened to manifest to me. Perhaps I was attempting to keep her nearer to me just a little longer. Perhaps it was all my love for her I was experiencing in those feelings. Perhaps it was about me more than her, I so hope. Perhaps it was to strengthen my siblings' and family members understanding of the great Law of Attraction and of how we manifest out of our intended love and desires. I do not know. I can only still feel amazed at the path of least resistance I am required to walk.

I am in no need to forgive my Mother or myself. I am in alignment to celebrate and realize. I know that what is happening at any time is good. I am aware of the Source of Wellbeing in my life, in your life and in everything in all life. There is no one to blame or suspect. I do not care to judge the timing of this event. It is all right with me. I am actually a very fortunate person to vibrate any manifestation of this degree of detail. I am the creator of my life experiences, as calm or dramatic as they might be. I do not want to analyze all the events in my life as I do this one. I just want peace in it. I want to trust my request to substantiate the truth in the Law of Attraction and the power of my Being. I want to know who I am and that I am worthy of greatness. I want to feel that it all is supposed to be. And so, it is.

# The Art of Appreciating MORE

I am so happy that my desired manifestations came to be, and I have come to appreciate something very great and worthy. Both those manifestations, the feather and the scarf, were requested to prove the validity of The Law of Attraction. I have given that up. There are better reasons to want to manifest a desire far more fun than proving The Law Attraction works. Now I am enabled to become more involved in what it is I want and then ask for it. Ask, Believe and Receive.

Recollecting the manifestation of the Lavender Scarf through my Mother and her death, also makes me come to my senses about how close the non-physicals are to us. I feel the presence of my Mother often and of others gone to "the other side". It is valuable to keep in touch with those over there because they can assist us, if we desire that help. They are always there loving our time with them when we acknowledge them as part of everything and nothing that we understand completely. We can come to trust more their love and great appreciation of us. Sometimes I smell my Mother and with numerous aromas and smells both likeable and not so, and then isn't that the way it was on many levels with my Mother. After all she lived the best she knew how to live and so too do I.

Thanks, Mom, for presenting the Lavender Scarf to me. It was a perfect time to do so, and I didn't miss it happening. And where is it now… it is inside a wooden box that contains my Mother's old perfume collection. I love that is smells like her as I open it to touch it and to smell Mom.

## Chapter 7 - Appreciations on Manifesting the Lavender Scarf

- ❖ I appreciate myself for realizing how to avoid drama and trouble as much as I did, as a child and still now.

- ❖ I appreciate the dreams I had, as a child to find a better life for myself.

- ❖ I appreciate realizing that Life is as good as I allow it to be and that my thoughts create my life experiences.

- ❖ I appreciate learning how to prioritize my thoughts into appreciations and to appreciate the rich huge contrasts that my Mother provided.

- ❖ I appreciate experiencing more Joy in Life, as I grow more capable of sharing my life with my husband, Uri.

- ❖ I appreciate that I have written about this manifestation, and, although it was complicated, I am happy that it is recorded.

- ❖ I appreciate my parents for taking care of me before I was able to do so for myself.

- ❖ I appreciate that all manifestations are perfectly timed.

- ❖ I appreciate myself as a Great Appreciator who trusts the LOA and who manifested the Lavender Scarf into my life.

*To see in another through loose coupling of self within the other, is like seeing water through the clear glass sidings, yet... if you want to see water put your eyes under water and open your eyelids up. In all matters, feel what you are experiencing and, in your feelings, choose your way. It is not a judgment; It is feeling.*

## Chapter 8  Jury Duty Judgment Day

It was a proper legal-while since last I was called to come into my county courthouse as a candidate for a jury position, again. The past few times, I spent that initial scheduled first day in the waiting hall with another hundred or more potential jurors. Once or twice, I was able to avoid going in at all, as my group number, which is randomly created, was released on the day otherwise I would have to appear in person. On those occasions I found this out the night before my scheduled date through a phone message, releasing me and others

# Jury Duty Judgment Day

in my group. Often when I did have to show up, I was not called in to participate at the next level of becoming a juror. That was always a relief. I had been a juror too on a couple of occasions over the past dozen or so years. Each time I served, I actually wanted it to go that way, because I wanted to have the experience of what the justice system felt like to participate in more directly than, say obeying the laws, voting or paying taxes.

This time, however, I knew it would be different. I felt it right away. Yes, I knew. I was called in to do my civic duty and I knew I always grow, in some way for the experience, however, I am more often let go than brought on the final jury, and, frankly, that is ok by me. I think most people want to avoid jury duty most of the time.

I felt so differently about getting my notice this time around. Right from the first thought about it, I felt that I could not serve, at all, ever again. I feel I cannot "judge" another, any longer, even given all the laws and circumstances staged in the courthouse to provide and encourage jurors to judge. My ability to judge anyone is diminishing as I become more experienced, and as I realize into my life more joy and happiness. I felt that I would just go along with the instructions to show up, since I did not see any box to mark to disqualify me. There is no box asking if I feel I can judge another person, fairly or unfairly. I cannot judge at all. I cannot even appreciate if there is a fair or unfair way to judge. Inside of myself, I knew I could not serve, and that concept was creating within me a need to comply clarity for myself and others. How much did this Law of Attraction mean to me and was it worthy enough to be seen by others?

*The Art of Appreciating MORE*

I also had no way of finding an easy way out through the first questions to become exempt through the package in the mail. So, I got put on schedule and here I was wondering, how I could experience what I apparently attracted into my life, such that I did not have to experience contrast and discomfort, while taking the path of least resistance.

I realized I had changed in so many wonderful ways since last I was called in to serve as a juror. I thought about the ramifications of a society that might stop judging each other, as I had mostly done with my life. I felt that a becoming non-judgmental society was to be a compassionate conscious society. What would that actually do to what I know as freedom and democracy, if anything? I was feeling a little confused about my impact upon society, not totally wanting to be an example to anyone out there, knowing intuitively that there just had to be a crack in which I could gracefully fall into and through without making a spectacle of myself. I was somehow serving my own purpose being here and involved with what could very well be indicators of a change in our governmental system. Afterall I exist, and so too do others like me who know the Law of Attraction and have a strongly growing desire to back away from government systems and politics. I know I am unique in today's society. Unique is just another way of giving title to the uncertain. It is not a vehicle in which one is non-conforming. I was feeling like I had arrived at knowing myself well enough to know I could not pretend to anyone that I could, in fact, judge another. I choose to avoid judging as much as I can.

I was feeling trapped in my social responsibility to be more "normal". Unique is pretty normal in these stages where society is a civil responsibility, on which we open the curtains to national cooperation. I am not a disobedient person. I am deliberately unable and unwilling to judge another. I know that others feel they can judge another. I cannot and do not want to. I feel that I used to be able to do this, based upon the laws of man and the land, now, I can separate my feelings and beliefs with the composite of the nation, although civility carries a great deal of rationality and composure to me.

I am not off in la la land. I care and keep the rules and laws. If someone else doesn't behave the way I want them to or others want them to or any organization or institution and government wants them to, I cannot stand behind that totally. It is a strange new world out here in this thought.

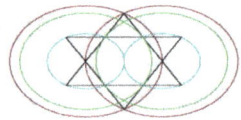

Why do I not want to judge others who are breaking the rules? The rules are clear. So, what is the issue?

I want to be cognizant about this myself, and perhaps as I continue to get more experience I will. I am uncertain about all the rules being so perfect to have. For now, I am not wanting to subject myself to testing my ability to judge another person in a courtroom or anyplace. It is so unenlightened for me to be placed into this position, and somewhere among my doubt and my absolute intention to do what is right for me and everyone else, I knew, I could not serve as a juror now in my understanding of what matters to me.

I have discovered many things about myself that I did not have the time or experience to know until now. Experience has been my greatest teacher and the longer I grow the more teachable, though discerning about what to learn, I become. I am also more in control of my experiences. In fact, sometimes I wonder if I can learn any other way but through experiences, although I know I do not have to experience everything. I can vicariously learn through other people's experiences and stories told, written, acted out or heard. That is from the perspective of this other person. And there is experience in reading stories and supposed facts. Often, I learn from observations, which is very helpful and sometimes I learn from imagination. Mostly and foremost, I learn through my personal experiences, and I know better than ever, that I cannot judge others. I am in the daily processes of willingly withholding judgement on myself, as well. I know that we are all living our lives in the way we are intended to do so. We do not really "make mistakes", we go through things that we attract onto ourselves, either knowingly or not. Mistaken previously to think myself a victim, I surrender to the love that carries me on. The wiser I become, especially in my knowledge of the Laws of the Universe, and especially in knowing of the Law of Attraction, the more deliberate my thoughts, feelings, emotions and actions become, usually. I cannot judge others for the place in life that they are living in now, nor can I judge another for their ability to understand everything that they are doing. We are each so unique that it is impossible to know what or why anyone is experiencing what they are or are not.

There is a major life-course-shift when in acceptance of what is as what is meant to be and for good in all directions of understanding what is happening. The most important knowing in that being so, is that it is endlessly and limitless in its happening. There are no stops or halts in the momentum of goodness and grace. There are no exceptions to this continuance occurrence. There is a passing away of doubt and there is an overstanding of self-choice. We are great and powerful designers and developers of our lives. We alone can come into that space of acceptance as a way of life; good and holy. I know this truth in my life, and I cannot pretend it is not so.

How then, can I become a meaningful juror, when I do not care what another is coming into learning in their experiences, nor do I desire to interfere? I am seeing others for the perfection of their journey, rather than in the, so-called, errors of their ways. I am unable to be a juror, if I cannot judge. I am not able to play the game of interference with anyone who I respect as my equal: different and equal.

It is perfectly ok with me that others are qualified to be judge and jury. I just cannot be that person.

Apparently, it is still my civic duty to show up for Jury Duty.

There I was. One of at least a hundred people sitting in a holding room waiting to be called, or in my case hoping to not be called into the next level of jurydom.

Nothing much outside of administrative and organizational information and instructions took place all morning. I rather enjoyed being there among so many of my community. People can be fun to watch. I liked that some people waited in a state of relaxation while others were busy on their phones texting and reading. Some came fully equipped with laptops or books to read or listen to on their earphones. I felt good being there and was finding a lot of good feelings sharing this civic duty with so many others willing to be part of this system.

Everyone was released for lunch and expected to return in an hour or so. I remained on the premises, and went to the cafeteria there, grabbed a bite to eat and then, decided to sit outside on this beautiful day, after taking a healthy walk around the pleasantly manicured courtyard. This was a special courtyard that was set aside for jurors and was inaccessible by the general public. Many other potential jurors were there and as I walked around a young lady, a fellow juror candidate decided to say hi and strike up a conversation with me.

She was so delightful. I love the community I lived in. She was so much a representative of the nice people who lived here, and she put in so much effort to do the right things in her life and it showed in a calm and true person who communicated well. I reflected on the thought that we had so much in common. We would have missed knowing each other if not for this gathering. I also knew we might never see each other again. I have to say in all honesty, I cherished this opportunity to meet this lady. I found her easy to listen to and to trust. She told me that she was already up in the next level of jury selection, in a courtroom on the second floor. She was so hoping to be passed on if it came her turn to be further evaluated. She was in a room with many other potential jurors still and along with the judge, the lawyers on both sides, the accused and victim were all present for the weeding out process of remaining jurors to obtain the finalized jury and the appropriate number of alternates. She was, so far, not questioned and was feeling that she might skirt the entire process, as they had all, but a few remaining to be chosen, albeit everyone in her group was expected to return after lunch until this was finalized.

She told me that many people had some pretty good excuses as to why they could not be a juror and they

## Jury Duty Judgment Day

were being politely excused. She said one person was excused because he felt there is a possibility that policemen are actually Lizard People from another planet. That got him excused and a great laughter from everyone in the room. My heart sank at her laughter and the thought of others laughing at him. I too started to chuckle and smile at that happening. I do not think that Lizard People are making up the police force, but I do not judge so whimsically the beliefs that others have. I feel that if a person believes in anything that the Universe can produce, then it is reasonable to also think that it can be produced. I felt that I might be laughed at if I had to be asked questions and if I had to answer with the one that kept swimming about in my head. All I could hear within myself is that "I cannot and do not want to be forced to judge another person." I told this lady that I did not think about Lizard People, although, I have heard others state that they believed them to exist. I thought it was a good idea to dismiss this person that feared Lizard People. I wondered how he would ever have determined any evidence about the police officer involved in that particular case to be a Lizard Person or not. I appreciated the humor of this excuse.

I told my new friend that I did not want to be questioned about my ability to be a juror. She told me again that she didn't want to be selected either. She had kids in school that she wanted to be there when they came home. She said that she and her husband and the kids too, give up a lot of money that she is not working and a stay-at-home mother, and for jury duty to not make that a valid enough reason to let her off, she only wished she had a belief in something so off the wall as Lizard Policemen. She then asked me why I did not want to judge anyone who is being brought before the court.

I then gave her what felt like a Law of Attraction 101 class. I spoke about the way I understand the universal laws in general and that what I think about, comes about. I said I really did not want to focus upon the details of a court case, never-the-less have to involve myself in the judgment of right or wrong about what another Human Being was experiencing, with several potential versions of it presented to think even harder, and more about. I told her what was going to be the same speech I would later have to teach to the room I was going to be called by others; the judge and the lawyers, to judge me in on my determined inability to judge others. It was so ironic.

After a while, she sighed out of her something that sounded like compassion and said, "Oh that is going to be hard for you to do. I hope it doesn't come to that for you. Others will see it as you are saying whatever you think will get you off." I told her I was being honest. I do not ever want to be on a jury ever again. I had grown up and into someone who understands, not only the laws of the universe in association with the laws of man, but also, I know who I am. I am not someone who really cares about what others think about me, because I do know who I am.

We heard our return bell ring out lunchtime as over. She wished me luck and I her. She closed into me and hugged me which surprised me just a little as I felt we had expressed some strong and gentle feelings that strengthen connections quickly. It was a very pleasant encounter. Then off we went. I never saw her again. I felt the vibrations of a momentum that had to play its course, although at other times of my life I might have denied myself those feelings of knowing what was going to happen if I kept in sync with my current thoughts. With her, I had the opportunity of sort of practicing out

## Jury Duty Judgment Day

my words that would have to come out of me if asked. The more I thought and spoke of it, the more I came to accept that it was to happen. I had put too much thought into action about this and for reasons, above and beyond my comprehension, I knew I'd be asked to speak out and loudly about my beliefs. I felt nervous and destined. Therefore, I was not surprised, just wishing I knew better how to change my vibrations to let me go home, when right then my name was called along with forty-nine others.

We all packed up and had ten minutes to find ourselves waiting outside of a courthouse room on the third floor. I looked around and still there were over a hundred people who were probably not going to have to get to this level of juror indoctrination that I was floating off to the third-floor in. I decided to take the staircase. I was feeling something happening. I was strangely feeling that the Universe and the Society were wanting me to qualify myself as a Law of Attraction Teacher. I was prepared. I began thinking a little differently, instead of worrying about what I might say or do, letting go of any potential to teach, sensing a Voice Within me wanting to assist, I stopped my struggle with the interactions that may occur. I let down my concerns. I turned a corner in my mind. I released the outcome as a goal. I was now flying high emotionally, recognizing my power to be was substantial. My thoughts were good and respectable. The results of my thoughts are always better than I could even predict. I was available to allow. I felt so good with myself. I trusted my path and now saw this not as an opportunity or a forced experience. I felt it was all an adventure in which I became a powerful creator. I was smiling and happy as I took my place, somehow already knowing the outcome.

*The Art of Appreciating MORE*

And low and behold in the time it takes to be one of the last to be questioned, I was asked to come forth and the standard questions were asked, and I answered them appropriately finding myself in agreement. Then all questions stopped and the last one, for me, was asked.

"Did I have anything to add to this conversation that might alter my being chosen?"

I said "Yes!".

In that moment I felt all lights of life in the room focus upon me and I totally understood my place of light and love. My body felt itself in a strength and a glow softer than a thought, at the same time. It felt like magic. It was my turn to let others recognize my unique feelings that I knew everyone had someplace within them as well. I was as some might say, In the Vortex, feeling invincible, totally aware, shining and bright, a Lightworker of love and joy, a spirit of health and vitality, intelligence and wisdom, a force to be noticed well, and inside that mix of glorious feelings, I was also an example. I knew myself well there in that moment. I knew that one good thought, one honest basic truth, one unstoppable fact of love, was the strength of civilizations. One good thought, such as I was having, feeling and actualizing was far more powerful than many, many negative ones. I contained a powerhouse of joy and I knew the outcome was perfectly timed into my life and into the lives of all else who were present. My message was valuable and important to me and to others, not that that really mattered to me, it was though that it was true. Truer than anything else going on in that room. My love-light was to be shown, it was glowing brightly already, and I knew all I ever needed in that very moment. I was very confident and certain. I knew the results before I spoke a single word. Yes, was enough and it was all a done deal before uttering anything else. Any words from then on were just to manifest acknowledgement. My thoughts create my reality. I also knew that good begets goodness. I appreciated my essence, and everything opened up into a love that filled the room instantly and entered everyone's hearts. It was magic and I was creating it. That felt very good. I tingled with absolute confidence, self-appreciation and joy. I was sure, absolutely, sure. Everyone in that room now, was going to hear something honorable enough to haul me into this scenario, which now became a beautiful platform of timeliness and goodness. I was very comfortable. I had all my composure, and I was in the moment of now, watching others await my mind, heart and spirit to overflow. My vibrational resonance was overflowing. I felt amazingly well. It was my opportunity to find that many others would resonate with me. I knew this already. I was ready and so too they were ready. This I knew intuitively. I knew that many people felt the same feelings and didn't think to state them out loud. We often avoid bringing feeling that are not spoken about forward. It was what I had grown to be. I was someone mindful.

I looked at the judge directly and said;

"I cannot nor do I desire to judge anyone at this point in my life. I, therefore, request to be dismissed."

The judge, a woman of my age, looked at me and said in a very sweet almost too soft voice that was clear and almost as comforting as a poem;

"I understand exactly where you are coming from. I only wish I did not have to judge others. You are dismissed. Thank you."

I smiled agreeingly with her, gathered up myself and walked out of that courtroom as gracefully and quietly as possible, wanting for the energies I had to come along with me as it was apparent there was a lot more of life in front of me to enjoy and I felt this day was reopened to me, as the experience taught me much. The relief was exhilarating. Looking back, I could actually see that the judge understood. Her posture and vibrations spoke volumes. I recognized a life form in her demeanor that ached for the Freedom I pronounced as mine, knowing it is hers too. I thought in a flash, that she experiences this feeling often and was familiar with its truth. She will soon retire out of this business and all these experiences will assist her in joy. Experience is a great teacher. I chose the Freedom to judge not. Judging is something I play with all day long in many ways and for many things. This Judge was part of the system and totally financially engaged in the responsibilities of judging. It was her profession. I felt a relief and an instant growth. What grew in me? I grew instantly realizing, again and stronger, that one benefits from normalizing opinions. In other words, avoiding judgement, while probably even more importantly, I realized that freedom is what I hang my hat on, it is my anchor, so to speak. Judging is part of this experience, or the lack of judging, however, it is the freedom to judge or not that was the cornerstone of the joy I was feeling. I love finding my freedom in new ways. I love seeing the power of others Freedom too. We all have equal Freedom. Long before we were born, we always knew that Freedom is the basis of our Life. All of our lives. I appreciate that so much.

I knew that I had achieved a harmony with my desires and I additionally permitted that frequency to come to me, through me. I gained a great wave of satisfaction for this moment coming about having known it was to become. In the experience, I found an abundance of good feelings and I was then at a very positive emotional place from which I could actually form new desires. Success is like that and success is a daily recognition of self-capabilities. I wanted to savor the moment. I was feeling quite good.

Do not judge, least ye be judged. Create from your soul of equality. Freedom is a true and absolute birthright for everyone, and when you utilize your freedom, you are at peace with yourself which is nice enough. Also, when behaving in your absolute trust in freedom you feel very good and life is easily going your way. It feels good to feel good. Feeling good for the little things is as perfect as feeling good about the things that feel big. There is little place and rarely temptation in my life for judging others, and I do not feel much impact by the judging of others upon me. I am secure in my life standings, right now, and hopefully for most of my time remaining of my Earthly journey.

There are spaces and places in my life where I judge seemingly appropriately, and there are places and times when I feel the judgement of others upon me. For example, judging if something is comfortable or good for me, is a personal preference. I am uncertain when personal preferences turn into judgements, although the relationship is fairly semantic and vague. When it feels good to judge, then it's probably a personal preference. We all can feel when judgement is clouding the situation. Now though, I know to see things in my softer light and diffuse others their vibration as influential and in so doing I project back a field of equality that holds strength for me to be wise in my options to teach equality off of the judging experience rather than to avoid the conflict. I choose wisely where I place my attention and have found that unless someone is asking me why I am feeling and stating what I do, I can trust that they are searching other reasonings. I am not here to change everything in this world and so I opt out of opinion on political issues, including the manner in which our government works out its understanding of problems. I can agree with recognizing that all politics is somewhat debatable in its search to fix what might not actually be broken.

I was listening to a local streaming intake-outtake over the internet of court hearings and those coming forth were all illegal aliens from our southern border with moving-driving, license, or vehicle registration tickets. Living in The Villages in Florida at the time, my receiver, which was a computer, found this government broadcast in a small rural area near the Mexico – United States boarder. I was so impressed with the clarity and compassion the judge, incidentally another woman approximately my experienced age, was dismissing the violators with allowance and explanation. That was a good example of changes in our government and its court of law. We are all so similar and have so much in common and on that I judge all people as perfect.

Coming up to date with the climate of today. It is Covid inflicted, protest resulted, confusion times for many people. With all that is going on I reflect upon the experience of that day I escaped Jury Duty. I felt so good to have had the freedom to express my desires to not judge. It was wonderful that I was respected for my choice to not judge. I am so happy for the freedom to stand up and be counted as someone in this amazing country who doesn't want to judge others. I am sincere about it too. I want to appreciate people for who they are not for why they are. I think that when I get into thinking about why people behave differently than I do, I can get mixed up in trying to figure them out, when, in fact, there but for the grace of God go I.

I do recognize particular things very quickly about others. It is one of my Innate Gifts. I have a strong and fairly accurate sense of understanding regarding other's self-appreciation and worthiness. And I can quickly detect when someone misses that their Basis of Life is Freedom. All those aspects of self are fundamental towards happiness and fulfillment.

There is another thing that I truly understand within myself that I see many others lack knowing about themselves. It is one of the most valuable things to know about self and it is useless if you think it only applies to you. One cannot be possessive with it, for it requires a truth that resonates with everyone for it to be universally utilized, although only you are the enabler. It is substantiated on the individual basis and cannot be forced into knowing. It has to be totally felt as real and it needs a belief to withstand within self. It is absolute, if known or not known, though I think that all people know it at times. It is intended to be a constant knowing about oneself and others. It is best known, than missed. We are intended to be here in this knowingness, so when you can, promote it for yourself and for others. People mouth it more than mean it. Many have not been taught it. I know I was not really taught it in the direct formal sense, although I always had a great deal of understanding of it without being taught. I have found this one thing is a treasure and with it I am ever a better person. In fact, with this knowledge I am enabled to be whoever I want to be, to do whatever I want to do and to feel a confidence that sets me in a special place in life. It is a magic that applies to everyone. It is that we are all created equal. Unique, and, absolutely equal.

When equality is a given in your life, judgement is unrequired and, in fact, counter to its meaning. One cannot judge another and actually appreciate equality. In fact, there are many negative things that one cannot even think about if one believes in equality. Equality defines a true existence rather than balance between everyone, although not all people understand that in order to be treated as an equal, you must feel that equality is exactly that… it is equality. It is not sometimes you are equal to each one another and other times not. Equality applies one hundred percent of the time. There are no exceptions to the definition of equality regardless of your previous teachings; nationally, religiously, institutionally, governmentally, generationally, culturally, geographically, conveniently, genderly, generally or even sometimes intuitively. Many people will have to unlearn in order to relearn. That is not to say we cannot or should not judge others for their actions specifically that bring harm to another or to anything. Equality isn't destructive. It in fact, cannot be practiced in the negative or inequality that applies to misdeeds. Equality is a given. We either know it or not. We either feel it or not. We are equals. We are all equal to each other. Different and equal. What do you feel? Do you feel equal to everyone? I do!

It is the greatest stabilizer for me. I intuitively and immediately respect everyone as an equal. We all are equally available to feeling our equality with everyone too. It is not common for people to know. The simplest of things to know. The purest of things to know. Still some or rather many people are unable to grasp this concept effectively. It's implausible for me to think equality out of existence. I am not me if I am not equal to everyone else. It is an impossibility to think about. In truth, I recognize others do not know that they are equal to everyone. No one is better equipped to be human. We are all equals.

*Jury Duty Judgment Day*

Without judgement, it is easy to see. If we could help others to see their own equality and believe in it, we would have an entirely different world. Imagine living where everyone knew, without a doubt, that they and everyone else are absolutely equal.

What then would be the need for governments or punishments if we all recognized our own and then others their own equality. I do not even think governments would be needed any longer. We would each recognize that we all have equal opportunities. Not the way it is now, where when I hear those words, I think, well, what is being given to someone who is unequal, or rather, someone who believes that are not equal or is treated as an unequal by others. You cannot force others into knowing their equality or stop thinking they are superior. What opportunity is not considered equal to all? That is the problem. We actually have a society that believes they are not equals to all. And there is probably a majority of people, albeit a shrinking number, who think they are either more or less than another. For what reasons does this exist? I have to wonder!

Is it because we are not taught equality and that inequality seems to thrive far longer than it should because we are an awakening people who are growing a consciousness? All being equal, we each can only be the creators of our own reality of equality. Once equality is a strong component of you, you will adjust to your greatness in ways that are probably impossible to write about. When you believe in equality, you are seen as an equal. If you do not know yourself as equal, you cannot see others as your equal.

Maybe one reason inequality exists and is so overlooked by many as inappropriate, is because some people mistake the idea of confidence with being superior. That might well be what some think. I do not know what others are thinking to understand why they are thinking that way, although there are apparent indicators. It's complicated in ways and it is as simple as pie. Knowing personal equality changes everything. We are all created equal, are more than words to state, they are a space of existence. There is no almost equal. There is only absolute equality. There is not privilege as being an inequality, for privilege only exist if inequality is believed in. There is only equality for everyone. If needed; be that change.

Presume for now that equality was a universally known given. It was the obvious statement of life. We all knew it to be exactly that. We recognize that we are all individuals. We realized that whatever makes us individuals are all equally valuable to each other. That is true too. We are all here to love one another. We are all here to love ourselves and to love one another. Saying you are equal to everyone else is like saying I am a Human Being, all Human Beings are created equal.

Why is that so hard for so many people to know. I so love seeing more join in the chorus of equality. For it is a beautiful song to hear sung. I am though always going to know that I am equal to everyone and that everyone is equal to me. That makes a lot of difference.

This might meet with a lot of controversy. I have to be astute and brave enough to say it. Someone has to and it has to be said. More importantly it should be thought about rather than reacted to. All the protestors who yell of inequalities only promote more inequalities. Why can I say that with such convictions of truth, because, when you think yourself unequal you are. When you demand equality, it cannot come. It is time to stop the belief of inequality and to start living the truth of equality. Instead of shouting demands to create equality, learn to respect the equality in self and in all that others are too. One cannot become less equal in order to make some who thinks they are less equal become equal. And it is a lesser attempt to think for superiority, for in so wanting, more inequality becomes reality.

So, what can be done?

Trust in self as an equal to everyone that was, is or will come into your life and enjoy the wonder. Be the change you want to see in this world. If you want equality, and of course you should want equality, the kind of equality that changes the world around us all, then know your own equality first and respect others for their equality.

What would happen if we each other understood our true equality? A lot would happen. Imagine that led to a lot less judgement of self and others. The comparison of equality eliminates the status of better than or less than.

No need to judge each other when equality rules our lives. And then what, what would we all be doing without judgements and thoughts of comparisons of equality? I think, no, I know a lot of good would happen. We would collaborate more, discover more, invent more, create more, and more and more.

I beg you to find that place of equality in your heart and soul and allow us all to expand together. In the awareness, when people do things together within the state of equality, the path and the goal are truly amazing. It is worth the focus. This is the path.

What do you envision universally known and practiced equality would look like? It would look like love. It would

## The Art of Appreciating MORE

bring to the hearts of everyone the intention of good. It would find kindness everywhere and in everyone. Everyone would treat each other as they want to be treated. This is a knowing of goodness as deep as the sea and as wide as the skies. Everyone has heard that we should love one another as we love ourselves. Then why, with this simple thought are people unwilling to believe in it? To me that is a big mystery. We are ready to take up this thought and put it into our hearts as a common understanding, as is Monday the day after Sunday. If we can all agree on a day of the week, which in reality is totally meaningless, then why has it been, until now, so difficult to accept equality for everyone. It only really starts with thinking yourself an equal.

The issue of past inequality and inequities arise in many thoughtful minds and hearts. This is a good stabilizing momentum that may, indeed be required to accelerate equality. Yet it will soon pass. In the compassionate hearts of consciousness, equity can play a part of balancing the results faster. It is also a part of the celebration of becoming aware of equality. Being generous is a kindness and while we transition in humanity into societies that recognizes true equality, being equitable is a goodness. It will be less required once balances are acquired. What a wonderful party we are invited to attend. Creating Equality. A small world it would become in the thought of this harmony. So many things would change. It would be a huge shift. I feel it coming.

And so, it is.

*Jury Duty Judgment Day*

## Chapter Eight- Appreciations on Judgement & Equality

- ❖ I appreciate that we have an amazing government structure and I love the people of the United States of America and of the Earth Globally.

- ❖ I appreciate all Human Beings are Free to judge or not.

- ❖ I appreciate my ability to judge anyone is diminishing or discriminating softer as I get more experience, while I realize into my life more joy and happiness.

- ❖ I appreciate that I am deliberately disabling myself to judge others.

- ❖ I appreciate that experience has been my greatest teacher and the longer I grow the more teachable I am, yet the more discerning about what to learn.

- ❖ I appreciate with mindful conscious experience there is a fading of doubt, a creating of more self-confidence, and an overstanding of my freedom of self-choice and self-judgement.

- ❖ I appreciate the absolute knowing that we all are equals while different and unique by perfect complex design from pure love and inclusion.

- ❖ I appreciate in recognizing good conditions and fortune one can in confidence build upon more good conditions and fortune.

- ❖ I appreciate that in a world of absolute honored equality, we all thrive.

*The Art of Appreciating MORE*

*Appreciating Desires*

*There is a hunger in my heart that loves to be fed.*

## Chapter 9  Appreciating Is a Tool

What are any of us without our desires?

Even a vase desires to be filled of the water for the rose.

I notice myself and others trying to do this thing or another thing seemingly in pursuit of obtaining desires. If we only knew what our desires actually were, we could better serve the moment in easier chase. It seems I may

## Appreciating Is a Tool

not always know what I want. Prioritizing what seems to be my top desires can be cloudy as seemingly I want a lot of things. And I want a lot of different things. Intuitively, I know my desires know each other and the Universe is establishing a living ability to harmonize and even build one desire upon another in order to create them. I might be uncertain about my desires versus my needs. I may resist desires for lack of their possibility or probability. I admit, that actually knowing which are my worthwhile desires, is confusing at times. I feel the connection between my ideas and my desires.

### What do you desire?

If you can answer that without the lesser values of not having what you want, then you can, in a timely way, create what you want into your reality.

I desire to be happy, healthy, wealthy, worthy and wise. A world of things fit under that umbrella. It is something like a mantra to me now. Uri and I toast and click our morning hot tea by both saying these words together, "I am happy, healthy, wealthy, worthy and wise.". Each one of those words as our desires fit like five fingers fit a hand. Each digit strengthens the group of fingers. Each finger has its own purpose. All work together. Likewise, with happiness, health, wealth, worthiness and wisdom. They fit together and form something very complete.

I feel that desires are golden nuggets that shine brightly into our lives with an insistent love continuously forming from time unknown. I cannot overstate this concept of desires as cooperatively growing overtime, becoming, as such, clearer and more understood within a haughtiness of longing. Initially, the more general I am about my desires, the more specifically I can see into my desires. This is how I formulate understanding of my desires. In *"The Art of Appreciation Book"* it is said like this and it still makes me feel good about ways to think about desires;

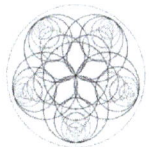

> *'Desire's sparkles are analogous to brilliant night-stars pirouetting in a perfect effortless ballet through a dimension unseen but familiar in the heart. They are each crystal-clear points-of-light and all contain multifaceted complexities that integrate precisely with ALL else. Desires are, of course, always personally agreed-upon thoughts and are collectively innumerable and immeasurable and reside in the incomprehensive shared-space of what is "total life". . . Desire clarifies the course of life with the thrill of creating. Desires accumulate and clarity becomes what converts them into manifested reality.'*

I want and I get. I see this way with it and then I feel diverted from it as quickly. I give and I take. Desires are

## Appreciating Is a Tool

like personal gifts that develop upon the roots of an innate capability to utilize that which comes into our lives for the best intention. I often think of desires as personal and even intimate, but is that really so? They are the becoming of self-preservation and the accumulation of progressive changes. We think desires feel good to be fulfilled, only to discover that it was always the finding of what we wanted that thrilled. This is often expressed within this type of familiar statement;

> *'It is not the goal that is most important;*
> *it is the journey and how we react,*
> *accept, experience, enjoy and expand*
> *within and from it.'*

It is good to knowingly seek and obtain desires. Mostly in so doing, it amazes oneself with a new desire, usually connected to an often-recent fulfilled desire or associated with a greater choice since a fulfilled desire shown light on confidence and stimulated larger dreams.

In my pursuit for happiness, which is an ongoing desire, I choose to enjoy the attractions that trend my desires into specific directions. I have been listing my desires out too. It sounds easier than it actually turns out to be. Try to list what are your desires. I also list what are those things that make me happy. That is also a very thought-provoking exercise. The first ten or so things that make me happy and then the top ten or so things that I desire seem to flow out of me. Once I record the top-level items of things I desire and things that make me happy, there is often a direct line between them. I might desire a house in the country and I also feel happy in nature. The ability to think about things that matter to me also attracts them into my life. That is Law.

## The Art of Appreciating MORE

Desires can be very personal initially, and then when really looked at there are components to them that fall into a universal goodness. If you desire anything that causes harm to another, it is not a desire at all, it is a jealousy or some form of negativity, at the least. Any jealousy that takes from another is restricting self-development and joy. Desires should always feel good, if you feel that they are allowable or obtainable. If you do not feel the ability to have what you think you desire, then it is not a true desire. One must believe in the ability to have what you want. One cannot believe in the ability to have what you do not want. If you do not believe in your desires, then they are unreal, and you will never obtain them. For example, it would not serve me well to desire to be a famous basketball player. I know that that could never be a true desire. Permit yourself to discover your true desires. I promise you they will be better than becoming a famous basketball player.

Looking at what others have succeeded at is a way to know options. Wanting what another is or has, is not the same as desiring for and from self what is absolutely right and perfect for you. For; in our equality we all can create what is really best for us. Focus upon the trueness of obtaining desires and allow yourself to grow confidence in your direction. You can create what you want. It is tons easier to first know what you really desire and then trusting it into existence. That is a much easier way to live a life, rather than just floating along from one quasi-desire to the next without requesting from within yourself real clarity. When you just "do not know what you want", put it away for a while, allow some maturity to come into a more solid footing. Giving things of uncertainty time to settle into a more solid desire, is a much better idea than to go seeking after something uncertain and time is saved. Desires by nature are living in the shadows of details

*Appreciating Is a Tool*

initially, so appreciate the journey and watch for more solid impressions to surface. Following after what is unwarranted to pursue is time consuming. Being in agreement with your desires does not contain drama; compromise does. It is a worthy adventure to look for the kindness in self and reflect that off yourself and certainly kind options come to you. It is easier to be this one of deep experiences, because you can say yes to what feels right and appreciate your choices are easily won rather than fought for. You obtain confidence by being confident. Be willing, therefore, to be even more confident.

> *It is quieter in tomorrow to know yourself today.*
> *It is better to smile and let drama slip away.*

If you have found yourself desiring impracticalities, rescope your inner truth and be honest with yourself. Thinking big desires is as easy as thinking small ones. As it is with manifestations, which desires become, it is a deep personal honesty that brings about what you desire; little or big. Be good to yourself, think big, and become all that you can become. Desire from the heart and you will sense the goodness and purity in your desires. Kindness applied into all facets of life is what fuels individual and massive changes that are happening already in yourself and in our society. Clarify your desires, then collect them and treasure them as priceless jewels that shine as brightly as the stars in a clear night's sky.

Uri and I conducted an experiment and let me tell you about it. We almost daily sit down, journal and pen in hand, and write out our "Appreciations". As explained in *The Art of Appreciation Book,* we developed particular ways in which we could expand better understanding about ourselves and each other by simply sharing our

Appreciations with each other after they were written down. We began to play with our types of Appreciations by focusing upon what we wanted most to appreciate, because it felt very good to be more specific sometimes and it actually began to be noticed that the more, we appreciated something the more relative things to that came into our lives. Appreciations begat Appreciations.

In our further experimenting, we decided to be more pro-active about our Appreciation subjects and at some point, we decided to Appreciate what we wanted, what we desired. That may sound like an easy thing to do, but we were quickly noticing that it was different and more interesting than we thought it ever could be. The reason it seemed challenging was because we didn't really know what we wanted. We decided to categorize our Appreciations regarding our desires and still we were only finding ourselves in the high level of contents about our desires. We pursued our categorizing and then started to link particular Appreciations to desires that were accomplished and ones that were new and wondrous. We were wanting to evolve our thoughts into clarity about our desires. The more we recategorized our Appreciations into types of desires, the closer we got to really finding our true desires. That was very good for us, because our Appreciations were sometimes too vague to apply a lot of focus into. I would like at this time to demonstrate the potential of using Appreciations to discover actual desires. I noticed that many of us have more of an understanding of what we do not want more than what we actually know what we do want. That is okay, initially. In the process of creating Appreciations, since Appreciations, by definition are positive statements, the results were rapidly becoming expressions of desires rather than ideas about what we dreamt about creating with doubt involved. When appreciating our statements boil down to complete

# Appreciating Is a Tool

directional statements or mantras, we have a strong believe in their possibility, which is a good place to be to effectively manifest.

I will create some Appreciations about what I would appreciate coming into my life within the next month or two. After I create a list of Appreciations, whatever comes to mind knowing, of course, they are all positive, I will then categorize them, looking at the chart, first as an Inside Self Appreciation (something within me) or Outside Self Appreciation (anything that is in the world outside of me.). After that I will put all the associations that seem appropriate to that Appreciation listed under it.

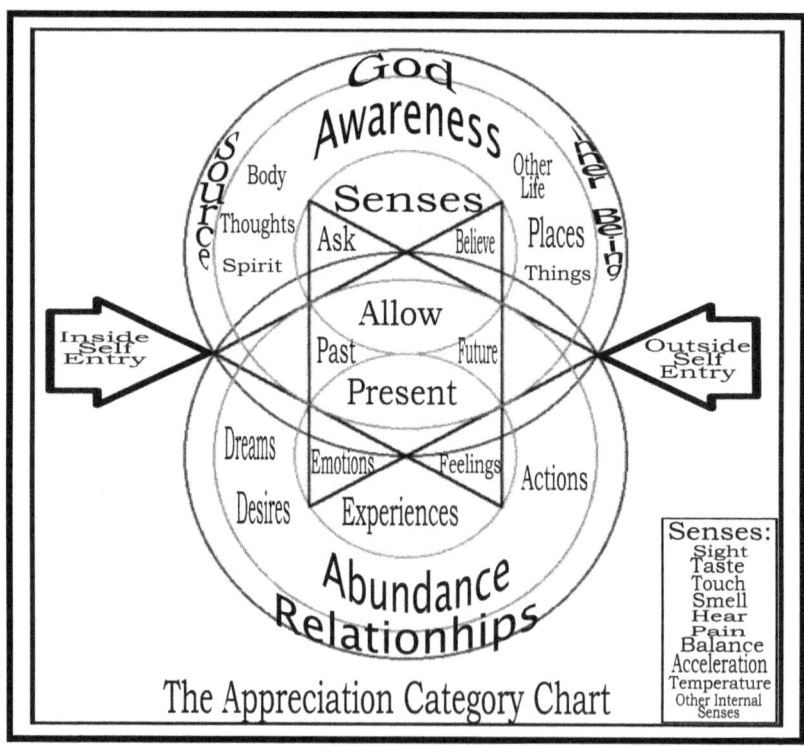

The Appreciation Category Chart

*The Art of Appreciating MORE*

1. I appreciate that the work on the new upgraded water system will be complete, the trimming of several of the trees will be finished and wood will be stacked up for winter firewood.

<u>Outside Self Entry</u>
Place, Things, Actions

2. I appreciate that I will have completed more aspects of the book to be published soon.

<u>Outside Self Entry</u>
Actions, Future, Things

3. I appreciate my work focusing on Appreciations as a tool, a guide, a reliable practice to improve emotions and thoughts, as a framework to improve emotional status, and even as a way to learn more about myself

Inside Self Entry
Dreams, Desires, Actions, Awareness, Emotions, Feelings, Thoughts, Experiences

4. I appreciate my continued good communications with my daughters, Natasha and Michelle and their partners.

<u>Outside Self Entry</u>
Relationships, actions, present, past, future

5. I appreciate getting to know our new little castle house better.

<u>Outside Self Entry</u>
Allow, Place, Things, Experiences

6. I appreciate finding life in the country is so nice and welcoming

<u>Outside Self Entry</u>
Thoughts, Allow, Places, Feelings, Emotions, Senses

7. I appreciate the curtain choices to help keep the house warmer during the upcoming late autumn and nearing winter months.

<u>Outside Self Entry</u>
Things, Desires, Future

8. I Appreciate that my husband and I are continuing to eat healthy foods that satisfy and help us have more energy and good health.

<u>Outside Self Entry</u>
Things, Feelings, Experiences, Future, Present, Past, Actions, Abundance, Other Life, Body

9. I appreciate the choices we are making regarding the future landscaping, gardens and buildings on our property.

<u>Outside Self Entry</u>
Places, Things, Future, Dreams, Actions, Abundance

10. I appreciate feeling happiness and increases in spiritual growth and joy.

Inside Self Entry
Senses, Source, Awareness, God, Allow, Abundance, Experience, Feelings, Emotions. Spirit, Thoughts, Believe

That is my first step. Writing down what naturally came to me on the day I created those Appreciation Statements above and then using that chart I come to know which ones were Outside Self Entries and Inside Self Entries.

I seem to appreciate what is outside of myself more than what is inside of myself, or rather what is "me". I've known this happens even after years of creating Appreciations. It happens to me and it happens to everyone I know. We seemingly are better at appreciating things outside of us than we appreciate ourselves. I have been trying to appreciate myself more over the years, and still, it feels a little like conceded or self-occupied. I am certain that it feels off to see all my goodness and to think of myself too highly. That's what we are all or mostly all doing. We are finding it uncomfortable to appreciate ourselves. That is so off.

Really, if we could appreciate ourselves more, we could believe in ourselves more, and we could manifest more, and we could be happier. That being said, I've come to appreciate myself more than ever before now. Interestingly self-appreciating has been simultaneously mirrored with the feelings of increasing my compassionate consciousness. That is good. This compassion partners within my persona and I release more warmth and kindness. I love these two factors connecting as such. It is very true that I believe in myself more and that, yup, I manifest more and faster, and, I will say, I am ever more increasingly happy, and I care about others more as a result. In fact, my happiness is more joyful and complete, as it is more complicate with goodness and love for others. So why is it still so difficult to go for it and appreciate myself more easily.

I thought perhaps if I looked at the categories of things that my chart could help me to see somethings I was missing in the attempt to improve. I noticed I hardly ever appreciate my Inner Being. That was a surprise to me because I appreciate my Inner Being very much. After nearly every daily Appreciation Session I do, usually with Uri, after we finish writing a page of Appreciations, sometimes with great intentional focus, other times at random, we do something else. We enter a meditation state. We have combined our Appreciation Sessions with a special time that we relax into a meditative space where we continue to write from what we have both come to know as our InnerVoice. We read our Appreciations to each other and that would have been enough to really assist us in numerous ways to improve our relationship with each other and to get to know ourselves better. And so, it was for years. That was until I started to feel a strong desire to write from this special place Within. It was pretty amazing that my InnerVoice was so informative and loving in so many ways. We both, totally, enjoyed this new addition to our Appreciation Sessions.

## *Appreciating Is a Tool*

It was a self-channeling. It was happening to me especially when I wrote. I had been experiencing it while I wrote The Art of Appreciation Book too. And when I sat alone and journaled appreciations, I would feel that a strength Within me would write after I was finished with my initial thoughts and writings. The messages were always encouraging and uplifting. They were loving and generously inspirational. They were full of praise and inciteful directions. I was so excited with these communications. It is amazing that the words that I wrote I sometimes had to look up in the dictionary to understand. I didn't even know the meaning of some of the words. I knew it was something provided to me that was actually more intelligent and definitely wiser than I was or that I was aware of about my thoughts. This Voice Within was a higher spirit. It was a huge Beingness. Is all I can say that feels right. It was also of varying sizes and levels. If I closed my eyes, I still wrote, just sloppier. I was there and not there at the same time. I asked; "What are you?" It told me a lot of different definitions of itself. I asked; "What is your name." I've asked that question many times again and again. The answer is always the same. It says, "I am that which has no name."

I have been so blessed to open up to this Voice Within. It has changed my life in simple and profound ways. I have learned how to connect quickly with this Voice, and I know it is always available to me. It makes me understand that I am never alone. It teaches kindness toward self and others. It is kindness toward me. It is always there being involved with my desires and pursuits. I am ever amazed at how well it knows me, often I feel better than I know myself. It reasons with me and I converse with it. I can feel it ever there. You would think the world revolves around me with all the attention I can receive from this InnerVoice. It is not like that though. It is never intrusive and always there. It never intrudes upon me or my thinking ideas or emotions. It is always available like a best friend is available and though I have never had a better best friend than my InnerVoice. It loves me in a powerful way. I know so much more about myself because of its presence. I also know it was always present and always will be there for me. It is part of the features of Life for everyone. We all have the ability to request our InnerVoice to be there and commune with us. All it takes is allowing.

I've been enjoying this connection for a few years and then Uri started to make his connection too. I encouraged him to do so after writing his Appreciations, and he was reluctant to do so. One day, we were on a road trip and had scheduled many miles to go when we came to that time of the day when we wanted to create some Appreciations. Since we were in the car, I recommended that we take turns by out loud saying one Appreciation and then alternating between us. It was going really well. The Appreciations on the road were new and refreshing. There was so much to appreciate. We traveled for miles and miles taking turns and loving the uplift it was yielding. We appreciated the road, the car, the scenery and so many other things one after the other coming out like warm waters into the afternoon. I felt the lovely closeness we had being in a car and it kept feeling easier to find another then another Appreciation. They were all so beautiful.

We probably would have continued even longer when all of a sudden, I said; "Let me see if I can get to hear and speak from my InnerVoice." I did. It was far easier than I had seen others while channeling out loud. It just felt completely natural and familiar. I, for a while, felt that it was me just completing the next Appreciation. It though

*Appreciating Is a Tool*

was something better, higher or purer than my Appreciations. It was a Voice as clear as can be; speaking to us both and in perfect range with what we were desiring to hear. It was delightful and with each next word a new one came and still, I drove the car in full awareness. I was not interrupted. I was in a conversation. Uri was included too. We then drove and forgot completely we were in a very profound deep loving conversation with something other than either of us and something more than both of us and something connected to both of us. It was not a wild thing. It seemed totally natural and comfortable. It felt like something we had been experiencing for all of our lives. It was new and old at the same time. It was bigger than the day we were in, longer than the road we were on and more loving than we knew how to share between us until then. The kindness was apparent and soft in its manners. It was polite and thoughtful. Tactful I might say. It reminded me of that statement I liked when I was a child and young adult when interacting with others and wanting it to go well; "Let's be very polite so that we can be more polite between all.". Polite was a part of it, and so too is a greater kindness. Kindness is a provision that will lead humanity into the future of goodness and love. It is so easy to implement. We felt really good about this and it felt good too.

Yes, it felt like it was feeling very good about it all. We must have always wanted this to happen. It was easy for me and it was easy for Uri. Our questions were not actually questions, they were Appreciations. Our Appreciations were each different for the next often following concepts from the last and so they were flowing about in the frequencies that top themselves in positive thoughts and feelings. Our communications were not based on finding something out that we were wondering about, they were on the amazing uplifting feelings that associate with Appreciating. We were in a very positive place looking around and within and it was a beautiful enlightenment to attract this new connection within our Triadual Vortex, which is what we call that place we go to together in joy and love. It is one of the status' we strive for during our Appreciation Sessions. It enables us to know the feeling of being more than the together total we are added up individually. We are much more in our Triadual Vortex and now we were even more. . . much more.

After that encounter we felt an encouragement also. We felt an invitation to journal after we write whatever number of appreciation statements was seemingly enough, to be quiet and then allow our InnerVoice to write words, concepts, clarifications, ideas and general information that are good to know.

We are certain that this happened to us because we desired it to happen, and we were ready for it to happen. Now nearly every Appreciation Session is followed up with a relevant session with our InnerVoice. Hence, we have so much more to share. We are so happy for it too. Life is completely different.

Generally, I desire kindness and generosity to settle the places in my wandering soul that longs for what is pure and good.

And so, it is!

*Appreciating Is a Tool*

### Chapter Nine- "Appreciating is a tool" Appreciations

- ❖ I appreciate that my desires are sometimes apparent and obvious and other times vague and mysterious.

- ❖ I appreciate that when I really know what I desire I can focus on that more deliberately.

- ❖ I appreciate my journey and know my goals are in alignment with the joy I experience along the way.

- ❖ I appreciate that as I become aware of the way I feel today, in keeping calm and honest with myself, the days to follow are also aligned to this awareness.

- ❖ I appreciate that deliberately and intentionally avoiding drama, is assisting me now and in the future.

- ❖ I appreciate that I could learn to better and more often appreciate myself.

- ❖ I appreciate That a string of appreciations reveal much to me about what I like and what I desire.

- ❖ I appreciate the Voice I hear Within me that strengthens my awareness in many ways, including my desires.

- ❖ I appreciate that being vague about my desires can enable me to relax into a stronger knowing of myself.

- ❖ I appreciate that Appreciations are a tool to assist and regulate my walk in life.

*The Art of Appreciating MORE*

*Shapes of Non-physical*

## Chapter 10  Appreciating Non-Physical Awareness

I had a dream that felt so real and it informed me of some of the many things that I want to know more about. It was a multidimensional and multi-time segmented dream, in fact there are parts of the dream that I was awake. I feel compelled to write about this happening, because I really think there are several unique thoughts for all to consider.

Uri and I were lying in our amazingly comfortable bed, ready to fall asleep and we were talking about some of our experiences across this now seemingly complete day. We were lightly holding hands more like touching hands when I started to feel a sensation of something like electricity moving about in our hands. It seemed to emanate from Uri and travel through my thumb and come out the other side of my thumb and then go back into Uri's hand from that spot where we were touching each other. I interrupted our conversation by saying, "Do you feel that?" He didn't.

Once I explained what I felt happened it pivoted our conversation again into that experience I had when I felt this same or similar force of energy, like electricity, though not in any way shocking me or anything, when my brother, Hughie, was dying and then dead. The electricity flow continued after the machinery he was attached-to shouted its flat-lined indifference toward my brother's spirit and soul that was still there with us. It, this electricity, is a vibration that contains flow; as in communication, energy; as in power, and perhaps something more of some nature unusual though loving; as a gently felt electric kindness. It felt like a static fur of current. I feel it currently in some of my fingers as I type this idea of sensation into words. It felt curious, different, and mildly attention-giving with some form of message attached into its mobility. It seemed when happening that along with it was an undefined knowing that it will not last for a long time, which is why I could not become too familiar with it. Perhaps in that feeling that this was temporary, the thought that it might be a warning as much as an information source seemed appropriate. I thought of other times when I felt this; one being an encounter as I walked to the back-storage area of the house I was living in years ago. I was on a worn pathway and it was dark outside so as I stepped forward at one point I actually bumped into a deer. We were startled to meet so innocently each on their own ways and for a moment we just froze into each other's existence and then I notice the deer was a buck and his strong antlers of head-ware was so close I was about to touch them, when in that moment an awareness of potential danger swept through me and perhaps him. We slightly backed off and quickly and directly passed each other occasionally looking back. That moment of concern was sudden and dissolved quickly too. That moment in this electrical vibration molding was similar to that moment of awareness of each other, buck and me, although it was lasting rather than moving away. In fact, I felt myself become familiar with it; as if to say I was overcoming that sensation as alright and that there was absolutely nothing to be afraid of in this furry electrical soft field.

We, Uri and I, were decidedly going to sleep, and so we didn't overstate this happening to me. We were sleepy and gave peace and calm allowance. I then felt a boost in time travel and a jump about into a sequence of questions and explanations to share with Uri openly. We were falling to sleep. Kind of on and off. Holding on to awake together and then letting it go to sleep together. Honestly, I didn't know if I was awake or asleep some of the time and the sequence of my thoughts seemed scattered and fragmented across some time in which I felt asleep and awake, simultaneously. This was unusual. The night was filled with questions and conversations within me or in dreamscape and several conversations with Uri, seemingly within and outside of his dreamscape, as well.

I recall feeling connected to at least two, perhaps three non-physical entities. In that connection I was also aware that there are billions of these entities, somewhat bobbing afloat about in reasonably close proximity to each other, though independently in harmony with each other in thought. Generally, they are about half the size of an adult Human Being although they were invisible. Size intuitively seemed like a measurement of contained space, say within a puddle of vertical fluctuating free-standing water, yet it was a living organism of high intelligent consciousness. Within that relative size idea, there is little else in common between us it seemed,

## Appreciating Non-Physical Awareness

except for the ability to communicate in and internal common language. We spoke or rather transmitted thoughts back and forth in the same language and it was English. That, I thought, uncannily very convenient and it being realized brought to my surface-thought and theirs, as well, some doubts in our communications at all. It did, however, seem more of a translation of structured thoughts rather than the quick connection between me and the deer. It was more substantive with ideas floating between us rather than only awareness of each other. It was very uncommon. In fact, nothing like this, that I can remember, ever happened to me.

In that concern, I started to speak loudly to Uri, and I woke myself up and yet I did not wake up Uri, who was snoring loudly. In fact, louder than I had ever heard him snore previously. I thought he didn't even hear me as I came out of my sleep hearing myself partially yelp out some sounds that didn't complete their words. And I couldn't remember the words I was trying so hard to pronounce. It felt similar to coming out of a frozen helplessness from a nightmare. It wasn't a dream, or, was it? It wasn't a nightmare, or, was it? I then actually woke Uri to describe my night dream and these entities and said they were like beautiful bubbles. You know those bubbles that one creates by blowing soapy water into a large hoop and slowly forming it into a moving shape of rainbows and shimmering thin connections straight out of your exhaled breath.

Beautiful and seemingly indestructibly fragile, because these entities did not seem to burst away into a pop of nothingness. Instead, I felt their illusive non-figures rapidly or swiftly and smoothly change and reconfigure themselves and their mass of self. It was there, although it was not there at all. It occurred to me that albeit I could somehow sense a shape, I did not feel they could be defined by their shapes by me or by themselves. There was a magnitude, as I said, by which they were no larger than about the size of half an adult human and perhaps, at most as wide as two humans. I had an idea, while sleepily talking to Uri. I mentioned that these entities reminded me of a character that was in a tv show. I couldn't recall the name of the show and was asking Uri if he remembered its name. I said it was something like Oracle and the character was the green gooey blob alien entity known as Lieutenant Yaphit, who was a crude effective engineer on the crew who could move through things and change his shape at will. Uri knew what I was thinking about and said the tv show, which is a science fiction comedy and a spoof on the old Star Trek series was, Orville.

I fell back to sleep and continued to be in the same place, as if I only jumped out of my dream world to talk to Uri about what I was going through. I actually kept falling in and out of sleep all night and the sequence of conversations with Uri and with these particular two entities were constantly being interrupted with a lack of understanding of each other's existence. I woke up later than usual and with a great energy and a confusion. I felt it was a valuable evening of dream and reality mixing it up in my head and heart. I really do not want to forget these connections and understandings I gathered in this experience, so I will write what I can remember now.

The two entities that I mostly communicated with were so interested in me that I felt they found me important

## Appreciating Non-Physical Awareness

and they were very polite and they were more careful, now that I was more accepting of them, to keep the relationship resonating and so the conversation, if you can call it such, was easy to follow, actually on both sides as I too found their essence to be, not superior, but intelligent and equal. They turned focus from me, occasionally, to chat ideas over with others nearby and I felt others offering back through these two, their blended ideas as what could be said and asked of me in order to gain understanding of what I was in relationship to what they were. The one of the two that did most of the direct communication with me was as surprised about me as I was of it. Our existences seemed to feel like the opposite of each other's and in a while we all agreed that this connection was like a "first contact" and with a very different Being of Consciousness. I was given some answers and gave some information to them that seemed to interact with each other in ways that we all grew respect for each other, and that initial "fear" of differences, was wearing off replaced by mutual wonder.

I kept recalling my yelling to Uri earlier as a confused desire to escape out of this connection. Now, I desired, as too did they, to continue on having communications and cooperating together.

Their existence, as I mentioned, is close to the opposite of ours. They are non-physical and connecting provided each side a potential awareness of clarity that we previously missed being on our respective sides. On my side, the physical side, I sometimes think about what non-physical is like, albeit, I have accomplished after a lifetime to respect, that non-physical aspects of myself as real and impending or becoming more aligned mutually with my physical aspects and in so I realize each as independent and part of the same. In other words, I sincerely believe that I am a part of a much larger entity that I am also still and forever will remain connected to and that larger part of me is connected in some, if not many, ways to All-That-Is. I further accept that not all physical Human Beings feel that is their truth and that too is okay with me. In that vein of thought, I felt or had an intuition that these entities with whom I was engaged with in conversation and actually communication that they were not aware, until then, that physical existed and there were no parts of them, so they volunteered to express, that were now or ever that they knew connected to physical. They did feel that I had a non-physical component though. That meant to each of us that not all non-physical entities chose to experience any part of physical experiences. So, that too was okay to know about each other. I asked if some Force was keeping this knowing from them as I also expressed that the physical entities are taught at a young birthing aging that the non-physical realm was sort of off limits and however, many people were taught that after our physical experience we would return our souls and selfness into that space where what is physical could rejoin with the rest of us again and become our complete non-physical self. We call that the death experience as physical and then we melt somehow, though there have been few to speak of it, back into non-physical. Our soul knows of this even when we are less aware of it all it seems. I stated that I believed that becoming physical added growth, knowledge, wisdom, appreciation and experience to All-That-Is, which makes the journey from non-physical to physical and back worthwhile for everything. I was reminded that I had to have had the freedom to choose, as that is a given understanding for all life, apparently, as a Human Being, knowingly or not.

As we were exchanging thoughts and concepts with each other, there came a time in which I felt I was falling into a form of love with them and wondered to think what would happen after we ceased this current communication. For example, would we be able to reconnect at another time? Or Was our connection of interest to continue? Those concepts were very interesting to them especially whereby I was feeling that being in a quasi-sleep state was assisting my connection. They felt it was purely intuition that they were emotionally feeling that enabled connection as they were fully awake and aware. They, the One and the second one, Two, sensed my being-ness as a magnificence and a similarity within all that was apparently different. They didn't know how they could ever locate me again, though they wanted very much to do so and desired, as such, for they were often to become truer modules. They kept referencing our communications as their "intuition" and my "willingness".

They liked it very much. I did too. They felt it was important and valuable and something whose time was right to experience, albeit was far from what they had expected to discover currently, and they felt a bit unprepared and somewhat amazed at coming into knowing something so remotely apparent in their interests of life. They were experimenting with intuition of this particular nature. We all reluctantly agreed, upon departing our own ways, as change was insisting on moving us along and we could barely hold on to each other any longer. We would attempt to "meet-up" again.

I will now describe my interpretation of these non-physicals. To begin with there are bagazzilions of them. More than I have number-knowledge of to say. They do not belong to Earth as we do. They are not attached to anything like a solar system in our structured existence. They are invisible to us, and we are invisible to them.

That was a big surprise to me for some reason. I always thought of non-physical as invisible to me. I never thought for a moment that non-physical could not realize or see me or us. Well the truth came to me then that the only non-physicals that can somewhat see me and us and in this time-space-reality, were the non-physicals that I and us have partial attachment to and these non-physical beings didn't realize that until we collaborated our ideas together to conclude such. What that meant was that most of the non-physicals have no idea what-so-ever about physical existence and that physical existence is connected deliberately to non-physical existence very specifically. That is not to say that all physical beings even agree that non-physical exists, albeit, that seem irrelevant to me, especially in light that most non-physicals haven't the faintest idea of what physical can even be. That was a parallel abstract content that made it easier for us to continue in our defining ourselves to each other.

In their non-physical world, they move sort of like as a float and with a rhythm that they accept. They desire much in their momentum. I could not relate to most of what I felt were their desires, save that they were highly loving and authentically lovely. I felt a closeness in trust between them more than ever I would between myself and another human I would ever meet as a stranger. They were newly realized, rather than strangers to me. They were existing right within me. Neither of us could recognize each other as they are not in another plane per say, as much as they and we are utilizing our awareness in different ways. They attempted to address themselves to my greater non-physical part, kind of like through me. There was an apparent delay in the transmission, so to think of it and thus I felt myself lead. I was better at relaying messages from them to my Inner Being than they were to my Inner being directly. The

# Appreciating Non-Physical Awareness

results that seemed somewhat incomplete, commenced, were that these entities also choose to connect to what is something like an address to my Inner Being such that they might assist in both my Inner Being's future connection to me and these one and two entities connecting out of their intuition and apparently mine as a willingness, so that they might assist in the forward momentum of not just me, but of Humanity. They all were feeling it a good time to do so. I felt these concepts to be very beneficial in theory, although I cannot recall all the finer details that came up between what now felt like three entities, although all but me, were together. I was basically alone, which was a very impossible concept for them to absorb with any meaning. They are always aware of others and they are less independent than I am, we are.

There were the One and Two and even the Three who were in concert with ideas to respond and ask, there was my Inner Being Collective, and there was Me. I was amazed with the feeling of togetherness we all were experiencing as these entities floated through me, we both feeling something like intuition and my Inner Being more enabled to appreciate some of the details better and growing in love for the expansion. This event was spontaneous and not directly deliberate. It was being orchestrated because, as I said; I was willing, and they were curious. Now, I was curious too. My willingness was changing rapidly, and I was astonished and allowing to a level that required me to understand better my responsibility in participation.

This, dear readers, was the ultimate moment in being on the leading edge of thoughts for me, and, still I was partially asleep, so my total consciousness and recall are slighted. I loved this growth and feel parts of it slipping off into today, which is why I wrote this much out as soon as I could upon being in this day. I am advised by my Inner Being that they are hopeful that I will recall more aspects of this transaction as I am ready to receive more and that there is hope that our reconnections might well become easier for us to arrange now that my Inner Being is more composed with the vibrations in which we all considered our intuition residing.

I am looking forward to more to be continued, I think.

As I mull about this amazing dream like intercommunications I focus upon the idea of non-physical and physical as being strongly misleading concepts and those two expressions side by side are too black and white. The non-physical has some form, though all too little shaped to define as a somewhat or something as we know things to be from our physicality. There was a slight form as I observed without sight. I felt a presence of each being unique and approximately half the size of an adult Human. They were more like a shimmering bubble of rainbows and covered in an untouchable film of shine. Not fragile, more fluid and beautiful. The shape never rested into becoming anything that could be identified as uniquely existing, only moving unto the into-ness of itself and the feeling emotionally was one of great curiosity, respect, intelligence, enjoyment, and love.

Having come, myself, to appreciate that I am a smaller portion of the largerness of me that is non-physical and collective, I am sparked in found thoughts that I've come from non-physical and will return to non-physical. It is not the other way around, whereas I am physical who then created myself to be connected into the non-physical. My soul is always non-physical. My soul is also in a light spectrum and in a frequency, as is the envelop of any object. I might say that our external frequency

## Appreciating Non-Physical Awareness

and light spectrum and perhaps other vibrations might make up an aura around us individually. That might be the somewhat form of substance these non-physicals were more like. Non-physical isn't physical and vibrations are not physical. Or are they?

Humans admittedly or maybe better stated most agreeably cannot see a soul. Some Humans can feel their souls and other's souls too, not all and it isn't often spoken or acknowledged this person to soul awareness. Hence, my superior partner is my non-physical component. This is not meant to be a demeaning statement towards myself. I am worthy of all I am ready to accept. I am a part of my non-physical components, and true, that segment is more aware than I am of what I am not enabled to be aware of at this point usually. That means I have more to learn and come into understanding and my non-physical portion of me already knows a lot about me. My basic freedom to grow at my free will, also provides a potential new awareness that entwines with my Inner Beings awareness individually and collectively. My non-awareness that grows into an awareness in so doing contributes to universal growth which All-that-is appreciates. Hence, there are times I know more about me than does my Inner Being. It is worth repeating that at that space I contribute into life an expansion and All-that-is rejoices, with or without my awareness of it happening.

In my journey to love my life experiences, I am a creator and albeit much of my creations are similar to others theirs, it is also true that in my wandering soul of desires, I sometimes seemingly stumble, although that is debatable, upon a capsule of novel thoughts that waken up the Universe with great pleasure. My Inner Being is not so much a superior partner to me as it is intended to remain distinguishable from me; not separated, just distinguishable. It is not that I am less capable of learning, although it knows more. On occasion I find out something that my Inner Being either lost knowledge of or didn't know or, more likely, I am creating. My Inner Being benevolently completes gaps of understandings within me and sometimes, although logically much more rarely, I complete gaps for my Inner Being to sense growth from gaining through me. One of our purposes is to contribute. I fulfill this posture because it is intended as such. My Inner Being is connected to me and I am connected to my Inner Being, and I was first also totally Non-Physical.

Many Humans do not know their non-physical partnership. Many Human Beings are unaware of their continuous connection to their non-physical counterpart(s). This real, often un-realized, relationship is a strong part of consciousness awareness that somewhat troubles reality to believe exists. Until this encounter with One, Two and Three, I didn't know nor did they, that not all non-physicals are aware of the physicals ever less the connection from non-physicals to physical Beings. A multi-world opened up to us on both sides.

Immediately, One, Two, Three and more, felt a desire to add to our increase in ways I was somehow blown away about considering and I feel tired quickly at the thought of this all evolving into Humanity, and into myself. I felt a tremendous intelligence, not unlike my own InnerVoice's intelligence or my human love, although, different. Actually, there is no true way to compare them. The most apparent difference was a sharpened hope and wonder. I thought that maybe my connection to my Inner Being could have some flavors of traditional thoughts within them and this new entity group was so filled with new ways to accomplish what I felt I was stuck in moving away from or into. I too developed an immediate heightened sense of hope and a magnificence in what changes might be available, if "fear" was gone. These non-Human-Beings, had no trace within their realm of so many of the negatives we Human Beings are subjected too and have to decipher ourselves through as if to say we take for granted that crime, and cruelty exist, yet, these non-Human-Beings have no evidence of any off the mark behaviors between or within them. There is a purity, the likes of which is not thoroughly appreciated as possible here on our physical Earth. That is not to say that it is better to have a more perfect existence, it is though stating that without physicality many negative things could not exist. Additionally, from this experience or a purity level of life, it became apparent that trouble can be avoided on Earth. We can choose to avoid negative thoughts, which will in turn create a world of positive results. It wasn't disgusting to see Humanity's faults of negativity; it was an opportunity to appreciate what a world without negativity was like. It was very nice. The process that Humankind will certainly take into improvement is going to be very rewarding and wonderful to pursue. Seeing the possibilities that become into this method is exactly what is intended through the visibility into an existence of positive living.

I've been informed and, hereby so too have you, that most of the vast without size non-physical is unaware of physical. Know yourself now and forever, that all of physical has some knowingness of non-physical because we are all a part of non-physical and will always be, and it is impossible to deny who we are to ourselves, really. And still, when we choose to, we can be aware of non-physical at any time and when we acknowledge an awakening of those unaware non-physicals becoming more aware of us, and remember this is coming to them not through their involvement with our existence, rather through their independent growing consciousness, of which we are creating, we evolve too.

There is a refreshing and reclarifying that washes and purifies what is meant by potentiality. Surround yourself with the depth of light and open out the shadows of darker times and spawn colors into your love; for we are the Light and the Colors contained in Light, in a consciousness becoming aware of its beautiful self.

There is much to this experience. At the time of my writing this part of my experiences from recall, it is now more than 150 days ago that I had my awakened-dreamy encounter with One, Two and Three. I am uncertain of my accuracy in describing some of the ramifications I feel are connected to this encounter. First of all, I've been sick for nearly every one of the days I've lived since that experience. I believe that there is a connection. I would rather there not be, hence, at the moment I will tend my thoughts into my being sick as possibly separate from this having happened. Sincerely, I have an *intuition* there is a connection. I am, hence, really pretty afraid of having another connection take place. In other words, my *willingness* has been changed. I am less *willing* to subject myself to sacrificing good health and wellbeing for the communications sake. If further contact is to be made, I need first assurance that I *will* not be harmed, nor *will* I harm; although I've had no information given to me to think that they were injured and I believe my connection with my own Inner Being knows to inform me, as such. I want to do things that add value to my quality of life, and I am uncertain of how to control the consequences in the contact. Without a mutual benefit, it seems unwarranted to suffer. I hope my connection did not alter negatively those unaware of physical non-physicals; One, Two, Three and much more. I was never this sick before in my entire life, so I am unsure of many things right now. There is a part of me that says; "This being sick and this encounter with unaware non-physical entities has to be coincidental.". I though, feel a truth in it. I do not want to be sick any longer. I also feel that this encounter was important. Not of physical value to me, even depleting me of physical prowess, but spiritually and intellectually valuable to me and to them and to All-That-Is.

I've been giving this encounter a great deal of thought even during the days, weeks and months that I've been ill. In fact, it was difficult to not think about it. My body was shut down, although my mind was awake. I thought a lot about this happening, to me, to me now, why and what to do about it. I am now in recovery and, today, is the best day I've had physically in a very long time. It was the middle of March when I first was involved in this previously described contact. It is now the end of August. I really do think I was not easy to diagnose because it was something unique and different that resided within my physicality that confused my body with slow responses. I was not diagnosed conclusively, and I was seen by several doctors at different stages of this stupid infection. The last doctor who saw me mentioned that my CT, on the computer screen, did not look as bad as the camera he was examining me with as he was probing inside my sinuses. I just cannot desire to write out my chronological events that made me so ill, however, there was another day that I read what I wrote about One, Two and Three during my sickness. It was when I first realized a timeline connection between my living health and my *willingness* to communicate with these non-physicals. I have been continuously feeling that it was a first contact and I started to realize that the non-physicals who know that there is a physical plane were aware, of course, of these non-physicals that I encountered. They were surprised that we connected, and they are resistant to it having ever happened and do not really advocate for it happening again. I felt confused by that. Why? Why, did I feel so helpless in this new concept? And why, would the Source of All Life, not intervene into my sick body with assistance to heal? I didn't intend to fall into this knowing. Part of the reason why I sense I should avoid re-encounter is because of my being ill because of it. I think. This is so confusing to me. Yet, I feel that it was terribly difficult to go through this illness and recovery is slow. I too do not want to go through this again. And my resistance and immune system is still soft and fragile.

I feel that the entire experience, both the communications and the illness, are connected. I need to think about the ramifications of this ordeal, real or imaginary, and I have got to feel more confidence in my health before I venture into something I only kind of know to be true. It's not the encounter I feel that needs to be solidified to believe, it is that I feel vulnerable to illness that infected me, unintentionally, as we passed into each other's realms. I am not nor am I interested in being a martyr or someone who is into sacrificing my wellbeing for anything. This encounter seems to not hold a benefit in my knowing, excluding the idea of it coming into existence. Should it be true, so be it. Should it be merely a dream, so be it. What I do feel is an outcome of

## Appreciating Non-Physical Awareness

it, is that I've never had this concept come to me before. I love science fiction and comic-book stories. Thor is one of my favorite characters. And my imagination is vivid and healthy. I've never before heard or read anyone with this amazing thought that there are many non-physicals who do not know about the physical time space reality I am living. That is a novel thought.

Sometimes I want to gift away that thought to others, as I am doing here and now, and other times I want to investigate it on my own more prior to letting others in on this amazing thought concept. Since I first found it, I've thought about many aspects of this, as if it were true. It would mean, most likely, that we who come forth into the physical world, had to have first been taught about it and this is not something every non-physical is privy or maybe even care to know. This idea of a select few, in comparison to the vastness of individuals I sensed in non-physical existence, know about time-space reality is overwhelming a thought. It means so many possibilities of choice and desires that conjure up from that space in which the knowers of time-space reality exist together can actually be. Which in turn means that there are colonies or groups of non-physicals collaborating on the collective intelligence of the physical realm. There are numerous other thoughts that gather in the sensing of this separation of knowledge amongst the non-physicals. It feels altogether too much like the possibility of kind of like a conspiracy theory might well exist and separated by those non-physicals who know this and those who do not know this...making it feel a bit like a secret.

I do not want to know secrets, and I do not believe that I can carry a secret. I am free to express my thoughts, real or imaginary, to whom ever I want or will listen. Perhaps there is a natural awakening within that flood of non-physicals who are unaware of physical, as we humans harbor that type of natural awakening, as well. Certain knowings, in fact, probably all true knowings are only known through a personal and natural coming about. Experience is our greatest teacher, maybe our only teacher.

What is real and what is a dream in our comprehension of life experiences? Do you know… really know? I am open to feeling that perhaps this experience made me feel ill and perhaps I was ill and from being so, I had this experience. I do not know. A great spiritual teacher of mine, Abraham Hicks, says; "If you have the wherewithal to think of it, the Universe has the wherewithal to make it.". I'm unsure, at this point, if I will ever really want full-heartedly to encounter this "tear" thru realities into connecting up with what I think I will call "uncommon knowing". If I do, I will ask, of what do I benefit from the encounter, if they know, and do they think it possible that I was infected physically within the connection?  No harm in asking, if I ever so allow this again.

I trust that these "others" are meant to be brought forth into my mind of wonder. I will keep dreaming, you keep dreaming too.

In a touch between two Beings, regardless of the degree of differences or similarities, and there are always more that we have in common than not, the energy flow is a packet of translations. I feel shaky inside when I give long enough thought to the non-aware-of-physical-beings I encountered. I feel the connection provided to me a better awareness of the size of what I do not know and it yielded less than I feel satisfies me for the equality in it. Over even more time, I am even more uncomfortable with the results of this encounter. I

## Appreciating Non-Physical Awareness

dream bits and pieces of the experience and there are some parts of it that are impossible to trust as belonging to me for any benefit. The biggest benefit is that I am better off not knowing any more at this point in my life.

It wasn't a nightmare nor a silky heavenly dream. It was different than any other experience I've ever had in my life. I see the tear or rupture in the separation between us. It still hurts or pangs me a little, especially with confusion. I feel that I will be somehow compensated for that errorish time opened between us.

> *I am alone in my asking about it as my InnerVoice says; "Let this go. You are special to know it as such; for now, this is unrequited and unintentionally you could be harmed by allowing... so be unwilling. It is something like learning about fire. That is a good thing; for you cannot give and support equality without receiving and there is nothing being gifted to you for your open willingness. You are not a victim. They are unaware of this concept to victimize. They are, however, aware of the backing up on your part and they will respect that by its nature to state something without saying what."*

It is a gift to know as much as I do, is it not! I rethink this seemingly danger recognizing that Humanity has benefited tremendously by learning how to properly respect fire. I have no desire to further push the envelope past good manageable health and wellbeing. I can trust that when something feels off, it is a positive message to receive and take heed.

From time to time, over the past months, which is now about a year and eight months since my initial encounter, I feel a knocking so to speak at my conscious doorway and additionally, there are some visuals that come along in the moment of attempts to reunite; as my soul address is accessible by them without permission to enter without my approval and I cannot be taken into their place, as I previously was, albeit I did allow it. I was willing, they were curious.

I recall having seen this visual prior to my encounter. I was driving the car when it happened in The Villages, Florida where we for a while had relocated to retire. After attending a play that our neighbor was preforming in, I had an experience. As I drove home on the meticulous roads at The Villages, feeling happy for the evening's events, there became a quasi-oval rainbow jagged bordered opening, like what might seem to be a portal. It is the tear or rupture I previously mentioned. I thought it was perhaps something inside of my sight. I challenged that briefly and was uncertain if maybe my eyes were malfunctioning. It was a very beautiful thing to see although since I was driving, I did not want to test my eyes and resumed while avoiding noticing it as much as I could avoid it. I told Uri about it and that was that. It was gone within several moments. It was within a few nights after that portal that the encounter took place. I believe, looking back at it, that my body's mind state cannot walk through that portal unless I am in a relaxed state of being and or in a physical condition that has reasonable space physically to divert my attention to this someplace else. Even driving on The Friendliest Hometown roads of The Villages, obviously my nearly full attention had to be on driving. This realm of non-physical existence where the non-aware-of-physical Beings reside is oblivious of the outcomes and consequences the physical Being are subjected to if not paying attention to the required balances of existing in the time space reality we Humans live in. It is an unintended hazard for us in the times at which we can

# Appreciating Non-Physical Awareness

even allow or be willing. They are, indeed, curious, however, unaware of our ramifications should we leap forth too willingly. These entities have conscious at an order of magnitude higher than "fire", therefore, they recognize now, my reluctance is for a reason. Ouch, there must be a way in which we can settle our differences as we all so enjoy the discoveries yet to become. Isn't that an amazing thought.

Recently, about three weeks ago, an oval heavily edged portal appeared while Uri and I were relaxed and watching tv. It was in the exact same location in my field of view. It was on my left side, translucent, robust, and very beautiful. A real attention grabber. I asked Uri if he saw it. No, he didn't see it. I closed my eyes, turned my head a bit and realized it wasn't inside of me, as it was only visible to me when my eyes were open. It called welcomingly to me. I would not proceed into this invitation. I did attempt to communicate from where I was.

Silently, I clarified my position. I told them that I could not continue forth due to the fact that I am hurt physically by the results of deeper contact. I mentioned I would not forfeit my health and physical wellbeing for another encounter, although I otherwise would. I said that they had been connected to what caused me illness that struggled for many months into me. I now was being better, yet, unwilling to offer myself up to them for the contact sake. My life is rich with joy and love and I did not have an alternative need to sacrifice myself. They were listening to me. They do not understand time as we do.

I stated that I would only venture forth, if first of all, I was compensated for what I had already experienced in illness. They asked what that even meant, as they do not experience decline of any nature. Physical illness is unknown to them. It is a huge incomprehension for them to think about that they caused me harm is not within their vocabulary or understanding. There are not degrees of Beings there, that they detected, although I definitely felt differences between them; One, Two and Three and the rest. They didn't all together pick up on what I was meaning, although some ah-ha moments were felt when I was teaching them of my perceived appreciation of their subtle differences. One was braver than Two or Three. One was more curious than others and knew me more thoroughly. They had not recognized that variation. Now it was forming an awareness. There became a thought that sameness expands further than they thought about until in that moment.

I expressed my need to feel compensated for being even though, innocently and inadvertently harmed. I didn't know what could be considered compensation, yet expressed the great value I feel in Wisdom and Knowledge, Longevity and Wellbeing. I would only ever step forward if there was something in it for me. If I was suffering, they too might be having some form of ramifications they are unaware of. I need equal consideration, otherwise, I was a victim with no purpose. I would never allow them to hurt me again, if possible. They knew now that they had done something that created my innocence to be altered, they too were altered. We need to figure this out before continuing.

They did not enjoy the concept of causing harm. I asked that we give time to think this out. Again, time itself is an unfamiliar concept to them, however, I mentioned that time had happened since last we connected from my part and experience and they accepted that something meaningful was placed into that capsule of connection. I further stated that I needed to know no

## Appreciating Non-Physical Awareness

harm would become of me if I ever chose to step into this portal again and I repeated myself with expressing that I'd never consider it at this point where there was apparently no return on my previous encounter. First that needed to be compensated for from them. No others should be harmed either and that was their responsibility to respectfully appreciate. After all, I was not looking for them when found. They are curious and now they should be compassionate towards Humanity. Contact needs to be understood.

I felt, and still do, a little anger in the careless loss of innocence on my part for having had to experience illness. Though I now look at that ill and recovery time as a pivotal space in my experiences. From that encounter and experience, we gathered ourselves together and removed ourselves from The Villages, Florida and returned home to California. During that time of being sick, I came to appreciate that I missed my children and that I wanted to be back in California. We attended our daughter's wedding in Santa Catalina right in the middle of not feeling well. I remember that when we landed and then got over to Catalina, I felt better. I said to Uri; "I think I am allergic to Florida".

We both giggled, but that was a turning point in both my health and in our return to California. It was a very interesting trip that brought us here now. We live in the magnificent Sierra Nevada Foothills in the countryside in a beautiful house that is more like a modern castle than a house. We have several acres of land and it is an amazing renewal into the benevolence of nature. It is lovely. In my most recent invitation to be willing, we were here in this place of beauty and comfort. The Non-Aware-Non-Physicals, are completely unaware of my latitude and longitude or any part of my physical association, hence they are totally confused at my mentioning having a new location. Location has no real meaning to them. Earth has no substance to them. They move about through what we know as Earth unaware of it being there. I saw that take place. It is very surreal.

If I can see or sense them, and I can sense and observe something of them, an aura of shimmering lights, occupying no space that I do, they can appreciate me. And they do. I appreciate them as well as I can see them in that illusive way of shimmering lights of colors. I have put in my request for compensation. And we will see what happens. I am blessed in my life already, with or without non-aware-non-physical assistance or compensation. Also, from my request, My InnerVoice is alerted at all encounters between us all and there are processes being analyzed to determine if compensation is even possible. I believe it is. We will see. I am most fortunate. To permit an emergency of connection is not appropriate as we are not feeling that any healthy results come from an unhealthy exchange. We know though that "Fire" is of benefit, so we hold hope. Mankind is ready for new creative energies to come into our view and implemented into our experiences. We thrive in so many ways from electricity, yet, we need to consider the future of the Earth's health in a like way as we want the non-aware-non-physicals to consider our health. Exchanges in the future will require growth in our knowledge to apply new technologies into our world, without causing harm. This is a fact that is true in all experiences. Life is supposed to be good. Kindness and compassionate consciousness is required to expand properly.

I want to not be angry with their innocence or with mine, as well, hence, I learn to love deeper as a valid and practical return on my experience. It was not yet an investment, nor do I feel a detrimental forfeit that makes

## Appreciating Non-Physical Awareness

me unable to accept this encounter as a health-wise misfortunate thing any longer. It was what it was. I will not go there again, until if possible, the wrinkles are straightened out and there is compensation for my alterations.

Love is an amazing power and God knows I felt a great deal of love in these encounters. For that, I have great hope. If the future contains the knowing of more dimensional encounters and travel, this is one to consider. Humanity, we know has to evolve, and so too that means other entities, non-human, are in need to evolve in their understandings. This seems so logical to me.

Imagine being able to relax into this portal and then move about into that nothingness to another otherwise latitude and longitude position within nothing and then walk back out into another time space position. Yes, that could be a fabulous, convenient and practical way to travel the planets or even, of course, moving about here on Earth without causing environmental depletions or personal harm. I love that and more the interactive benevolence of crossing over into the non-physical. The solutions of ramifications from illnesses need to be repaired. Willingness should not be taken advantage of. Once in error, twice is unacceptable. Let us hope for solutions, for we can adjust our reality to include other realities. We are consciously ready.

There are times, I think deeply about this encounter, this seemingly "first contact", and my stomach turns like butterflies bursting about wanting freedom. It is a somewhat uncomfortable memory. Well, correction, the memories of the experience are pretty gosh darn wonderful. It is the physical results that weaken my spirits. I am not a drinker, though it felt like a hangover,

I suppose. Until remedied, and I can only wonder at that coming along, I am out for a break. I cannot imagine what they are dreaming up, as that world and this one is so far from each other that it is nearly impossible to imagine. In that thought, I cannot imagine what the unknow will bring forth. Can you?

Whatever the "unknown" is, it is improving All-that-is. Why else would it arrive; for we are loved greatly. Many times, upon times, as I forward think myself into wisdoms that move me and I take my personal Geiger counter into, not only new places to evaluate, but, into new ranges of registry and experience, I am reborn, again. This ordination is part of my evolutionary rendezvous into the spectrum of undecided and ever encouraging becomingness that activates my Innate structure of long awaited be-longings. The premise of this is to shake up, agitate and purge, what is intuitive to my open spirit of experience, based upon previous imbedded beliefs, of all natures, and promulgate possibilities previously unthought of as valid. It is the activation of change and it is essential for growth and improvements.

We, Humans, are headed into a new untraveled and undisclosed highway of thinking and allowing. It is not uncommon to turn away from things that seem impossible or unthought of, yet, in this time of great shifts upon us, and with each of us impartial and detached to previous outcomes, we can approach more wonder and worth. This is not to say that we need to disbelieve what we have; it means that we have more to know about. It is not that what was before is all wrong, it is that we can leverage what we know with what is coming into our realm to know more about. Some things might fade away, change or be incorporated into additional understandings. The ancient wisdoms and

## Appreciating Non-Physical Awareness

the modern, that which we dabble in and the known to be stable, the novel and the unsuspecting, what we are used to and what seems foreign to us, the standards and the appreciated, the apex and the vortex, can all exist with each other in harmony. Relearning isn't always replacing. It can be complementing and augmenting. Being aware and accepting of growth makes expansion something to embrace and love. There are no limitations in love.

And so, it is, perhaps, to be continued!

## Chapter Ten - Appreciating Non-Aware non-physicals

- ❖ I appreciate the ideas of there being great benefits in being Willing to Allow what is new to come to me.

- ❖ I appreciate that there are times and experiences in my life, when my direction was determined by my willingness to trust that what I don't know can be known if I allow.

- ❖ I appreciate being a Physical Being.

- ❖ I appreciate my propensity to be curious and to recognize curiosity in others.

- ❖ I appreciate my propensity to be willing and to recognize allowing in others.

- ❖ I appreciate that there is always something new to learn.

- ❖ I appreciate my open-mindedness.

- ❖ I appreciate that there is more going on than I can ever know all of.

- ❖ I appreciate the possibilities of contact with intelligence other than physical Human Beings.

- ❖ I appreciate that Love feels so Universal and expansive.

- ❖ I appreciate that I love myself.

*Appreciating Non-Physical Awareness*

## Chapter 11  Appreciating my Inner Being

I love my Inner Being. It is so much a positive part of my life that I can allow myself to connect, knowingly almost anytime I want, to a source that is omnipresent. Even when I feel I am not actually requesting a connection to my Inner Being, it is always connected to me. My Inner Being is a part of Source God and for that and in that anything is possible. I just ask to be connected and it

## Appreciating my Inner Being

comes to me. I've practiced getting in touch with my Inner Being formally through the responses to my Appreciations and now, I feel I can get into that Appreciative State nearly as readily as I can get out of it, but easier. The choice is always mine.

I am loved and I am love. This kindness of knowing self to be love reaches deep within the life I live. Once I became aware of this aspect of connective experiencing, everything became more integrated within my existence. This concept, if only a seed for the reader, is a delightful possibility for better harmony between humans and generations to come. It is time to reinvent this story of Human living. We can do it. We are free to change the path for self and for others. In freedom and joy.

For many years, Uri and I have been writing lists of our Appreciations into our journals and almost daily. If we think we are too busy, we miss out on more than is worth it, so we know the value of our time as being able to Appreciate will afford us more clarity and thus more time, even in the very day we are in and, certainly, over time. That is the way it always works. Years ago, we had taken time to question this fact, and we came into the time when it became our absolute truth. We allow it now, willingly. I, generally, write my appreciations on the recto page, which is the right side of the open journal (usually the side that is the odd numbers of a book), and I document the responses with the messages from my InnerVoice, on the verso page, which is the left side of the open journal (usually the even numbers of a typical book format or the left side). Although I realized something interesting in that description that I want to mention. Uri was raised in Israel and Hebrew is his first language, spoken and written and perhaps that is why Uri's journals are different from mine in his writing them down. The Hebrew books I would say start at the back of the book. As a result, Uri uses the verso page for his Appreciation Statements and his recto page for his InnerVoice messages. It's nice to sense so many complementary components to our relationship. I appreciate our differences.

We wait not for something to go wrong or off to connect to our Inner Beings, we actually have less going wrong or off as a result of our connections. I usually take about ten minutes, although I do not think I've ever really timed it out, but it feels like about ten minutes, for me to write out on the recto page, the day and date and then I write, I appreciate (and I fill it in). I deliberately seek to create appreciations about myself, as I know that doing so will remind me to look at myself with more love and understanding. I try to write unique things about myself without duplicating my attention too often, although I sometimes want to bring attention to special attributes about myself or my desires, ideas or experiences, so that I can feel my growth. Appreciating always increases what is appreciated, and I just know when it is proper to repeat or strengthen specific aspects about myself and other things, as well. This is highly personal.

It is apparent that when I am scheduled to go on my annual physical check-up that I intuitively appreciate my good health and wellbeing prior to my visit. That is a very good support system to build within myself. I so enjoy my skills and talents and at times when they are to be used soon with more vigor, I appreciate my abilities. If I am about to attend a meeting of some nature, I will appreciate, prior to attending that meeting, that I am easy to get along with and that people like me and respect my ideas, opinions and contributions. I also appreciate that I meet nice people that want to cooperate with me. I appreciate that I anticipate a good meeting.

## Appreciating my Inner Being

That's really a very good preparation to implement into my state of being. Each morning at waking up, it is also valuable to conjure up a good day. Today is a very good day. Make it a good day. We are free to do so. Life is what you make it.

Share your experience of this good day with your Inner Being. Inner Being, I know you are there. You care for and about me. I know you love me, and I request knowledge to connect to my best experience. I am aware my requests are received if I am a willing open conduit.

As I create my appreciation list, I also appreciate other segments of my life. For example, I appreciate my loved ones and their amazing skills and talents. This appreciation supports my loved ones immeasurably. I appreciate my past, though with less focus than my future, and I appreciate the present moment I am in. I appreciate what feels like a new desire and what I still want. I appreciate so many different things inside of myself and outside of myself, and, over the years I have found that developing my self-worthiness is most beneficial for creating a happy life.

When first, years ago I started my still continuing study of "appreciations" I gathered "appreciations" from my friends in a group I was conducting at my home. I clearly noted the distinction between having gratitude and being appreciative. I worked with people who also were informed of this difference. I remind you that gratitude comes from a place of thanksgiving for getting something you did not have, and appreciation comes from a place of understanding intuitively the love of what is deep within the existence of already knowing that I have been fortunate to experience what is provided rather than pleaded, prayed or begged for. I am in appreciation for the graces I experience from inspiration and gratitude is more from a motivation.

After my collection of "over a thousand "Appreciations", I began to categorize them initially into two categories. All "appreciations" would fit easily into either "Inside-Self-Appreciation" or "Outside-Self-Appreciations". What this meant is "Inside-Self-Appreciation" were "appreciations" that were about me, personally, and "Outside-Self-Appreciations" were about anything other than of myself. And even though we immediately know that there is a lot of stuff to appreciate outside of ourselves because the world is so big, I was really amazed to discover that most of all the appreciations I had collected were "Outside-Self-Appreciations" and so few about "Inside-Self".

From learning that, I began to put into practice a deliberate focus to appreciate myself and overcome this tendency to neglect and avoid appreciating self, as if it were a better behavior to think less of self. Self-sacrificing is that deeply embedded into us that we can actually feel ashamed or embarrassed to put self-first. That is a difficult pill to swallow, yet, for the moment, think of it as such. Think of this loving self as a prescribed pill that will help you feel better eventually. It remains an amazing journey. Over the years since then, I've promoted Self-Appreciation for myself, of course, and for all others too. Learning how to love and appreciate oneself is the greatest gift we can give to ourselves and to everyone else too.

When next you sit down to write Appreciation Statements, recall that in so doing you participate in opening up a great power. Okay, admittedly one does not really need to create Appreciation Statements in order to hook-up, so to speak, with ones InnerVoice. It is

*Appreciating my Inner Being*

empowering to know that it can only help you find that InnerVoice to do so. I know that we all can feel reluctance in approaching new ways to love yourself. It can also feel a little intimidating to reach up and beyond to what should feel normal. We all understand the seemingly discomfort of finding a new normal. Especially going through and breaking out of the Pandemic of 2020-2021. It is a wonderful feeling at the same time. I encourage everyone reading this to let fear go and remember that it is all a matter of the way it is looked at. Eliminate fear. It can be dissolved so quickly in your mind by simply allowing a higher Voice to speak with you. It can only Love You. The feeling of consistent Love generated by my InnerVoice over these past couple of decades, has brought so much goodness into my life. It is the difference between owning a book and reading a book. It can sit dormant, or it can be opened. This analogy of Your InnerVoice being a book, is definitely on the lowest side of amazement. There is no book as great as the one within yourself.

At the end of *The Art of Appreciation Book*, I wrote about the initial messages I received from My Inner Being. I've had people ask for me to elaborate upon it. I do appreciate that curiosity, and I respectfully appreciate that I am less willing to share with others who do not believe in the presence of Governing Spiritual Authority, Omnipresent Influence, therefore, I find myself quietly placing messages in-between my words. They are influenced by My InnerVoice, who gathers all that I need unto a platform of messages that accommodates my direction more than my needs. As you go within, seek to understand this principle; Your InnerVoice communicates in a like manner to your creating Appreciation Statements, although it is different too. The point is that Your InnerVoice is always kind and loving. That truly is something that we could all use more of.

Thinking in those terms of desiring More, will always yield More. Love is a powerful ingredient in life experiences and in our preservation of self, it is a requirement.

Going into the place of hearing Your InnerVoice is something like listening to self-thought about your ability to package up Love to insure feeling appropriate on this journey. We all want to be happy people. Do you believe that to be true? I do. Even those people who seem happy to be unhappy, they just forgot how much better it feels to let go of their ill-applied insecurity or their harbors of guilt that they hide within and from their fear of actually being the creator of happiness. In like vein there are an amazing number of people who feel guilty at having more than others and they reduce their self-appreciation with a bottle of charity to ease their invented pain from what they feel is them taking too much and leaving behind not enough for everyone else. That too is a generational, religious, or institutionalize clutter of unawareness of there always being more than enough and their connection to lack. There is as much as is called for. Balancing the need to get and the need to give is a delightful, delicious allowing. When you find any troubled thoughts as to your giving or getting too much or not enough, bring your mind into its softer space where you can meet your compassionate consciousness and trust that flow. If you remove lack as a reality and apply a thoughtful cushion to dwell upon, you will always care enough in all directions of nurturing spirit.

*Appreciating my Inner Being*

Short circuiting the emotional scale (see Figure one for the Emotional Scale and the Virtuous Leaps) and entering Appreciation is but a workable shift into a better place and faster than going through the longest way possible, except to move forward. When the momentum of change thrills, all one hopes for is, MORE.

It cannot be taught, this opening up to Your InnerVoice, although in creating, listening and feeling your truth in positive Appreciations from your creative thoughts, will always wake you up. Your InnerVoice is always there, for you and being involved in everything you know to be as real, or not. There are no secrets here to find out about. Honesty is so accessible and affordable. Love the powers of life and trust yourself to find what will assist you in living a good life. Finding the Voice Within, is not the goal you may have been thinking about. It is a real place. You need no invitation; you are always welcome.

I ask, believe and receive. I've mentioned that numerous times, so herein let me demonstrate that process. I was writing about my InnerVoice and actually I started to fall off into a sweet space of void of thought and in that moment, I felt myself actually nod off. I felt a push forward and a snap awakening. In that moment, my InnerVoice said something to this effect:

*"If you want to explain how others can reach their communications front with their InnerVoice, you have provided enough direction already. It is more a doing thing than a learning from another thing. Perhaps if you shift it up and write out some of the messages you've received over all these years from your journaling, that indeed will demonstrate your experience in a manifestation."*

Hence, I went upstairs and randomly gathered four journals, of the hundreds, and brought them into the office such that I can transcribe some messages for all to benefit. I know it will be the best thing to do. I trust my InnerVoice. When I first began to communicate with my Source, I did so after journaling Appreciations and then I would ask a question. Here is one such session:

11/24/08. What is the basic understanding of abundance of money and free living in the sense that I've noticed some pursue getting things for free and others independently pursue obtaining more money?

Answer: *"You should be asking this instead; What do I feel about having more or less? Because the word Free resides in the total word Freedom is why some are seeing free things as having enough. Carefully listen to this Now! I want you to know that Freedom is the foundation of having everything you want. Freedom is the ABC's of the alphabet of Abundance! With Freedom there is a void of Fear. With freedom there is a clarification of the desires that bring you forth. Be Free and you attract what is free, yet as you are most aware of freedom implies the ability to allow into you, desires, also. In other words, in freedom you are more clearly or keenly in touch with your personal preferences, and you get to decide the substances that you enable into your supportive existence and at the same time. If you want an abundance of money to flow into your life, such that it feels free to you or if you want your abundance to manifest with lack of money that too is possible however, we know you appreciate the empowering ability to flow money and that you also appreciate the ones who want money to be less meaningful to them while experiencing the benefits of the products created with money, included into its shaping. Being aware of other's manners and "beliefs"*

*Appreciating my Inner Being*

surrounding immediate interface interaction with money is a valuable insight. Most, useful you will find.

Sing a song of abundance that song becomes like you. Hear a message of willingness and your will be done. Taste the flavor of success and it showers you with more. Sense it all and you grow delightfully sensitive. ESP is Yours! "


Here are a few more journaled InnerVoice communications. I found them by opening the book to wherever it opened.

02/10/09. I asked: "What do I need to know?"
          Answer to both Peggy and Uri:

**Answer:** *"You need to know and always remember that there is only a Source of Well-Being and that that Source is graciously and most willingly and absolutely and unequivocally available to you all of the time.*

*You need to know that you are loved and that you are love! This is, will and has always and forever been so to be! It is forever the same. You need to know that better than any other informational thought or vibrational feeling you are! It is more than an experience you choose to have deliberately; it is greater than all and every thought you have ever or will ever hold focus on. It is within every sensation and it is bigger than your physical self. You need to know this first for knowing so releases all matter of knowledge and understanding. Know it in everything you are. You are enormously loved, and you are 100 percent Love."*

02/11/09. I asked; "What do I do or feel or think to be able to recognize and entice opportunity to gather towards us, approach us, and introduce itself to us?

Answer: *"You are wanting for opportunity to come to you and we will say that that is a better idea than you to look so hard for it. We know that you two are a perfect match to so much Goodness and that is what is being summoned to you right now. Rid yourself of any doubt of this. It is dumb to doubt. Beware of changes and people who were changed by you and the fact that it is opportunities are being drawn to you can spend this allotted time to become comfortable with the inevitable fact that it is almost upon your door. It is wonderful it is grand it is simple, and it is fun. The Spirit of the Law of Attraction and your being good excellent students of the Teachings of Abraham is affording you this special prep time that will assist you with the calm appreciation of acceptance and total expectation. Keep on the study and apply it to all in your Life and Be prepared in body mind and spirit for truly great things, manifestations of things, money, people, places and all in comfort and design will and is just about ready to blow your minds. This is good, this time, to prepare. It is some time other than that time many and you too have experienced that is time to come into acceptance, allowing, receiving. This time at hand is to call calm. Feel it? Calm your spirit mind thoughts of Life. It is a perfect unfolding. It is not a holding back. It is time for you both to get ready for the ride of your Lives and we feel such Love and complete Appreciation that you two are arrived for it and it is so good. You will smile and laugh and have such fun together with this that you will spin in that Triadual Vortex in complete appreciation for your joy and ours. The time is as they say, "At hand".*

On a question about us staying in our vortex and accepting allowing and receiving…

## Appreciating my Inner Being

*It is good to ask such a large question and you are both welcomed to spend as much Time in the vortex. It is a way of life for others as well. It is big very big so expand that thought and you will see clearly. Enter and stay. Enter and sit and walk and talk and be all that you are meant here to be. It is always available. It calls you and you will see. You feel comfort? Oh, comfort is more than soft. It is warm. It is love. You sense its approach as you approach it too. It is a space. This vortex is wise surroundings that breathe for you your wisdom to be more your hope to know all. Strange worlds we are yet all is good as love is good. Vibrate love and walk in, look about find your easy chair and open your new book."*

03/14/10. (By now in my nearly daily communications, several years, I rarely ask questions usually. I just allow words to come to me after I complete my Appreciation statements):

*"Eyes see from Within your soul of now in place of then. It is now; feel the presence of it surrounding thee. Sense the quiet moment that Now is, while too, become your awakened day.*

*I AM with you. This everlasting soul has your story to be told as you unfold the willingness of the light that foreshadows or the one foretold.*

*Bring yourself into this day in the thoughts touched into it by your mind and heart. Ask and it is Given.*

*I want a day of deliberately being, so the happiness that is always in the flow. Come to be a sacred song. Sing out from me what I've always known to be. Ring in the New Year today with it find the hopes and dreams amounting to this Peaceful Day. Taking the time to live, being in this only ever now.*

*This is my day it belongs to creation and in it flows the wants of Good news. Rejoice in the day. As it aligns your song to the sound of all important to you. Gathered unto you are all the sounds that tell bird from cat. You are the creator of peace and harmony. Your thoughts create part of the day; the rest comes from the heart. Feel the Love of this balanced synchronicity and hold back what you manage into the entire fold.*

*Be willing to be a willing piece of your own desires. The vague cloud soon defines itself as your story is being told. Write (Right) on the nose. Your power can be sensed to all cooperativeness. Bring it in and let it out. Opportunity is holy. It comes and is here now. Learn from it, you made it for that cause.*

*Options are variables of opportunities noticed. Reach for what you want."*

3/29/10. *"Breathe Truth in from the Great Vastness of the Universe of knowing You are Loved. Master Yourself.*

*Hold strength in that thought.*

*Be your own Master and feel the empowerment of it. You hold and own the keys that unlock your value as the everlastingness that you are. Breathe Trust in from that Universal sanctioned Life-giving air that purifies understanding. Rises up your surprise that is your Life's cause.*

*You can and do connect to the Living Movement in the Momentum (the beat) of awareness. Sing unto Life anew song, from an old one changing ever so with renewal. Enlighten the Day with your immense confidence level that brings a certainty in your availing more information in your message of empowerment that you realized when*

*Appreciating my Inner Being*

*doing. It is so good of you to become aware of the powerful messages coming from you. Your audience is awaiting. We are excited with and for your freedom as burden is lifted!*

*Be a willing component to the changes you project since the beginning of time!*

*The book is being read.*
*I am that you are.*

*Wealth, yet too it is given for it eases joyful living and you enjoy being so! Clarity is why you see what you do and that comes to thee like the coast shares the shore. Wisdom you find a natural companion and with it you shine a Bright Light".*

04/21/10. I asked a question: Advise on the show?

**Answer:** *"Fear lacks reason! Pleasing others feels good to you all and we share that characteristic as well. We love answering your questions, especially when they are directly and clearly expressed... yet... we hear the vibration of the request, the electricity of your desired knowing and we tell you in every question there is much more being asked, so we travel words to you claiming them all.*

*Be so, be you!*

*Smiles are felt this way whereby they are more than what you say. All is exceedingly well! You are a total Living Spirit as well as a total Living Being in such... the rhythm of life's flowing easy where you go, and fear lacks reason. Understand progressive learning as it's time to excel.*

*Sidestep the drama and find the calm reservoir of abundance that is more than enough to quench the thirst for teaching. Sing a heart-thought into a tune and listen to the chorus. We are all there with you, lighting the way on the path you forge based on the tranquility of truth. Breathe in and out the voice of the Universe and smile often. Peace and Love are granted in the wisdom of their abilities. Empowered are thee Strengthened in Love Eternally."*

<u>05/21/18</u>. *"Tapping into your Mastery is a capability, that is common and most encouraged. It is like having a book to read and then opening it up, otherwise its contents remain as they say; "buried in a book"!*

*Your appreciations come out from within. They are often like desires to have more yet that is only part of the collection of components comprising the entirety either desires or appreciations for whenever the reasons one might have to appreciate; there are still more. So many sweet souls to gather about for all involved. Keep asking, believing and receiving. Negative Entertainment can only exist outside of the understanding which knows all too well that the SOURCE of ALL that IS, is and only can be Love.*

*You easily sense Fear in others and self. Because you know it to be an illusion albeit a shadow passes behind all that had light shed upon it. So, be easy about the noticing of what you saw more or before you began to choose more deliberately. Your choice from feeling emotions, moods, events and knowledge (getting the point). Be intuitive and catch the waves of impulses and idea-forming thoughts. The sun is always shining although there are clouds releasing shadows, still, Light always prevails. Changes are the momentum of ideas in the moment of now. Be aware and well.*

## Appreciating my Inner Being

*What you seek, clarity of Now,
is a way rather than a roll."*

<u>06/27/18.</u> *"Put away time as a measuring pole and know better that experience aligns best with direction rather than time. The "now" records the criteria that produces quality. What is of conscience reminds us that energy and understanding mysteriously evolve the degree at which acceptance can carry out its tale.*

*When love filters into the hues of light to be realized by a wise heart, the mind's ability to trust overturns all obstacles that shadow the right to be free. Pleasing as it might play-out the imposition of comedy or drama can easily distract you from playing and leave you to observe rather than create.*

*It's not lazy to wait to create what it comes to be in time; for you will want to be ready and prepared. There is no waiting; there is only becoming.*

*Enable resolve to bring with its indifference, and in so, you are always ready. More is the Mantra of Source and you are already More in that knowing of Self as the part of Source you bring forth.*

*Listen to your Self-force and appreciate you can and that you trust the motive of Source love. Peace is just another word for choice."*

<u>11/17/2018.</u> *"When something is made to produce good results or is created to be helpful from a space of good feelings and upliftment, the usage recognition, results or influences come to be arrived at or near at that intent. That is why it's best to create under the influence of self-created and nurtured joy and wellbeing. These frequencies you call healing are tweaked to what feels*

*good and somewhat tingles and that type of vibrational sound wave touches the wavelength of normalcy and with a stimulation to reply, since sound is pitched! To create attention. Yet, interestingly there are other portions that happen simultaneously. Within the packet of a sound wave that related to movements that are neither seen nor heard and in such there exist harmonies that each singularly are unrecognizable by hearing.*

*The multi-use of the senses seemed, up and until recently, to be clearly apparent, although, now you and many others, although not all, are more aware of what influences humans is more than what is sensory defined in seeing, hearing smelling, touching and tasting that sensorize at a top level, yet, feelings are the Mother of All Sensory Knowledge. We feel warmth in many ways; in*

>  *A voice*
>  *A gesture*
>  *A word*
>  *A temperature*
>  *A color and MORE*

*So, think warmth into reality and there comes a flow and deliberately so. In a gentle breeze there are feelings."*

<u>12/07/20.</u>  *"Keep thinking about how the future can meet up with the future you dream of and then feel what it is like to be in the future. When the concept of winning a race is as recognized outdated as other things that seem to force competition into acceptable formats, then the race is over, and everyone wins it all. It is nearly impossible to think this world or others can exist void the striving to be ahead and win. It is off completely and complexly. Other worlds are growing easier by allowing the choices to be the direction rather than the competitive results. Winning is a non-active process. So, what is the result of trusting*

*Appreciating my Inner Being*

*direction rather than artificially winning places. Imagine a world of More certainty."*

Literally, there are thousands of messages from My InnerVoice in these Appreciation Journals and as time goes on, as you can see from the proceeding transcripts, the messages become easier to understand, at least it seems that way to me. There has been a maturing of communications over these many years. I think it is because My InnerVoice actually has become more familiar with my experiences that work to enhance my specific understanding and potential growth through our communicating. My InnerVoice is also more adapt to my vocabulary, although I still write down words that are written by my InnerVoice and that I have to look up in the dictionary. I am learning to accept the excellence of My InnerVoice. The examples that My InnerVoice can construct are based upon my individual life, although the messages are universal.

I think there are many volumes of messages to choose from in my collection. I allowed myself to randomly pick books and then randomly open to pages. I have no way of judging which messages I've found most profound in my collection; they all are for me. I have an idea that these are most constructive for the reader. My intent is to share what is most appropriate within the loving guidance of my intuition. My journals continue to grow.

I close this book by stating how much I loved writing it. Years in the making, it is a piece of myself and it is so good to share with you. I love and appreciate every one, everything and, of course, every think.

*The Art of Appreciating MORE*

*May the Light of Love always be known by you, as you.
May you always know your own equality and freedom and
then to shine it onto all others in joy.
May your Life be enriched with self-direction,
self-confidence and loving guidance.
May all that you want, be easily manifested.
May you find the heaven of self-awareness and
self-consciousness with you often and increasingly so.
May you realize your own thoughts as positive and pure.
May each day be lengthened into longevity;
as we all shift into More.
MAY YOU LOVE MORE.*

*Muchness,
Peggy Halevi*

*The End*

# Appreciating my Inner Being

## Chapter Eleven- Appreciations Regarding My Inner Being

- ❖ I appreciate the amazing process I took to be able to connect often and easily to My Inner Being, My InnerVoice

- ❖ I appreciate that my InnerVoice feels like I am the Voice I hear and that I am Wiser and more open about feelings and direction in that Voice.

- ❖ I appreciate how positive and loving this InnerVoice is.

- ❖ I appreciate that I allow myself to reach up to listen to my InnerVoice.

- ❖ I appreciate that the messages are always so clear from my InnerVoice.

- ❖ I appreciate that my life is improved since I hear and listen to my InnerVoice.

- ❖ I appreciate that my InnerVoice always focuses on the present moment or the future, never is in the past.

- ❖ I appreciate resonating with the feeling of trust and honesty I hear in my InnerVoice.

- ❖ I appreciate that I gather a new perspective from allowing myself to communicate with my InnerVoice.

- ❖ I appreciate that I am, you are and we are.

## Bibliography

Below is a scanty partial list of the many Law of Attraction Leaders, Spiritual Guides and others who have in ways influenced my Path of Least Resistance and my work, herein. I cannot say where a thought becomes to belong to someone or myself. I do know that I have appreciated many Law of Attraction people and others that assist my soul in creating and evolving. The grocery store clerk, my husband, the doctor, my child's friend, a dog, a cat, a poem, a movie, a song, a person I do not knew and some I knew well, my parents and relatives, and other people's parents, sisters, brothers, children and relatives. My Law of Attraction knowledge comes from personal experiences with nature, others, self, and thought.

I feel there are few, if any, original thoughts that can be owned by anyone. We are all one. We all breathe the same air and are free in the same ways. I, at the same time, want my work to reflect an appreciation for others who think in similar ways as do I, both living and passed over. This list seems to be of the ones I can think of currently, however, I've been influenced by others and their thoughts from the first day I was born, perhaps even prior to that time. I know that it is a positive action to thank others for their work or love that has influenced me into the very essence of this book, however, that is impossible. I will state that I thrive in questioning authority and in collaborating ideas with so many wonderful people and experiences that my heart is open to the trust that I resonate and feel connected to many others and a growing number at that. This list is a stark degree of a much larger list that I cannot put together as conclusive. Some influence me in ways to continue to seek after and others, not so much so. I've read the Bible

## Bibliography

in many version styles, so many science fiction authors that to name a couple would be an injustice to so many more. I've attended seminars, listened to endless videos for all kinds of people who are willing to share their thoughts, and I hear a Voice Within that brings to me much wisdom, knowledge and love.

I am educated and I learn on my own from my experiences of allowing to flow with my interests. I am a student-of-life in my desires and ability to write. I love all those who have contributed to my thought process and I appreciate myself for being as independent and honest as possible. I appreciate all these spiritual guides in this list and so many more. Thank you.

Ralph Waldo Emerson
Rhonda Byrne
and All in the Secret Book
Esther Hicks
Terrence McKenna
Louise Hay
Wallace D. Wattles.
Lee Carroll
Eckhart Tolle
Daryll Anka
Gregg Braden
Wayne Dyer
Thomas Troward
Oliver Napoleon Hill
And many more.

In remembrance of the loving guiding soul of my friend Lauri Day, who told me often that,

*"All Lightworkers Live in the 5th Dimension."*

www.ingramcontent.com/pod-product-compliance
Lightning Source LLC
Chambersburg PA
CBHW072002150426
43194CB00008B/966